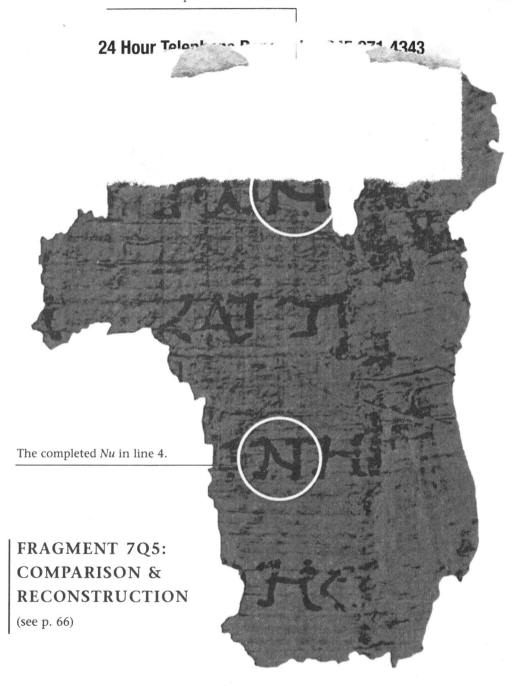

The reconstructed *Nu* in line 2. The tend
straight strokes in an almost arch-shape
the second *Eta*, is obvious in the reconst
and the *Nu* in line 4 are as different in s
the two undisputed *Etas* in lines 4 and 5.

The completed *Nu* in line 4.

FRAGMENT 7Q5:
COMPARISON &
RECONSTRUCTION

(see p. 66)

THE
JESUS
PAPYRUS

THE
JESUS
PAPYRUS

CARSTEN PETER THIEDE &
MATTHEW D'ANCONA

Weidenfeld & Nicolson
LONDON

First published in Great Britain in 1996 by
Weidenfeld & Nicolson

The Orion Publishing Group Ltd
Orion House,
5 Upper Saint Martin's Lane,
London, WC2H 9EA.

Published by arrangement with Doubleday, New York

A catalogue reference is available
from the British Library

ISBN 0 297 81658 6

Typeset by Selwood Systems Ltd

Printed in Great Britain by
Butler & Tanner, Frome & London

Dedicated to my three-year-old son Frederick who said that he would like as many heaps of paper on his desk when he has grown up as I had when writing this book.

Carsten Peter Thiede

Dedicated to my darling wife Katherine, who explained to me why the papyrus mattered. As on our wedding day, I still 'count the ways'.

Matthew d'Ancona

CONTENTS

THE GREEK ALPHABET

UPPER CASE	LOWER CASE	NAME	LATIN EQUIVALENT
Α	α	*alpha*	a
Β	β	*beta*	b
Γ	γ	*gamma*	g, n
Δ	δ	*delta*	d
Ε	ε	*epsilon*	e
Ζ	ζ	*zeta*	zd, z
Η	η	*eta*	e
Θ	θ	*theta*	th
Ι	ι	*iota*	i
Κ	κ	*kappa*	k
Λ	λ	*lambda*	l
Μ	μ	*mu*	m
Ν	ν	*nu*	n
Ξ	ξ	*xi*	x
Ο	ο	*omicron*	o
Π	π	*pi*	p
Ρ	ρ	*rho*	r, hr
Σ	σ, ς	*sigma*	s
Τ	τ	*tau*	t
Υ	υ	*upsilon*	u, (u, ü)
Φ	φ	*phi*	ph (f)
Χ	χ	*chi*	ch
Ψ	ψ	*psi*	ps
Ω	ω	*omega*	o

ILLUSTRATIONS

A section of photographs appears between pages 82 and 83

St Matthew[1]

Charles Huleatt, ordinand, Wycliffe Hall, 1887[2]

Charles Bousfield Huleatt - missionary, scholar, Magdalen man[3]

Luxor Hotel: Charles Huleatt's home for a decade of winters[4]

The little-noticed plaque to Charles Huleatt's memory at the Luxor Hotel[4]

The Magdalen Papyrus[5]

The Qumran scroll fragment 7Q5[6]

The Nile at Luxor[4]

Luxor Temple[4]

The Old Library at Magdalen College[4]

Carsten Peter Thiede with Dr Christine Ferdinand, Fellow Librarian of Magdalen College[7]

Photographic credits

[1] The Bodleian Library, Oxford

[2] Reproduced by kind permission of Wycliffe Hall, Oxford

[3] By kind permission of the Intercontinental Church Society and Guildhall Library, Corporation of London. From Guildhall Library MS 15726/9

[4] Matthew d'Ancona

[5] The President and Fellows of Magdalen College, Oxford

[6] David Rubinger Israel Antiquities Authority

[7] Georg Masuch, Paderborn

For truly, I say to you, till heaven and earth pass away, not an iota, not a dot, will pass away from the law until all is accomplished.

St Matthew 5:18 (RSV)

Biblical quotes are from the New Jerusalem Bible,
except where specifically indicated.

PREFACE

Any scholar or journalist who enters the extraordinary terrain of this book needs all the friends he can get. This has been a collaborative venture by the two of us, spawned by a series of interviews in late 1994 and subsequent meetings in London, Paderborn and Oxford. But our work has been made easier and more stimulating by the support of others.

In New York, our editor Mark Fretz was a patient and sympathetic shepherd to a project that was often logistically complex. In London, we received energetic help from our nonpareil agent Giles Gordon and our editor at Weidenfeld & Nicolson, Ion Trewin, who made very useful suggestions.

At *The Times*, the Editor Peter Stothard was extremely generous in his support, while Martin Ivens, the Executive Editor, provided welcome intellectual encouragement.

Pursuing Charles Huleatt through the Victorian mists would have been much harder without guidance from his descendants, Captain Julian Williams, Thomas Huleatt-James and Vere Wilcher; the historian of Wycliffe Hall, the Revd J. S. Reynolds; and Jill Lomer of the Thomas Cook Archive. In Egypt, Dr Mary Masoud and Nael El-Farargy of Wena Hotels were very helpful in our quest for the origins of the Magdalen Papyrus.

In Oxford, Anthony Smith, CBE, the President of Magdalen College, gave freely of his time and intellectual energy. We owe him a great debt of gratitude. Dr Christine Ferdinand, the college's Fellow Librarian, and Sally Speirs, the Assistant Librarian, were untiring and self-sacrificing in their patient assistance.

Among those who have offered indispensable criticisms, advice and help are Joseph Zias, Curator at the John Rockefeller Museum, Jerusalem; Dr Ulrich Victor, Reader in Classical Philology at Berlin's Humboldt University; Professor José O'Callaghan of the Seminari di

Papirologia at Sant Cugat del Valles; Professor Dieter Hagedorn of the Institute for Papyrology at the University of Heidelberg; and Professor Georg Masuch of the German Institute for Education and Knowledge, Paderborn.

Neither of us would have been equal to the task without his family's love and support. Above all else, this book is meant for them.

Carsten Peter Thiede / Matthew d'Ancona
Paderborn / London
St Matthew's Day, 1995

INTRODUCTION

Jesus was at Bethany in the house of Simon the leper, when a woman approached him with a bottle of very costly perfume; and she began to pour it over his head as he sat at table.

Matthew 26:6–7 (REV)

We may start with the fact, which I confess I did not appreciate before the beginning of the investigation, of how *little* evidence there is for the dating of *any* of the New Testament writings.

John A. T. Robinson, *Redating the New Testament* (1976)

On Christmas Eve, 1994, *The Times* reported on its front page an extraordinary claim made by the German papyrologist, Carsten Peter Thiede. 'A papyrus believed to be the oldest extant fragment of the New Testament has been found in an Oxford library,' the newspaper said. 'It provides the first material evidence that the Gospel according to St Matthew is an eyewitness account written by contemporaries of Christ.'

The story concerned three tiny scraps of paper belonging to Magdalen College, Oxford, the largest of which is only 4.1 by 1.3 cm. On both sides of the fragments appeared Greek script, phrases from St Matthew, chapter 26, describing Jesus's anointment in the house of Simon the leper at Bethany and his betrayal to the chief priests by Judas Iscariot. Though the verses concern a crucial moment in the life of Christ, the scraps looked unremarkable in themselves. Yet Thiede – Director of the Institute for Basic Epistemological Research in Paderborn, Germany – argued that they were of astonishingly early origin, dating from the mid-first century AD. He was shortly to publish his claims in the specialist journal *Zeitschrift für Papyrologie*.

The argument was complex, based upon expert analysis of the Greek

writing and extensive comparisons with calligraphy on other manuscript fragments. A scholarly controversy was bound to follow: Thiede
was challenging the orthodox view that the minuscule second-century
fragment of St John's Gospel in the John Rylands Library in Manchester
(P52) was our earliest Gospel text. He was also making a claim which
would have radical implications for our understanding of the Gospels
and their origins. And – most important – he was doing so on the basis of
physical evidence rather than literary theory or historical supposition.

The new claim clearly deserved a much broader audience than the
restricted one to which Thiede's learned article was addressed. Here, it
was alleged, was a fragment of the twenty-sixth chapter of Matthew –
remnants of a book perhaps 150 pages long – which might have been
written in the lifetime of the apostle himself. If true, Thiede's argument
had awesome implications. As one senior Fellow of Magdalen put it at
the time: 'It means that the people in the story must have been around
when this was being written. It means they were *there*.'

In its editorial column, *The Times* noted that many historians, theologians and linguists had speculated in the past that the New Testament
was written by contemporaries or near-contemporaries of Christ. 'What
separates Thiede from his academic predecessors is that he has identified
an artefact – albeit a tiny one – which seems to prove his point ...
This bold contention moves the debate on the antiquity of the New
Testament into new territory.'

None of this might have come to light had Thiede, whose wife is
English, not found himself in Oxford for a family celebration in February 1994. As a routine act of scholarly curiosity he asked the Assistant
Librarian at the college if he could take a look at the St Matthew
papyrus. He was struck and perplexed by what he saw – particularly
that such an intriguing fragment had been so neglected since last being
dated to the second century in the 1950s. Four more visits to Oxford
followed, in the course of which he was able to study the papyrus in
detail and refine his thesis.

When Anthony Smith, the President of Magdalen, learned what
Thiede was planning to argue, he made it his task to find out more
about the fragments and how they had fallen into the hands of the
college. How had this relic reached its twentieth-century home in
Magdalen? The records list the donor as the Revd Charles Bousfield
Huleatt (1863–1908), a one-time undergraduate of the college, about

whom almost nothing was known. Who was he, and what was his part in the story of the papyrus?

Not since the discovery of the Dead Sea Scrolls in 1947 had there been such a potentially important breakthrough in biblical research. Thiede appeared to have found evidence that St Matthew's Gospel was written only a generation after the Crucifixion – or even earlier. The papyrus itself, unearthed in Upper Egypt and bequeathed to Magdalen in 1901, might conceivably have been read or handled by one of the 'five hundred brethren' (1 Corinthians 15:6) whom St Paul declares had seen the resurrected Jesus with their own eyes. It was a claim that nobody with an interest in Christianity – spiritual or scholarly – could ignore.

Aware of the story's significance, *The Times* put its vast production halls in east London on security alert while it was printing to prevent the news from leaking to a rival publication overnight. Only a handful of the newspaper's staff knew the details of what was to be published. But discreet soundings in the scholarly world had already suggested to them how much interest was likely to be generated by Thiede's claim and how fierce the scholarly debate would be.

So it has proved. In the days after *The Times* ran the story, it was picked up by news publications all over the world, from Los Angeles to Delhi, while the British television channel ITN ran the story prominently on its prime-time news bulletin. On 23 January 1995, *Time* magazine's Religious Editor, Richard Ostling, reported the new research under the bold and evocative headline 'A Step Closer to Jesus?'

As expected, Thiede's argument provoked a powerful response, not least a vigorous correspondence in the letters columns of *The Times*. Some academics were hostile, arguing that the Magdalen Papyrus – or Jesus Papyrus as it is also known – had been dated quite satisfactorily, in 1953, to the late second century AD and that Thiede had done nothing to alter that consensus. In the *Sunday Telegraph*, Enoch Powell dismissed Thiede's argument about the handwriting on the fragments as unfounded and 'arrogant'. Graham Stanton, Professor of New Testament Studies at King's College, London, led the letter-writing charge and was so incensed by the redating that he wrote a hostile book about it called *Gospel Truth?*, which was published in the autumn of 1995.

Many other scholars, however, commended Thiede's approach and wanted to learn more. 'The problem is, this upsets the whole theological

establishment,' Ulrich Victor, a distinguished German philologist, told
Time magazine. Hugh Montefiore, a retired bishop and the normally
measured columnist of the *Church Times*, described the story breath-
lessly as a potential 'bombshell'.

It was not only in academic circles that the new research inspired
strong emotions. Thiede and the journalist Matthew d'Ancona, author
of the original *Times* piece, were overwhelmed with telephone calls and
letters seeking further information about the Magdalen fragments. In
his scholarly travels around the world, the papyrologist discovered that
his research had made an impact upon ordinary people, fascinated by
the questions it posed to them about the relationship between history
and faith, religion and empiricism.

Who would not be enthralled by the possibility that the fragments
might have been read by men and women who had walked with Jesus
through Galilee and wept as the storm gathered above the Cross on
Golgotha? But there was also interest in the methods used to reach the
new date and its implications for contemporary approaches to religion.
It seemed at times that everybody had a view on the Jesus Papyrus,
ranging from fanatical fundamentalism to almost pathological liberal
scepticism. Never before had a scholar produced forensic evidence of
this nature that the Gospel was written not long after the events it
described. It was hard to be indifferent about such a find.

The experience of Magdalen College itself was similar. Three scraps
of paper that had attracted little attention for almost a century were
suddenly being treated by outsiders as a uniquely sacred artefact, of
interest to people around the world who had never heard of the college.
The papyrus had long been stored in a display cabinet in Magdalen's
Old Library with other memorabilia such as Oscar Wilde's ring and
Joseph Addison's buckles. Now it required completely different care
and far tighter security. Overnight, a college treasure, one of hundreds
of precious manuscripts in Magdalen's custody, had apparently become
a relic of enormous significance. For the first time, Sotheby's was asked
to place a value on the fragments. For an academic institution to
discover that it owns what may be the earliest Christian document, a
tiny but crucial foundation stone in the literate culture of the West, is
a momentous experience. But it is not without its challenges, some of
them burdensome.

This book is a response to the flood of interest in the St Matthew papyrus. It is neither a religious tract nor an exercise in Christian persuasion. Instead, it seeks to make accessible to the general reader a major papyrological discovery and its implications for the dating of the New Testament and our knowledge of early Christianity. It seeks to bridge the gap between scientific investigation and the questions which every thinking person must ask about the Gospels and their significance. It seeks to promote debate as much as to answer questions definitively.

Indeed, such a book was overdue long before the Magdalen Papyrus was redated in 1994. Since the great philosopher and historian Albert Schweitzer wrote his ground-breaking work, *The Quest of the Historical Jesus*, in 1906, there has been a relentless effort by modern scholars to cross what the German thinker Gotthold Lessing (1729–81) called the 'ugly ditch' between history and faith. At the centre of this debate has been the New Testament itself and the question of its origins. When were the Gospels written, and in what order? And what exactly is a Gospel? What were Jesus's aims and would he have recognized and approved of early Christianity? From Schweitzer and Rudolf Bultmann – the most influential biblical critic of the twentieth century – to more recent writers such as E. P. Sanders, John Dominic Crossan and A. N. Wilson, scholars have tried in countless ways to assess the relationship between Christ's divinity and his humanity, between the Gospels as faith documents and their disputed role as historical sources.

It is central to our argument that the science of papyrology has played too small a part in the answering of such questions. To prove their theories about the life of Jesus and the early Church, scholars have produced archaeological, numismatic, inscriptional and literary evidence. They have happily imported the methods of interpretation offered by literary criticism, sociology and anthropology to support their own claims about the nature of the Gospels or the social structure of the early Church. A 1988 bibliography on the use of the social sciences in New Testament studies, for instance, listed more than 250 items. It has become fashionable to speak of the 'interdisciplinary quest for the historical Jesus'. Yet the rich seam of papyrology has yet to be mined in the same imaginative way by biblical scholars. This omission has been an intellectual loss for all who have an interest in these fundamental issues.

In the chapters that follow, we demonstrate the dramatic effect which papyrus evidence may have upon our understanding of Christianity's origins. The Jesus Papyrus is a key document in the long history of New Testament dating – a scholarly argument that has raged since the time of Papias, Bishop of Hierapolis (c.60–130). But it also has much to tell us about the first decades of Christian life; the multicultural, Greek-speaking society to which the papyrus was addressed; and the precocious development of the Church before AD 70 – the pivotal year when the Roman army crushed the Jewish rebellion and sacked Jerusalem. What can we know of the early Christians, such as those described in Acts 2:46 who 'with one heart ... regularly went to the Temple but met in their houses for the breaking of bread'; or the followers of 'Chrestus' in Rome mentioned by the Roman historian Suetonius (c. AD 70–140)? These fragments are important evidence of the institutional sophistication and ambition of the Church *before* the destruction of the Temple and even suggest that a well-developed ecclesiastical strategy was already at work in the mid-first century AD.

Above all, our book is a series of interlocking stories about the papyrus and the men whose lives it has affected. It explores the life of St Matthew and asks whether he might indeed have written the Gospel which takes his name and of which the papyrus is an early copy. It looks at the kind of men and women who might have been the first readers of this ancient codex and how they would have used it.

We follow the trail of the Revd Charles Bousfield Huleatt, the Oxford graduate, amateur scholar and devout missionary who found the papyrus in Egypt but tragically perished in an earthquake in 1908, leaving almost no trace of his life and work. Like the fragments he discovered and bequeathed to his beloved college, the story of Huleatt's life, scholarship and desire to spread the Word has remained obscure for almost a century. His is the enigma at the heart of the tale, a strange Victorian story of frustrated intellect and unequivocal faith rewarded by virtual eradication from history. It is also the story of Carsten Thiede and his modern academic quest.

Finally, our book examines the papyrus in the twentieth century: the last dating in 1953, and the redating four decades later. Much has been said and written since the original *Times* story about Carsten Thiede's research and Chapter 5 responds to the criticisms that have been made, explaining in greater detail than ever before the scholarly argument behind the new date. We conclude by speculating upon the place of the Jesus Papyrus in our own age, and its significance to believer and non-believer alike.

At first sight, this fragment could scarcely be less prepossessing. It amounts to little more than three tiny pieces of old paper, clasped between two slides of glass and labelled 'P. Magdalen Greek 17/P64'. History does not obviously cling to it, let alone faith. Yet this ancient papyrus, we contend, is one of the most important documents in the world. It is this bold claim which our book sets out to prove.

1

Portrait of a Papyrologist:
the Revd Charles B. Huleatt
Victorian Missionary and Scholar

Every one of us is a Magdalen man – the poorest, the least clever, the least conspicuous ... We are either worthy of it, or we are not worthy of it. Its name, its fame is in our hands: we cannot disown it.

> Lecture given by T. H. Warren to Magdalen undergraduates, June 1885

What further discoveries of the lost documents of early Christianity still await us in Egypt it is impossible to say.

> A. H. Sayce, 1896

It is far more the second-hand fallacies of Strauss and Renan that I have to combat in reality than any Roman doctrines.

> Charles B. Huleatt, undated letter

The name Charles Bousfield Huleatt means little today in Luxor. At the entrance of the hotel where he was Anglican chaplain for a decade of winters is a striking commemorative plaque to this forgotten man of faith and letters. It reads:

IN LOVING MEMORY OF THE REV. CHARLES BOUSFIELD HULEATT, M.A. CHAPLAIN AT LUXOR 1893–1901: WHO PERISHED IN THE EARTHQUAKE AT HIS POST OF DUTY AS CHAPLAIN AT MESSINA 1908. WELL DONE GOOD AND FAITHFUL SERVANT, ENTER THOU INTO THE JOY OF THE THY LORD. MATT.XXV.21

For the amateur scholar who found the earliest known fragment of the Gospel according to St Matthew, there could scarcely be a more apt scriptural tribute. Yet it has small significance for the locals who sit on the verandah of the Luxor Hotel sipping tea and puffing expansively on pipes as the impossible heat of the summer afternoon slowly releases its stranglehold. To them, the brass plaque is an attractive hieroglyph in a foreign tongue, rather than a stately record of a man who made a remarkable discovery. The earnest Oxford graduate who came to their land a century ago and sent home something extraordinary has left no folk memory behind him. Who was this man, and what brought him to Egypt to spread the Word and – perhaps – to seek truth? The most that the traveller who asks about Huleatt can expect is an indulgent smile and another glass of fierce Egyptian wine.

That this should be so is a melancholy irony symbolic of the chaplain's life, its frustrations and the recognition he was denied. Opened for the winter of 1877–8, the Luxor Hotel was for many years one of Egypt's most important institutions, a crossroads of scholars, soldiers and wealthy expatriates wintering on the River Nile. It was probably the finest achievement of the travel entrepreneur Thomas Cook, rivalled in prestige only by the neighbouring Winter Palace Hotel. Though its rooms do not look over the river, the hotel is but a stone's throw from the temple of Luxor, the awe-inspiring monument built by Amenophis III and other scions of the 18th Dynasty to the greater glory of the god Amun. According to legend, Jesus and the Virgin visited the temple during the Holy Family's Egyptian exile, by which stage its buildings were already a monument to the ancient past, its hieroglyphs meaningless to Nazarene eyes.

The grounds of the temple are an unparalleled museum to the religious history of a species, bearing traces of Roman, Christian and Muslim worship. Each era has left its mark and its mysteries, aside from less reverential curiosities such as the large inscription carved by the poet Rimbaud into the ancient stone of the south end's transverse hall. Turning to the north, one gazes down the Avenue of the Sphinxes which once led all the way to the yet more spectacular temple of Karnak. The powerful impression which this majesty must have made upon the Victorian mind is clear from an account left by one traveller in 1898:

> When the boat pulls up at Luxor the landing-stage appeared to be a colossal temple. Really this is across the road, but, even so, it was wonder enough. Arcades of huge pillars, some complete, some half broken down, some sprawling in hideous dislocation – they loomed grey and motionless and solemn in face of the ancient river and the flaming sunset ... As we went to bed almost under them they seemed to be rebuking squalid, modern

Egypt – rebuking modernity altogether, that was so small and fretting, while they remained so great and unsurprised.[1]

For a decade, this extraordinary place was the setting of Charles Huleatt's life and missionary work. Even today, a century later, Luxor Hotel still seems like a travellers' annexe to the temple, a place where those who are drawn to Egypt's past gather to see the ruins of Thebes, Homer's 'city with a hundred gates'. It was natural – perhaps even *de rigueur* – that Howard Carter and Lord Carnarvon should announce the discovery of Tutankhamun's tomb in November 1922 from the Luxor Hotel. Their portraits still hang in its gloomy lobby, tribute to the legends which quickly arose around their names and achievements. They are not forgotten.

The same cannot be said of Charles Huleatt. Humble though it seems in comparison to the young pharaoh's funerary treasures, the Magdalen Papyrus, with its handful of verses from the Gospel according to St Matthew, has far more to tell us about the origins of our culture, and the belief-system which has dominated it for centuries, than all of Tutankhamun's gold. Yet Huleatt has been granted none of the celebrity which fell so easily to Carter and Carnarvon. Indeed, his fate has been quite the opposite. The college to which he entrusted the papyrus in 1901 treated it with comparative indifference at the time. Its arrival at Magdalen stirred no scholarly debate or excited speculation; only since Carsten Thiede's redating in 1994 has the papyrus become the centre of collegiate attention. And if the young chaplain had a scholarly inkling of what he held in the palm of his hand, he was denied the chance to pursue his intuition. Seven years after he sent the fragments to Magdalen, he was swept away by an act of God which all but eradicated his name from history. Huleatt never saw the papyrus again, and his name was forgotten.

The redating has, of course, generated great interest in his life and beliefs among historians and theologians. Yet the fates have conspired against those who would reclaim his memory; the sources are fragmentary, thanks to an uncanny series of accidents. Huleatt, his wife and four children were all lost in the earthquake which destroyed the Sicilian port of Messina on 28 December 1908; so too were all his private papers, save for a bundle of personal letters retrieved from the rubble by his close friend, William Collins, the Bishop of Gibraltar. Two years later, the mud-brick Anglican church in the grounds of Luxor Hotel was washed away by flood along with its tombstones. Two trunks full of Huleatt family records went missing some years ago.

At the time of writing this book, the English missionary archive at All Saints' Cathedral in Cairo rema'ns closed – a matter of regret for all researchers into the connections between Victorian religion and Egyptology. To go in search of Charles Huleatt is like tracing the fugitive steps of a shadow. Yet his story – the story of a devoted Evangelical with an inquisitive intellect, who chanced upon the earliest Gospel text in the world – is integral to the history of the papyrus. Without Huleatt's scholarship, the fragments might never have left Egypt; without his filial devotion to Oxford, they would never have reached Magdalen, there to remain for almost a century before they would be accurately dated. Fugitive as it is, Huleatt's is a shadow that must be chased.

From Boyhood to Magdalen

Charles Bousfield Huleatt was born on 19 October 1863, in the Parsonage, Potters Bar, Hertfordshire,[2] second son and third child of the Revd Hugh Huleatt (1822–98) and his wife Cornelia. The Huleatt family – whose name is a variant of 'Hewlett' rather than anything more exotic – had its roots in Ireland and observed strong traditions of service in Church and army. Hugh Huleatt, a formidable patriarch who fathered eleven children, honoured both traditions as a chaplain to the forces between 1854 and 1879 (a role which, by coincidence, Carsten Thiede plays today) and served with distinction in the Crimea and China. In 1859 Padre Huleatt returned to England where he married Cornelia Sophia Bousfield, daughter of the extremely wealthy Charles Pritchett Bousfield, who was to be a powerful force in the life of his eponymous grandson.

In spite of his father's robust example, Charles Huleatt was evidently a sickly child and suffered from poor health throughout his life. The 1871 census describes the seven-year-old boy – almost certainly with exaggeration – as 'blind'. However poor Charles's eyesight was at the time, he was sufficiently able-bodied to enrol at St Paul's School on 1 December 1873. By this time, Padre Huleatt had moved from St George's Church in the Royal Artillery Barracks in Woolwich to the chaplaincy at the Royal Military Asylum, Chelsea. St Paul's was an entirely predictable choice for a well-to-do London family of means with high expectations for their frail son.

It was Charles's great fortune that this should be so, for at St Paul's he was to forge one of the most important friendships of his life. In December 1876, William Gunion Rutherford arrived at the school as a classics master, fresh from Balliol, which, under Benjamin Jowett, had become Oxford's most intellectually formidable college.[3] Rutherford's undergraduate career had been one of enormous promise and he was rapidly to make his name as a classical scholar, initially with the ground-breaking *First Greek Grammar* (1878) and then, three years later, with *The New Phrynichus*, one of the greatest works in English on Attic form.

Rutherford is best known for his later role as headmaster of another great English public school, Westminster. But it was in these formative years at St Paul's that he befriended and became an inspiration to the young Charles Huleatt, whom the *Oxford Magazine* later described as 'one of his favourite pupils'.[4] It was Rutherford who awoke Huleatt's precocious interest in textual criticism – a passion that always surpassed his dedication to his formal studies at university.

Indeed, their interests continued to coincide after both master and pupil left St Paul's. During the 1890s, Rutherford followed closely the emergence of new papyrus evidence from Egypt and in the last years of his life addressed himself assiduously to the text of the New Testament. He believed that the Greek used by its authors was radically different from the classical Greek he knew so well. In the preface to his 1906 translation of St Paul's Epistle to the Romans, Rutherford wrote of this distinctive biblical language:

> With every generation it changed, departing more and more widely from literary grace and logical precision, ceasing in time to be the cherished language of a race that of all races has best loved accuracy of thought and limpidity of expression, and becoming by degrees a tolerant speech whereby many races, all differing greatly in habits of mind and in national circumstances, sought for a time to eschew the curse of Babel.[5]

As we shall see in Chapter 6, Huleatt's erstwhile mentor might easily have been describing the multicultural Greek in which the Magdalen Papyrus was written. And, though there is no evidence that Rutherford knew of his former pupil's find in Egypt, it is intriguing that their academic concerns remained so similar. The fact that the *Oxford Magazine* thought their association worth underlining in Huleatt's brief obituary suggests that his revered teacher may well have assumed the role of muse in later life.

Huleatt excelled sufficiently at St Paul's to win an exhibition to read classics at Magdalen College, Oxford. Having achieved this distinction at a relatively youthful age, he stayed on an extra year at school, before taking up his university place in 1882, flush with an additional Pauline scholarship worth £50 for four years.

For a Victorian gentleman of Huleatt's background and academic promise to read classics at Oxford was almost a rite of passage. The school of Literae Humaniores was not only regarded as the most intellectually prestigious path for a young English gentleman to pursue; it was also thought to be ideal cerebral preparation for those who were to take up posts, clerical and lay, in the British Empire. The history of the Greek city-states and of the Roman Empire were considered parables of instruction for the elite charged with the government of Britain's dominions and territories; the classical model of the *vita activa* was held up to Oxford's young scholars for emulation in the glittering careers that lay ahead of them. In 1873 Jowett wrote to Florence Nightingale that 'I should like to govern the world through my pupils.' This was more than a donnish quip; to many of his contemporaries, it sometimes seemed that Jowett's influence did indeed stretch the length and breadth of the Empire.[6]

The talented young classicist from St Paul's spent four undergraduate years in a university where it was natural to seek dignified occupation abroad in the service of God and Empire. To take up a chaplaincy in Egypt, as Huleatt was to do not long after leaving Oxford, was to pursue an honourable calling rather than to submit to second-rate exile. More surprising, perhaps, is the fact that Huleatt performed so modestly in Oxford's examinations. In 1884 he gained a respectable second-class degree in Classical Moderations. Two years later, he was awarded only third-class honours in Literae Humaniores. This may well have been a disappointment to Huleatt, who took his BA in 1888 and MA four years later. Yet the importance of examinations to the Oxford system at this stage in the university's history is easily exaggerated. Since the Royal Commission of 1850–2 and the Oxford Reform Act of 1854, the clerical and nepotistic character of the university had certainly been addressed by committed reformers such as Jowett who had vigorously encouraged hard work in their undergraduates. None the less, the old habits died hard. Tom Brown, Thomas Hughes's fictional character, was bemused by the lack of academic pressure:

> First and foremost, it's an awfully idle place; at any rate for us freshmen. Fancy now. I am in twelve lectures a week of an hour each – Greek Testament, first book of Herodotus, second Aeneid, and first book of Euclid! There's a treat! Two hours a day; all over by twelve, or one at the latest.[7]

It was still said of Oxford that 'every freshman brings to it a little knowledge and no graduate takes any away'. Charles Huleatt probably performed as he did in university examinations because the pressure to do otherwise was still so relatively modest. More important to his long-term intellectual development and his later role in the story of the Jesus Papyrus was his continued amateur interest in textual scholarship – an interest he seems to have pursued quite independently of the formal studies on offer at Magdalen. His achievements in this field were such that in 1885 the *Journal of Philology* published an article by him proposing a series of textual emendations to Catullus and Propertius. That an undergraduate should have his work published in a learned journal was remarkable in itself. Still more impressive is the fact that Huleatt's suggestions seem to have been favourably received by his elders. In 1909 the *Oxford Magazine* described the Propertius emendations as 'highly ingenious' and noted that they had been accepted by 'several subsequent editors'. There is no reason to think that Huleatt had the application or inclination to be a professional academic. But his under-graduate flair in this field adds lustre to the theory that his interest in the papyrus which he found in Upper Egypt years later was more than that of the antiquarian hobbyist.

Why did Huleatt send the fragments back to Magdalen in 1901? Of all the questions posed by the papyrus, this is perhaps the easiest to answer. Founded in the fifteenth century, Magdalen is one of the most captivatingly beautiful of the colleges of the two ancient universities, blessed with a deer park, the imposing New Buildings behind cloisters, and a tower that is to many the architectural epitome of Oxford. Those who are undergraduates there never forget their youthful idyll in its quads and gardens. In 1901 the historian J. R. Green recalled the haunting experience of May Morning when Magdalen's choristers usher in the summer at dawn, a rite which Huleatt must first have experienced in 1883. It is a recollection worth quoting at length:

> We used to spring out of bed, and gather in the grey of dawn on the top of the College tower, where choristers and singing men were already grouped in their surplices. Beneath us, all wrapped in the dim mists of a spring morning, lay the city, the silent reaches of Cherwell, the great commons of Cowley marsh and Bullingdon now covered with houses, but then a desolate waste. There was a long hush of waiting just before five, and then the first bright point of sunlight gleamed out over the horizon; below, at the base of the tower, a mist of discordant noises from the tin horns of the town boys greeted its appearance, and above, in the stillness, rose the soft pathetic air of the hymn *Te Deum Patrem Colimus*.[8]

Such were the collegiate rituals that would have nurtured Huleatt's lifelong attachment to Magdalen. Indeed, he was fortunate to be a student at the college during one of its high seasons. Edward Gibbon had famously condemned his fourteen months at Magdalen as 'the most idle and unprofitable of my whole life'. But by the 1880s when the young Pauline arrived to read classics as one of about a hundred undergraduates, the college was in the full bloom of institutional renaissance. Building on the foundations laid by President Martin Joseph Routh – whose wig-curlers have been displayed casually beside the papyrus in Magdalen's Old Library for most of this century – his successor Frederic Bulley and the classics tutor Herbert Warren were driving the college to the forefront of Oxford life.[9]

Warren, like William Rutherford, was a product of Jowett's Balliol, where he had been a spectacularly successful classics undergraduate. From 1878 to 1885 he was a tutor at Magdalen, importing Jowett's strong belief that undergraduate teaching should be at the heart of college life. Warren succeeded Bulley as President in 1885 at the remarkably early age of thirty-two and held the office until 1928. The character of the modern college was shaped in those forty-three years during which Warren raised academic standards at Magdalen, increased the numbers of its undergraduates and – perhaps above all – defined its *esprit de corps*.

In 1932 Warren's friend and biographer Laurie Magnus described him as 'the second Founder of Magdalen', a worthy successor to Bishop William Waynflete, and noted 'his unforgotten method of making

"Magdalen men" out of sometimes reluctant material; of making the conception of a Magdalen man real and vital for life, as, by common consent, it had not been so made before his time'.[10] There can be no doubt that Charles Huleatt was one such Magdalen man. That Warren liked and admired him is clear from a letter he wrote while Vice-Chancellor of Oxford University, which appeared in *The Times* on 25 May 1909, five months after Huleatt's death. 'He was my pupil here,' wrote Warren. 'I had a very genuine regard for him. He was no common scholar; indeed he had a genius for textual criticism and kept up his interest in scholarship, both sacred and secular, in a way that not many do.'

What sense of collective identity and institutional loyalty would Huleatt have taken from Magdalen when he left in 1886? He would never forget the deer park, the lawn within the cloisters, the afternoons spent wandering down Addison's Walk. But there was more to it than that. The year before Huleatt left the golden stone of Magdalen, on 7 June, Warren gave a speech to the undergraduates of the college which does much to define the sense of mission with which they would have left Oxford.[11] Addressing the subject of 'College Unity' on the last Sunday afternoon of the summer term, he took as his text St Paul's Letter to the Ephesians: 'I ... beseech you that ye walk worthy of the vocation where with ye are called' (4:1, KJV).

Warren's speech was a hymn to duty, active living and a college ethos that celebrated the brilliant oarsman as well as the brilliant scholar. He singled out those 'leaders among us' who were leaving the college. He urged each of the fortunate few before him to make something exceptional of himself:

> It is not a question of each one of us being conspicuous, each one of us doing much, each one of us being a leader, distinguished from the rest; we cannot all be that. But we can, we must, all be something, and it is enough if that something is on the side of right.

Above all, he charged the undergraduates before him to remember that they were Magdalen men, citizens for life of a collegiate republic which he explicitly compared to Athens:

> Every one of us is a Magdalen man – the poorest, the least clever, the least conspicuous ... We are either worthy of it, or we are not worthy of it. Its

name, its fame is in our hands: we cannot disown it ... you go carrying the name of this place with you everywhere.

It was an injunction that Charles Huleatt would not forget. He would one day send the college an exceptional and sacred gift. He would try to be as worthy of his vocation as St Paul and Herbert Warren would wish. But first he must find where it lay.

Man with a Mission

What can we know of Charles Huleatt? He was married twice, first to Edith Bury in 1892 and then to Caroline Wylie in 1900. His first wife died in labour in 1897, giving birth to a daughter, Edith Irene, who survived. Charles had three more children with Caroline: Charles Percy, born in 1901, Gwyneth Cornelia Charlotte, born in 1903, and Rhoda Muriel, born in 1904.

From the wreckage of their home in Messina, William Collins, the Bishop of Gibraltar, salvaged a small bundle of letters, mostly from Caroline, which shed a little light upon her husband's nature.[12] They had first been engaged after he left Oxford, breaking off the betrothal in 1891. But Caroline seems never to have fallen out of love with her 'beloved knight', her 'Sir Galahad', and continued to write to him – often from St Petersburg where her family were in business.

The letters suggest that Charles was sometimes abrupt with her, intolerant of disagreement. 'I know that in essentials we think alike & you will forgive me if I cannot always think the same as you in minor matters,' she wrote on one occasion after their marriage, 'for you know that I would never try to teach our little one, or any other child God may give us, anything that was not what you thought and wished.'

In their long correspondence, Caroline endlessly reassured 'Charlie dear' of her love and trust, but referred in a letter in January 1900 to the times when he had been 'so outwardly cold'. It is clear, too, that memory of Edith often came between them. 'I think you will know that I can feel nothing but love for her,' she wrote, '& if I write as if I forgot this, I do not for one minute forget it in my heart.'

Charles's demands upon his second wife were great. He told her that he 'had failed in everything'. He scolded her for proposing he take up an 'easy post' in England and sending him a book entitled *Rest*. There are frequent references to his poor health and even to his 'trying exile'. But Caroline found reward in the fact that he treated her as a thinking person, quoted Ruskin to her in letters, and turned to her 'for intelligent intercourse on subjects of interest'.

Charles Huleatt was a difficult, driven man, whose yearnings could, it seems, only be satisfied by pious service to the Lord. If Magdalen College gave him an institutional home, the Evangelical movement provided him with a spiritual cause which was to shape his life. He was a man for whom the Word of God was the Alpha and Omega of faith, an implacable enemy of the High Church tendency, of the cult of priesthood, and of the taste of nineteenth-century Anglicans for ritual. He believed in the literal truth of scripture. If he ever suspected the true antiquity of the St Matthew Papyrus, this suspicion would merely have strengthened the deepest foundations of his faith. For an Evangelical of Huleatt's severity, the claim that the Gospels were written by contemporaries of Jesus was fundamental; it was not a matter for idle scholarly speculation. Every sentence in the Gospel was divinely authorized.

This aspect of Huleatt's character and beliefs is clear from those scattered remarks on doctrine and ecclesiastical matters made by him which have survived. While Anglican chaplain at Messina, he wrote to a friend deploring 'the second-hand fallacies of Renan and Strauss' which, he claimed, exercised an even more pernicious influence upon the educated than 'any Roman doctrine'.[13] Huleatt's choice of heretic was appropriate to his times.

In 1835 David Friedrich Strauss (1808–74), a tutor at Tübingen University, had argued in *The Life of Jesus* that the discrepancies between the Gospels showed that they could not have been written by eye-witnesses and that the miracle stories were simply myths invented by much later writers. Thus, for instance, the account of the Trans-figuration in the New Testament was regarded by Strauss as simply a mythical means of likening Jesus to Moses or – more obscurely – Socrates in Plato's *Symposium*. It was impossible, therefore, to write a meaningful life of Jesus. Strauss compared the sayings of Jesus to a broken necklace of pearls which 'have been worked away from their original position and like rolling pebbles have been deposited in places to which they do not properly belong'.

Seven decades later, in *The Quest of the Historical Jesus*, Albert Schweitzer (1875–1965) would write that 'In order to understand Strauss one must love him. He was not the greatest, and not the deepest of theologians, but he was the most absolutely sincere.' Strauss considered himself a true believer, confronting the reality of faith and its relationship to scripture. Yet to most of his contemporaries his work was at best outrageously iconoclastic and at worst pure blasphemy. Several attempts were made to ban the book, which was vilified in the press by writers often ignorant of his work. For his audacity, Strauss was expelled from his university and later became a schoolteacher.[14]

In his own *Life of Jesus* (1863), the French Catholic Ernest Renan (1823–92) had drawn a sharp distinction between the Jesus of history and the Christ of faith. He denied that any evidence for miracles acceptable to a historian had ever been produced. The life of Jesus was a purely human story of a man who more or less stumbled into martyrdom:

> Did he remember the clear brooks of Galilee at which he might have slaked his thirst – the vine and the fig-tree beneath which he might have rested – the maidens who would perhaps have been willing to love him? Did he regret his too exalted nature? Did he, a martyr to his own greatness, weep that he had not remained the simple carpenter of Nazareth? We do not know![15]

These ideas proved influential as well as shocking: eight printings were required in the first three months of the book's publication. George Eliot wrote of Renan's achievement that 'We can never have a satisfactory basis for the history of the man Jesus, but that negation does not affect the Idea of the Christ in its historical influence or its great symbolic meanings.'[16] Schweitzer dedicated an entire chapter of *The Quest* to Renan, celebrating his ability to make readers see 'blue skies, seas of waving corn, distant mountains, gleaming lilies, in a landscape with the Lake of Gennesaret for its centre, and to hear with him in the whispering of the reeds the eternal melody of the Sermon on the Mount'.[17]

This was the intellectual backdrop against which Charles Huleatt ministered and wrote. To a man of his unswerving belief in the Word, the campaign to drive an intellectual wedge between faith and history was to be opposed by all means available. Nor, it seems, was he afraid of the controversy which strong Evangelicalism tended to stir in the more sceptical age of Renan and Strauss. In a letter to the *Anglican Church Magazine* in 1904, for instance, Huleatt championed an openly sectarian approach to parish organization in the Church of England. 'Is it not time to face the truth officially,' he wrote, 'and admit in our theory of organization, what we all admit in practice, that the Church of England contains two sets of Christians, with views as divergent as the politics of Liberals and Conservatives?' He contrasted the church where 'the teacher bids his hearers to try his teaching only by the Word of God' with another where 'they are expressly warned against opposing their own private judgment to the voice of the Church'.

Better, he argued, that believers offended by the particular traditions upheld by their priests should be able to transfer to another parish, than that they slide into 'dissent or indifference'.[18] Huleatt's plan was ostensibly offered in the spirit of friendship; but it was only offered at all because he believed some of the differences in question to be utterly irreconcilable. The subtext to his letter was the pang of conscience which the true Evangelical felt in a congregation which did not share his values. Nor was Huleatt afraid of the fury which such views could provoke. Two years later, in the same publication, he prompted an angry exchange of letters with an outraged reader, writing under the pseudonym 'An Anglican', who was appalled by Huleatt's description of the Virgin Mary as 'a dead woman'.

Huleatt replied disingenuously that the Anglican's objection was 'quite unintelligible'. But the polemical nature of the doctrinal point which his adversary was trying to make was clear enough: 'I intended to signify that Mary is removed by God from the possibility of inter-vening in our aid.' In other words, Huleatt was sufficiently antagonized by the contrary belief in the Roman Catholic Church (as he observed it in Messina) to use language blunt enough to offend many of his fellow Anglicans.[19]

Uncompromising Evangelicalism was the core of Huleatt's adult identity. This was partly a dynastic characteristic. His wealthy maternal grandfather Charles Bousfield was a bounteous contributor to mission-ary organizations and was to fund Huleatt's theological studies as a candidate for the priesthood. The records of the Colonial and Con-tinental Church Society for 1899 reveal that Bousfield – whom *The Times* later described as 'a wealthy, and in his later years, somewhat eccentric philanthropist' – had contributed more than £10,000 to their work, a fabulous sum in those days.[20] Eight years later Huleatt himself, writing from Sicily, reminded the society that the late Bousfield's 'abstemious self-denial' had paid for the Sailors' Rest at Messina. Huleatt family legend has it that bonds worth £250,000 were found in his desk when he died.[21]

Though more often associated with Clapham and Cambridge, the Evangelical tradition was also a significant force at Oxford;[22] the movement formed, in the view of its historian, 'not merely a party, but a school of thought'.[23] Between 1807 and 1871, forty-five identifiable Evangelicals were elected to Oxford fellowships and tutorships, while twenty served the office of select preacher at the University in the same period. In 1877 the foundation of Wycliffe Hall, sister to Ridley Hall in Cambridge, gave Oxford a theological institution designed specifically for the ordination of young Evangelicals to the priesthood. Upon leaving Magdalen in 1886, Huleatt enrolled at Wycliffe and was a student there until 1888.

That he did so is a measure of his commitment to his beliefs. In its early years, Wycliffe Hall had great difficulty reaching its full complement; only ten students appear in the 1887 photograph, Huleatt among them. In Oxford, the new hall was regarded with a degree of suspicion; most colleges preferred graduates seeking ordination to do so at the diocesan theological schools or by remaining at their old university colleges. It was particularly unusual to spend two years at Wycliffe, as Huleatt did, although this may be a reflection of affluence as much as commitment.

What would Huleatt have learned there? Wycliffe, named after Oxford's greatest biblical scholar, was founded as part of an Evangelical offensive to counteract the spread of rationalism, ritualism and High Church practices in the Church of England.[24] The teaching, organized by its principal, Robert Girdlestone, was intended to be practical rather than narrowly scholastic and to provide candidates for the priesthood with a command of scripture, the techniques of preaching and other aspects of pastoral work.

There were fixed times for morning and evening prayer, for lectures and for meals, and students were expected to act as Sunday-school teachers or play a similar role in the life of local congregations. Typically, a week's lectures would include classes on Monday, Wednesday and

Friday on the Epistle to the Romans, textual interpretation, the names of God in the Bible, and sermon preparation. On Tuesday, Thursday and Saturday, lectures would be given on 'The Pentateuch; its Authenticity and Contents (Historical, Legislative, Theological)'. In the evenings, open discussions would be held on a broad range of subjects such as 'Personal dealings with the careless and the anxious', 'Reformatory work among London lads' and 'Illustrations of scripture from Josephus'. More important than the detail of these classes, however, was the spiritual backbone of the place. In an 1878 prospectus for Wycliffe Hall, Girdlestone warned of the expectations that would be made of a candidate for ordination:

> there is *one thing* about which he ought to be firm and clear in his belief and teaching. Knowing as he does that beneath the civilized surface of society there lurks worldliness, sensuality, superstition, and atheism – and feeling as he must the plague of his own heart, and his constant proneness to depart from the Living God, he ought to be absolutely certain that there is one remedy and one only for this evil state of things, namely *the Gospel* ... Other doctrines must be held in their due proportion, but we are bound to keep the Gospel of CHRIST in the fore-front at all hazards.[25]

This might be a text for Charles Huleatt's later life and the Evangelicalism that would propel him until his death. Wycliffe Hall lacked the venerable grandeur and social confidence of Magdalen; Girdlestone was certainly much less of an Oxford grandee than Warren. Yet Huleatt's spell at this theological college was surely decisive in setting him on a path that led first to the papyrus and then to an untimely death.

To Luxor

For a high-minded Oxford classicist to seek patriotic employment overseas was, as we have seen, natural enough; all the more so for a young Evangelical with a strong sense of vocation. There were frequent missionary breakfasts at the university, at which hundreds would gather to see off those who had chosen the evangelist's life.[26] Societies such as the Oxford Mission to Calcutta, founded in Christ Church in 1880, acted as a focus for such enterprises, while prospective missionaries like Huleatt could look for inspiration to the legends of great Oxford

Evangelists such as Henry Watson Fox (d. 1848), a Wadham man who had made his life's work in India, and Thomas French (d. 1891), Fellow of University College and Bishop of Lahore.[27]

This aspect of Oxonian romanticism was inextricably linked with the mythology of Empire. As the Warden of Keble College, the Revd W. Lock, put it in 1907: 'The British Empire is itself an expression of the Christianity which the Church has to guard, and Christians have now not only to teach that the powers that be are ordained of God, but see to it that they act as powers so ordained.'[28]

No organization better epitomized the sacred bond between God and Empire than the Colonial and Continental Church Society, to which Huleatt was to devote the rest of his life.[29] Founded in 1851 by the amalgamation of the Colonial Church Society and the Newfoundland School Society, the purpose of the C&CCS was to provide Evangelical clergymen, schoolteachers and missionaries for the territories of the Empire and Commonwealth and for British residents in other parts of the world. Its purpose was to minister to Greater Britain abroad; its doctrinal requirements simple and conservative. A recruitment questionnaire drawn up in 1842 asked the candidate's views on 'the sufficiency of the Holy Scriptures as the rule of Faith'. Huleatt's response would have been clear enough.

After Wycliffe Hall, Huleatt was finally ordained in 1888 in Hereford Cathedral and joined the ministry as a curate at St Mary's, Swansea, and then at St Mark's Church, Broadwater Down, Sussex. Among the papers retrieved from the rubble at Messina in 1908 was a letter of recommendation written sixteen years previously by J. H. Townsend, the Vicar of St Mark's, who described Huleatt as 'thoroughly loyal, reliable & hard-working. He has won the esteem of all in the parish in the short time that he has been here. The working men like him and the young men and lads have quite gathered round him. He is a good preacher & in preaching and visiting tries to reach the spirits of men and not only their understanding.'

Huleatt, in other words, might have settled down to a productive and successful life as an English parish priest. Yet his sights were set elsewhere by this time. He spent the winter of 1890–91 as English chaplain at Luxor, an appointment he was to take up every winter from 1893 to 1901. His enthusiasm for the task was evident from the start, in a report he sent back to the C&CCS from Luxor Hotel.[30]

'Any detailed report of the winter's work would have to consist chiefly of a record of the kindness of all with whom I was brought in contact,' he wrote. The presence of a resident winter chaplain in Luxor had, he said, become well known among travellers on the Nile, 'so that in very many cases they shape their plans accordingly, and arrange to be at Luxor for Sunday, both on the voyage up and when coming down.' Huleatt described the congregations as 'very satisfactory, though apt to fluctuate' and recalled that 'in one instance a gentleman, though in haste to reach Cairo, sacrificed two days' sight-seeing in order to avail himself of the ministrations provided by the Colonial and Continental Church Society'. The congregation had even held a successful Christmas service at which four or five carols were sung and the new chaplain was also able to report the arrival of a communion table, the gift of two lady worshippers.

What had led Huleatt to Upper Egypt? Once again, family connections had played a part. In July 1891 John Mason Cook, son of Thomas Cook, wrote to the society seeking further information about the young chaplain before he made a more formal appointment. 'The arrangement he made with Mr Huleatt was quite an exceptional one, he being the son of an old personal friend of his ... before a chaplain is appointed he would like to know something of the clergyman it is proposed to send.'[31] Evidently Cook was soon given the reassurances he sought and made the appointment a regular one.

This was a defining moment in Huleatt's life. In the summers to come he would hold temporary chaplaincies in Varese in northern Italy and Bad Schwalbach in Germany, and would intermittently return to England to see his family. But Luxor unquestionably became his home and the centre of his activities. Doubtless the dry heat of the winter was appealing to someone who was so often in poor health. The Cook's programme did its best to make Luxor Hotel sound a blessed sanctuary for the invalid, quoting a 'medical gentleman' to that effect. 'Here the sick man finds a friendly region where he can breathe the fresh outdoor life-giving air, and bask in the reviving rays of a generous Egyptian sun. Here he discards the respirator; here he has no need of the stifling stove-heated indoor refuge.'[32]

Egypt's fragile Christian inheritance seems also to have been part of the attraction to Huleatt's missionary soul. 'It is much to be hoped that the work of aiding the torpid Coptic Church to reform itself and to revive Egyptian Christianity may soon be set about with greater vigour,' he wrote to the society. 'It is much to be prayed and worked for that Egyptian Christianity may once more dominate the land and be a power for good, instead of remaining an obstacle to missionary enterprise, a reproach to the name of Christ, and so singular a specimen of an effete and fossilized church.' The Cook family, famous for their upright Evangelicalism, would have endorsed such sentiments. Huleatt certainly admired the 'real Christianity' of his patron.

To be chaplain at Luxor Hotel, and thus a significant figure within the Thomas Cook organization, was also to be part of an empire within an Empire. Since the nationalist uprising of 1882 and the British occupation of Egypt, Lord Cromer had been its consul and effective ruler. Yet many considered that true power lay with the Cook family, which had transformed Egypt's tourist industry and infrastructure, achieved control over the Nile steamers and established an unofficial dynastic cult.[33] It was said that the Sphinx had broken its silence to congratulate Cook Pasha on his success, while, at Aswan, there was a hieroglyphic inscription to the 'king of Upper and Lower Egypt, John son of the sun, Cook and Son, Lords of Egypt, Pharaoh of the boats of the north and south'.

The Cook organization was considered by the natives to be far more accessible and trustworthy than the Cromer regime. Indeed, its assistance was often needed by the British administration, not least during General Gordon's relief expedition when Cook transported 18,000 troops more than five hundred miles. In 1889 the magazine *Vanity Fair* wrote of him that the 'Sovereign becomes more and more potent as we get further up the Nile and here at Luxor, where a special hotel has arisen under the light of his countenance, he figures quite as a modern Ammon-Ra.'

Thus Huleatt – no stranger to grand institutions – had found himself a member of a splendid court as well as chaplain in a humble mud-brick church which lacked electrical lighting until 1898. The guests to whom he ministered were affluent travellers, some of whom would be staying in the hotel for their health or cruising slowly down the Nile on steamer or dahabeah. Once an unwelcoming village of mud huts, described by Florence Nightingale in 1849 as 'fearful', Luxor had become a winter playground. Beside Huleatt's plaque is a brass portrait of Albert Ferdinand Pagnon who, as Cook's agent, made the Luxor

Hotel a luxurious sanatorium for the wealthy, a civilized oasis of palms and acacias with a billiard room, tennis court, gardens, a smoking room and even a hairdresser's salon. Many of the guests were consumptives searching for respite from their condition in the dry air of Upper Egypt; others were unabashed pleasure-seekers. In 1892 the journalist Charles A. Cooper wrote gushingly of its charms in the *Scotsman*:

Days at Luxor were delightful, and nights in the Luxor Hotel dreamless ... Everything was clean and fresh and pleasant. The scent of mimosa flowers floated in at the window and open door. The sound of chirruping birds met your ear. The air seemed to be golden with the sunlight by day, and silvern with the moonlight at night. Tall palm-trees shaded you from the mid-day sun ... Truly, the Luxor Hotel was for me a place of delights.[34]

Life at the hotel was cosmopolitan rather than secluded. In 1898 there were reckoned to be 50,000 visitors in Egypt; Cairo was even referred to in the press as 'a suburb of London', a caricature which might as easily have been applied to Luxor. Huleatt would never have wanted for like-minded company.

The Cook empire was also avowedly paternalist in spirit, a spirit in which the young chaplain instinctively shared. It was traditional for Europeans to give medical assistance to the natives wherever possible and the Luxor Hotel's resident had made his services informally available to sick villagers during the 1880s. In 1887 John Cook began collecting donations for a native hospital, which was opened with great ceremony by the Khedive of Egypt, Tewfik Pasha, in January 1891.

Huleatt was evidently impressed by the Khedive's speech declaring the hospital open, in which he 'made a striking comparison between the colossal ruins left in the neighbourhood by the ambitious monarchs of pagan days and the less pretentious building which he hoped would remain for many long years to bear witness to the goodness of heart (he might have said also the real Christianity) of Mr Cook and the English-speaking travellers on the Nile'. The chaplain was to remain closely involved with the hospital, which by 1898 was seeing 32,000 cases a year. Such, indeed, was Huleatt's reputation there that the Luxor Hospital Committee lobbied to have a ward endowed in his name after his death.[35] The hospital still stands, a few minutes' walk from the hotel, but the chaplain's name is not remembered there today.

The Discovery of the St Matthew Papyrus

That Charles Huleatt led a worthy life at Luxor is not in doubt. Yet the chaplaincy was not only an opportunity for Huleatt to serve God and his fellow man. To be in Egypt in these years was to be at the centre of an extraordinary scholarly reconquest of the past. Napoleon's nine-volume *Description of Egypt*, published between 1809 and 1822, had reawoken the outside world to the majesty of Egyptian antiquity and heralded a century of ground-breaking Egyptology. In 1822 Jean-Fran-çois Champollion had provided scholars with the key to the door by deciphering the ancient hieroglyphs which covered the walls of Egypt's monuments. In his wake followed a generation of brilliant archae-ologists led by Auguste Mariette, founder of the Egyptian Antiquities Service, and Gaston Maspero, his successor. The temple of Luxor, the pyramids at Giza, the Serapeum at Memphis and the tombs of Deir-el-Bahari – all were excavated and investigated by men who were often left breathless by the pace of their own discoveries.

When Huleatt arrived in Egypt in 1890, major excavations had been underway at Luxor temple for five years and for considerably longer at Karnak. In one report to his society the chaplain wrote that the latter monument was 'said to be the greatest ruin in the world' and noted with Evangelical approval that the temple confirmed 'by the record on its walls the Bible account of Shishak's invasion of Judah'. He thought Luxor temple 'scarcely less noble' and was fascinated by the 'traces left of the time when Christians had consecrated these relics of heathendom to the service of their and our Lord and Master'.

But it was not only monuments that were being reclaimed from the earth and studied in the Near East. A wealth of manuscript evidence was also emerging, much of it early Christian in origin. In May 1844 the German linguist Konstantin von Tischendorf had found the Codex Sinaiticus at the monastery of St Catherine on the slopes of Mount Sinai, a fourth-century text of the Old and New Testaments which he instantly realized was 'the most precious Biblical treasure in existence – a document whose age and importance exceeded that of all the manu-scripts which I had ever examined during twenty years' study of the subject'.[36]

This Codex was written on vellum and would have needed the skin of 360 sheep and goats. Far more humble were the countless fragments of papyrus coming to light, preserved for centuries by the dry Egyptian climate. The natives considered the papyrus plant sacred, claiming that its stem resembled a pyramid in cross-section and its stalks looked like the rays of the sun. For visiting scholars, however, the ancient papyri were precious as historical sources. 'On the use of papyrus as rolls civilization depends,' wrote Pliny the Elder in about AD 70, 'at the most for its life, and certainly for its memory.' As a result, the scripts on papyri covered everything from the sayings of Jesus to laundry lists and receipts. Some were very long, such as the Prisse Papyrus (*c*.2000 BC), which the French Egyptologist Achille Prisse d'Avennes had bought and presented as a gift to his motherland. Most, in contrast, were very small, minute fragments of the past surviving to be puzzled over by posterity.[37]

Their survival was, of course, completely arbitrary. In the 1770s, for instance, papyri found at Giza were burned by natives because they liked the smell it created. But those that did survive were generating intense scholarly interest by the time Huleatt took up his post in Egypt. In 1877 Byzantine archives had been unearthed in the Fayyûm, while the great English Egyptologist Flinders Petrie had made major papyrus discoveries at Hawara. In 1895, crucially, the Egypt Exploration Fund decided to include the Graeco-Roman period in the scope of its research and funded one of Petrie's assistants, Bernard Grenfell, to search for further papyrus evidence.

In the years that followed, Grenfell's partnership with his Oxford friend Arthur Hunt yielded some of the most spectacular finds in the history of papyrology, notably at the former Hellenistic settlement of Oxyrynchus 200 kilometres south of Cairo. Trawling through the town rubbish dumps, they discovered verses by Sappho and part of a lost play by Sophocles. One day, as he sorted through the scraps, Hunt's eye was caught by the word *karphos*, Greek for 'small dry stalk' or 'twig', a word which occurs six times in the Greek Bible and part of a saying attributed to Jesus. The fragment, which included seven sayings, or *logia*, was quickly identified as a non-canonical Gospel text, about a century older than the Sinaiticus discovered by Tischendorf. Of this historic find, Grenfell remarked: 'I wouldn't have taken anyone else's word, but Hunt does know his Bible.'

Hunt was shortly to play an incidental but crucial role in the life of Charles Huleatt. There is no evidence that the two men knew each other. The regrettably poor sources for the Luxor chaplain's life have nothing to say about his reaction to these sensational discoveries. Yet it is inconceivable that he was not aware of, and intrigued by, them. This much can be guessed from the fact that one of his closest friends at Luxor was Archibald Henry Sayce (1845–1933), the distinguished Egyptologist and philologist.

Sayce had been a rising star in the Oxford firmament, a Fellow of The Queen's College by the age of twenty-five and a recognized authority on ancient inscriptions by the time he was thirty. In 1890, however, ill-health and the curiosity of an intellectual pilgrim drove him to resign his Oxford post and make for Egypt where he spent many winters in his large Nile-boat, the *Istar*, which had a crew of nineteen and a library of two thousand volumes. In Egypt and England, Sayce worked closely with Petrie on Greek papyri, an experience he describes in his memoirs as a private Renaissance of humanistic rediscovery and interpretation.[38] This autobiography records many visits to Luxor and at least two detours to Varese in the summer to see Huleatt. For his part, the chaplain later described Sayce as 'an old friend' who had given him 'an entirely free hand' to reproduce his books and disseminate them among the English-speaking flock at Messina. It was to Sayce that Warren would write after Huleatt's death, remembering him with fondness, and Sayce and the Cook family who launched an appeal in *The Times* to fund the brass tablet to his memory at Luxor Hotel.

In this scholar's presence, Huleatt would have experienced a boundless and infectious enthusiasm for the possibilities of papyrology. 'Countless manuscripts of priceless value have already perished,' Sayce wrote in 1896. 'But the soil of Egypt is archaeologically almost inexhaustible, and the land of the Septuagint, of the Christian school of Alexandria, and of the passionate theology of a later epoch cannot fail to yield up other documents that will throw a flood of light on the early history of our faith.'[39] It is intriguing to speculate what Sayce might have made of the papyrus fragments which Huleatt sent to his old college five years later, and what advice he would have given to his younger friend as they took tea together in the library of his Nile-boat. Sadly, the Sayce papers, now in the Bodleian Library, Oxford, include no correspondence between the two on this or any other subject. But it is reasonable to speculate that Huleatt would have maintained an amateur's interest in the emerging science of papyrology, if only to keep up with his scholarly friend.

*   *   *

At some stage during his time in Egypt, Charles Bousfield Huleatt found three scraps of papyrus which he considered very important. Before taking up his next post, in Messina, he arranged for his mother to send them to Magdalen, which she did by recorded delivery in October 1901, together with some rough notes by her son (now lost). Two months later, Huleatt himself wrote to the college librarian, H. A. Wilson, to check that the package had arrived, remarking regretfully *en passant* upon the recent robbery of mummies and papyri from one of the tombs at Luxor. This is the only record left to us of Huleatt's discovery and bequest of the Magdalen Papyrus – now the most widely discussed fragment of the New Testament in the world.

Where might he have come upon it? The market in such treasures was prodigious and still under-regulated, in spite of the efforts of the Antiquities Service to prevent the unauthorized sale of discoveries. Writing in 1895, the author Henry Stanley was scandalized by the contempt in which such regulations were held in Luxor and by the trade in mummies and other antiquities, many of them fake. 'Oh certainly Thebes is the place to buy souvenirs,' he wrote, recalling that one man had bought 'three men's heads, one woman's head, one child's head, six hands large and small, twelve feet, one plump infant's foot, one foot minus a toe, two ears, one part of a well-preserved face, two ibis mummies, one dog mummy'.[40]

Such grotesque and ghoulish purchases would never have been to Huleatt's taste, of course. But Stanley's example illustrates the easy availability of antiquities, authentic or otherwise. The antika-shops and bazaars of Egypt were full of illicitly acquired goods and scholars were frequently approached with papyri – those in Coptic and hieroglyphic script generally supposed by the natives to be more valuable than those in Greek. Sayce's memoirs make clear how liquid this market actually was.[41] Even a man as conscientious as Huleatt might not always have been able to distinguish between a sale that was fully legitimate and one that was not, especially if the papyrus was a gift from one of his many admirers and acquaintances amongst the guests at the hotel.

His overriding instinct was evidently to send the papyrus somewhere where it would be safe. This it would certainly be at Magdalen. His Alma Mater would indeed keep the fragments secure, safer than they would ever be in a land of grave-robbers, antika-dealers and tourists. But the college's reaction when presented with the papyrus was that of

the relaxed antiquarian rather than a fascinated scholar. Huleatt's letter
to the librarian of December 1901 reveals that the college had not even
acknowledged its receipt of the fragments in October. Arthur Hunt, a
Senior Demy at Magdalen from 1896 to 1900, was asked to estimate
their date, following Huleatt's own tentative suggestion that they might
be third century. Hunt, it seems, thought this too early, and suggested
that 'they may be assigned with more probability to the fourth century'.[42]

The fragments were laid in a display cabinet in the Old Library, a
magnificent but inaccessible room up a steep staircase in the college
cloister which directly adjoins the President's lodgings. Gibbon used to
labour over his books there and Magdalen Fellows still use the library
as a quiet workplace away from the busier parts of college. It is Magdalen's inner sanctum – although the papyrus was scarcely treated as
its holiest of holies. Instead, it lay among other college memorabilia –
the corrected typescript of *Lady Windermere's Fan*, a portrait of Henrietta
Maria – exciting little attention among the members of the college.

Arthur Hunt's verdict effectively ended the debate on the age of the
fragments until after the Second World War. He found a scholarly niche
at Lincoln College, while Grenfell returned to The Queen's College,
which has remained a stronghold of papyrology throughout the twentieth century. In 1953 the British papyrologist Colin H. Roberts redated
the Jesus Papyrus to the later second century and established its relationship to two scraps at the Fundación San Lucas Evangelista, Barcelona.[43]
That judgment was to stand until Carsten Thiede's redating, more than
forty years later. By this time, few Fellows of Magdalen even knew of
the existence of the papyrus.

Tragedy in Messina

The final chapter of Charles Huleatt's life – the postscript to his discovery
of the papyrus – was one of personal fulfilment ending in unexpected
tragedy. The chaplaincy at Messina in Sicily was perhaps one of the
least desirable posts offered by the Colonial and Continental Church
Society. Forty miles from Mount Etna, and facing Reggio Calabria,
Messina was one of the Mediterranean's busiest ports, a noisy, violent
town in which crime, disease and disorder were part of everyday life.

In 1895 the British consul described it as 'one of the worst that sailors can visit'. Yet Huleatt seems to have taken to his new pastoral task with relish. The spiritual poverty of the place ignited his missionary instinct as never before.

His despatches to the C&CCS became more frequent and more animated. In 1902 he reported 'the prevalence not only of gross immorality but of spiritualism, which has become a sort of worship of evil spirits ... there are families with English names such as Barrett and Hopkins whose members are unable to speak English'.[44] The focus of his work was the Sailors' Rest and the Anglican church on the ground floor of a large warehouse building, described by the Bishop of Gibraltar as 'the heart of the colony' of 130 people of English descent.[45] Huleatt's work was certainly more trying than his routine had been at Luxor. On one occasion, the chaplain was presented with a woman in his drawing-room, threatening to commit suicide unless he resolved a marital dispute with her husband.[46] On another, he found himself ministering in hospital to a sailor who had been viciously attacked by a Sicilian. Yet such trials were outweighed by the small spiritual triumphs of his work – not least persuading men of the sea to attend his services, teaching the English children of the colony the rudiments of Bible stories or baptizing a boy of fourteen whose drunken father had forgotten to arrange the sacrament when he was a baby. He also became independently involved in the conversion of Roman Catholics at Reggio to the Church of England, providing a small congregation there with subsidy as well as moral support.

One of the many consolations for the hard work at Messina was friendship with William Collins (1867–1911), the bishop with responsibility for European chaplaincies such as Huleatt's. (Collins's successor, John Hind, is responsible for Carsten Thiede's chaplaincy in Germany today.) Like Huleatt, Collins suffered from delicate health and was a scholar, Professor of Ecclesiastical History at the age of twenty-six. As Bishop of Gibraltar he was a tireless itinerant, and came to know Huleatt well, remembering him later as 'an indefatigable worker, large-hearted and tolerant, with a very true pastoral instinct'.[47] Collins passed through Messina on 20 December 1908, when he preached at the church, and was hoping to return before the end of the year. Eight days later, the town was obliterated, and thousands of Messinesi with it.[48]

The bishop was in Malta when the earthquake struck and returned at once on board the HMS *Minerva*. The scene of biblical devastation that greeted him early on the morning of 30 December was one he would never forget:

> Whole streets were so filled up with almost impassable masses of *debris* that it was often difficult to recognize parts of the city which one had formerly known well. It was a veritable city of the dead ... The survivors wandered aimlessly to and fro, with horror in their eyes, suffering agonies from thirst or hunger, and wearing anything they could lay their hands on.

One survivor compared the horror to Dante's *Inferno*. Grimly, Collins made his way to the ruins of the church where he found Huleatt's robes and the Christmas carol books lying open. The tall house on Via Torrente Trapani where the chaplain lived in a household of nine had collapsed. There were conflicting stories about the fate of the inhabitants. On 1 January 1909, *The Times* reported that the Huleatt family had been saved but had to correct itself five days later:

> The rescuers dug with frantic energy, being certain that Mr Huleatt, with his wife and four children, were under the ruins. The groans apparently proceeded from one person only. The difficulties encountered were very great, and in the evening another shock of earthquake rendered the work still more dangerous, for the tottering walls around threatened to collapse. Finally, Mr Huleatt and one child were found in bed, crushed but recognizable, death having been instantaneous.

On 12 January, Collins buried Percy Huleatt and Mrs Kirby, an English lady who lived with the Huleatts. On 3 February Charles and Caroline's bodies were laid to rest at Taormina. It was an ordeal from which the ailing bishop never properly recovered, finding solace only in faith. 'To those who see aright,' he wrote ruefully, 'sudden death loses its terrors, and fellowship in pain is gain.'

The grief expressed for Charles Bousfield Huleatt was widespread and sincere. The C&CCS reported that 'the personal tributes to our departed friend have been numerous and have come from unexpected quarters'. the *Oxford Magazine* remembered him as 'a genuine scholar and a most amiable and devoted man'. In time, the whole family was commemorated by a plaque in St Mary's Church, Shalford, headed FAITHFUL UNTO DEATH'.

Thus ended a life of scholarly and clerical pilgrimage, a quest for knowledge and decency which had led Huleatt thousands of miles from home. By some, he might be judged a mediocrity who had lived his life in the shadow of his patrons: Rutherford, Warren, Cook, Sayce and Collins. Yet in his quiet but determined fashion, he had crusaded to save souls and to spread the Word. And, along the way, had he but known it, he had chanced upon a treasure far more precious to the Evangelical than a Holy Grail or a Crown of Thorns; a treasure that would one day prove how ancient the New Testament Scriptures truly are and cast doubt on the 'second-hand fallacies' of Renan and Strauss. But that day had yet to come. For Charles Huleatt and the papyrus he rescued, decades of obscurity beckoned.

2

Dates and Controversies:
St Matthew and the Debate About
the Origins of the New Testament

'By the way, Sherlock,' said he, 'I have had something quite after your own
heart – a most singular problem – submitted to my judgment. I really had
not the energy to follow it up, save in a very incomplete fashion, but it
gave me a basis for some very pleasing speculations. If you would care to
hear the facts –'

'My dear Mycroft, I should be delighted!'

Sir Arthur Conan Doyle, *The Greek Interpreter* (1894)

There is a world – I do not say a world in which all scholars live but one at
any rate into which all of them sometimes stray, and which some of them
seem permanently to inhabit – which is not the world in which I live. (...)
In my world, almost every book, except some of those produced by Government departments, is written by one author. In that world almost every
book is produced by a committee, and some of them by a whole series of
committees. In my world, if I read that Mr Churchill, in 1935, said that
Europe was heading for a disastrous war, I applaud his foresight. In that
world no prophecy, however vaguely worded, is ever made except after the
event. In my world we say, 'The first world-war took place in 1914–1918.'
In that world they say, 'The world-war narrative took shape in the third
decade of the twentieth century.'

A. H. N. Green-Armytage, *John Who Saw* (1952)

This is a book about three tiny fragments of papyrus; it is also an
exercise in scholarly reappraisal. It calls into question the academic
consensus that the Gospels are the late creation of the Christian communities rather than the record of contemporaries or near-contemporaries of Jesus. Few issues facing the student of the New Testament
are so fundamental. How we approach these texts is in large measure
determined by our view of when they were written and in what cir-

cumstances. From the dating controversy flow many other questions.

Yet the most striking feature of this particular debate in recent times has been its timidity. Too often, scholars have feared to trespass on to territory staked out by others in the past. More than three centuries ago, Thomas Hobbes recognized the tendency of academics to make aggressive claims to intellectual monopoly. Writing to his French colleague Samuel Sorbière, he observed: 'Their public reputation demands that in the subject in which they teach no one should have discovered anything which they have not already discovered.' Regrettably, the same could be said of many twentieth-century New Testament scholars.

Only in recent years has there been a shift towards a more open-minded approach to the question of dating. The pioneers have included Martin Hengel, a theologian at Tübingen University and former President of the Society of New Testament Scholars, who has proved willing to question the orthodoxies of his professional field. At the end of his magisterial book, *Studies in the Gospel of Mark*,[1] Hengel reprinted an essay by one of the leading classical philologists and Homer experts of our time, Wolfgang Schadewaldt. In 'The Reliability of the Synoptic Tradition' Schadewaldt argues that the three closely related, or Synoptic Gospels of St Mark, St Matthew and St Luke (leaving aside St John's quite different approach) are far more authentic than we have come to suppose. Neither a theologian nor New Testament scholar, W. Schadewaldt instead brought his training as a classical textual scholar to bear on the Gospels – which, if nothing else, are clearly part of the literary inheritance of classical antiquity.

Schadewaldt's philological conclusions were striking: 'As to the substance of the narratives and sayings, I would say that if, as often in philology, we make a comparison in terms of good tradition, bad tradition, and very good tradition, on this scale of values we would say that the Synoptic Gospels are very good tradition.'

This does not mean, of course, that every word in these texts should be taken at face value. More than factual recollections, the Gospels are proclamations of the good message (the *euangelion* or good spell, gospel) about Jesus, in which historical facts are ordered with a clear purpose; thus, some sermons are omitted or given a different setting in different Gospels. The author of St John, likewise, had his own priorities, preferring the more intimate and personal remarks made by Jesus to his major public speeches. But such discrepancies are not necessarily evidence that the Gospels are unreliable or that they were written over a long period of time. The first evangelists and those who later decided to preserve all four canonical Gospels (as opposed to just one, as suggested by the second-century heretic Marcion) well appreciated that the transmission of four partially independent testimonies was a strength rather than a weakness. It would assist historical recollection and facilitate the spread of the Word.[2]

Oddly, it is academics working outside the New Testament field and with no axe to grind, such as Wolfgang Schadewaldt and the late legal scholar Sir John Anderson, who have done most to advance our understanding of the Gospels' reliability. The former writer realized, for instance, that modern assumptions about the time it took for the Gospels to be disseminated and widely used reflected a misapprehension about the speed of communication in the first century AD. For more than a hundred years, it has been taken for granted that the recipients of the first Gospel took at least ten years to produce the second. Thus, it has been assumed that St Matthew's Gospel must have been written in the eighties of the first century, accepting an approximate date of AD 70 for St Mark.

Schadewaldt points out that this 'error in the history of tradition', as he calls it, was once quite common in classical scholarship too. In Homeric studies, he writes, 'People have always acted as though it took years for the Ionian epic to cross to the mother country. In Homer himself Achilles said: "The day after tomorrow I will be at home in Phthia, on the third day." I have checked this out with old ships' logs and it is true: ships went as fast as that. But according to earlier Homeric criticism the epic took centuries to find its way round gradually. It is always a good thing for scholars – I put this quite generally – to use common sense as well as their methods.'[3] As we shall see in Chapter 5, the communications systems of the social world which spawned the Jesus Papyrus were far more advanced than might be supposed.

Many other arguments have been put forward in favour of a later rather than an earlier date for the composition of the Gospels. One is the claim that they were written only after the first Christians accepted that the Second Coming of Jesus was not imminent. The earliest communities, it is argued, expected the risen and ascended Jesus to return sooner rather than later, to herald 'the end of the Age' during their lifetime. Given this expectation, it has been claimed, these Christian apocalyptics would see no reason to preserve, collect and disseminate narratives about Jesus's life and works. Only later, when the first generation of eyewitnesses had passed away and disappointment at Christ's failure to return had given way to new doctrinal thinking, would it have seemed necessary to compile such texts – or so it has been argued.

Yet there is no real evidence for the messianic expectation upon which this theory depends. In Mark 9:1, Jesus says: 'Truly, I say to you, there are some standing here who will not taste death before they see the kingdom of God come with power' (RSV).[4] If one assumes that this *does* refer to a prospective Second Coming, one is left with a paradox: if Mark was written only when the first Christians had changed their minds about Jesus's return, why would they have recorded a prophecy which they had come to accept was not to be fulfilled? Why, in other words, commit to writing a prediction which had proved entirely mistaken? In fact, one can avoid this logical quagmire altogether because the reference in Mark is *not* to the Second Coming but to the Transfiguration of Jesus, which is reported in the verses that follow, 'six days later'. Here, Jesus is revealed as God's only son, in the full glory of God's power invested in him. The incident is recounted elsewhere in the New Testament, with St Peter's authority:

> When we told you about the power and the coming of our Lord Jesus Christ, we were not slavishly repeating cleverly invented myths; no, we had seen his majesty with our own eyes. He was honoured and glorified by God the Father, when a voice came to him from the transcendent Glory, 'This is my Son, the Beloved; he enjoys my favour.' We ourselves heard this voice from heaven, when we were with him on the holy mountain. (2 Peter 1:16–18)

Others have focused on St Matthew 10:23: 'In truth I tell you, you will not complete the towns of Israel until the Son of Man comes.'[5] Was this an unfulfilled prophecy made by Christ to believers who expected his speedy return? Again, the interpretation is questionable. In fact, the Greek text makes no reference to 'going the rounds of the towns', as the New Jerusalem Bible translates it. The phrase is fiendishly ambiguous. It probably refers to a process which St Paul also strongly supported without expecting its completion to be imminent: the conversion of the whole of Israel.[6] The first Christians were being expelled and persecuted, and as they fled from town to town, Jesus expected them to preach and evangelize along the way. Their execution of this responsibility is reported in Acts.[7]

Ironically, Matthew 10:23 provides stronger evidence for an early date for this Gospel: its reference to 'the towns of Israel' as an escape circuit excludes the non-Jewish town of Pella in Transjordan. Yet the Christians did flee there in AD 66.[8] This small omission has exciting implications, as Theodor Zahn, the classicist and New Testament scholar, pointed out in his 1903 commentary on the Gospel: 'Mt would hardly have written v. 23 if the escape of the Christians [to Pella] had already taken place at the time of his writing. Our gospel is written before AD 66.'[9]

In summary, the first Christians expected the Second Coming no more or less than their modern counterparts today. They did not regard it as imminent. Nor would this sense of expectation have been considered a reason not to record Jesus's sayings and to structure them into Gospels. St Paul, whose early letters are thought to have preceded all four Gospels, makes this quite clear. He is also quite explicit about the folly of speculation in 1 Thessalonians: 'About times and dates, brothers, there is no need to write to you for you are well aware in any case that the Day of the Lord is going to come like a thief in the night ... God destined us not for his retribution, but to win salvation through our Lord Jesus Christ, who died for us so that, awake or asleep, we should still live united to him' (5:1, 10).[10]

The question of Jesus's divinity has also been invoked to suggest a late date for the Gospels. 'I and the Father are One' (John, 10:30, RSV) was clearly understood by some of Christ's Jewish audience to be a claim to godhood. 'We are stoning you,' they declared, 'not for doing a good work, but for blasphemy; though you are only a man, you claim to be God' (John 10:33). The prologue to this Gospel (John 1:1–14) underscores this claim to divinity in more elaborate form: Jesus existed before the creation of the world, partook in the creation, and was at one in action with his father.

The claim to godhood also features in the other Gospels, as in St Matthew 16:19–20 where Jesus gives the keys of the kingdom of heaven to St Peter. But are they late additions, made long after the destruction of Jerusalem in AD 70 and the reorganization of the Christian life and mission? There is no evidence that the deification of Jesus was an afterthought. As we shall see in our analysis of the Magdalen Papyrus, belief in his divinity was prompt and unequivocal. In a letter written as early as *c.* AD 55, St Paul declares as much, doubtless drawing on teaching which had been passed down to him: 'for us there is only one God, the Father from whom all things come and for whom we exist, and one Lord, Jesus Christ, through whom all things come and through whom we exist' (1 Corinthians 8:6). In fact, the editors of the standard edition of the Greek New Testament are so convinced of the early, pre-Pauline provenance of this statement that they print it as a quotation.[11] The appearance of similar claims in the Gospels does not prove that they were written late.

Other scholars have focused on Jesus's prophecy of the destruction of Jerusalem and the Temple in AD 70, arguing that the Gospels must have been written after this date. Predictions of this kind were attributed to Christ after the event, it is alleged, to give him the aura of a prophet.[12] The critical importance of AD 70 will be discussed later in Chapter 4. At this point, it is worth mentioning a final argument put forward to establish the lateness of the Gospels. How could Jesus have foreseen the development of the Church, an administrative institution built in his memory? In Matthew 16:18, he appears to do so: 'And I tell you, you are Peter, and on this rock I will build my church [*ecclesia*]' (RSV). Could Jesus really have said such a thing in AD 28 or 29, to be written down in the lifetime of eyewitnesses?

The answer hinges on the Greek word *ecclesia*. This word occurs often in the Greek translation of the Old Testament, the 'Septuagint' which originated in the third century BC. There, it simply means the community of God's people, the congregation of God – a translation of the Hebrew word *qahal*. To Jesus, the use of this word in Greek, Aramaic or Hebrew would have been quite natural. To one hailed as the Messiah, the emergence of such a community in his name must have seemed all but inevitable.[13] But the claim that the Gospels could have been written only once that institution came into being – is unpersuasive and anach-ronistic.

What is striking is that the scholarly consensus about the date of the Gospels should rest on such precarious historical and philological foundations. In the final chapter we shall discuss the cultural and philosophical context in which this modern consensus has emerged and prospered. What, meanwhile, can be said about the authorship of St Matthew's Gospel? Few laymen take seriously the idea that the disciple himself might have written or supervised the creation of the text named after him. But should the idea be dismissed with such assurance? In addressing the question of the Gospels' origins, Martin Hengel noticed a technique customary in the making of scrolls which ensured that an author's name was likely to be recorded early in the life of a text.[14] Literary scrolls had tags glued to them, strips made of parchment, papyrus or leather. The tag – in Greek, a *sillybos* or *sittybos* – was affixed to the handle or otherwise attached to the back of the scroll in such a way that it was clearly visible to the bookseller or reader.[15] It fulfilled the same purpose as the spine of a modern book. Instead of unrolling the beginning of a scroll to discover its author and title, readers simply read the *sittybos*.

Hengel points out that such a tag would also have been attached to a Gospel scroll. When there was only one such text, the *sittybos* might simply have read 'Gospel' or '*euangelion*' in Greek. Until a second text was produced, such an identification would have been sufficient for readers seeking this particular, precious scroll. But, as Hengel notes,

> At the latest when the communities had two different copies of the Gospels, titles had to be used to distinguish them, in order to avoid confusion. Where the author was well-known to the community, a verbal reference would have been enough, but as soon as his work was copied, sent to other communities and put in an archive there, a title was absolutely necessary to distinguish it from other works. We may assume that at least the larger communities got hold of the newly composed Gospels relatively quickly because of the lively interchange between the communities ... If, as is usually argued today, the earliest Gospels were anonymous or lacked titles, because of the pressing need to distinguish them in community libraries a variation of titles would have inevitably arisen, whereas in the case of the canonical Gospels (in contrast to that of the countless apocryphal writings) we can detect nothing of this.[16]

Let us, for the sake of argument, accept the conventional dating of the Gospels: St Mark was written *c*. AD 70, St Matthew and St Luke in the eighties and St John nearer AD 100. By the time the second Gospel text was written – at the very latest – the tags on the scrolls would have had to carry the names of their authors. Even in the eighties, so close to the lifetime of the apostles and when so many first-generation followers of Christ were still alive, it is hard to imagine that anyone filling in such a *sittybos* would have dared to suggest the names of Matthew, Mark and Luke if these individuals had not written, or been in some way directly associated with, the books. A false attribution of this kind would have been even less likely during the sixties. And as we shall see, the first two Gospels, St Mark and St Matthew, existed in both scroll and codex form by this decade.

Who was St Matthew? The oldest tradition identifies him as Levi-Matthew, called upon by Jesus while he was sitting at his customs post near Capernaum (Matthew 9:9; Mark 2:14; Luke 5:27–28). Much more than a mere tax collector, he was a *telones*, a word which in Greek could be used to refer to an official who was responsible for a customs station. Levi-Matthew was in charge of a major border point. At Capernaum, the work involved two forms of levies: the sea tax which fishermen paid in Roman times,[17] and the land border tax levied on goods travelling along the Via Maris. This key trade route between Damascus and the Mediterranean crossed the tetrarchy of Philip and touched the border with the Galilean territory of Herod Antipas close to Capernaum, where there was also a junction leading towards Tyre and Chorazin. Recent research has established that Levi-Matthew was an influential customs official, perhaps even the leaseholder or tenant of the station, in accordance with the administrative practices of the time.[18]

St Luke, more forthcoming about Levi-Matthew than Matthew himself would have been, emphasizes his status and wealth in a cameo describing the scene after his calling (5:29). 'Then Levi held a great banquet for Jesus at his house' (NIV) or 'Levi held a big reception in his house for Jesus' (REV). Such a man must have had professional qualifications and financial resources. He would have been fluent in Aramaic and Greek, and, according to some scholars, might have been able to write shorthand – a theme we shall return to.

St Matthew may well have painted a kind of self-portrait when he quoted Jesus in chapter 13:52 of his Gospel: 'Well then, every scribe who becomes a disciple of the kingdom of Heaven is like a householder who brings out from his storeroom new things as well as old.' The late C. D. F. Moule, a Cambridge New Testament scholar, suggested that this 'scribe' was not a 'teacher of the law', as many translations have it. Instead, the Greek word *grammateús* refers to the well-trained writer. As Moule comments,

The writer of the Gospel was himself a well-educated, literate scribe in this sense. But so must also have been the tax-collector who was called by Jesus to be a disciple. Is it not conceivable that the Lord really did say to that tax-collector Matthew: You have been a 'writer' (as the Navy would put it); you have had plenty to do with the commercial side of just the topics alluded to in the parables – farmer's stock, fields, treasure-trove, fishing revenues; now that you have become a disciple, you can bring all this out again – but with a difference.[19]

Because of his position, Levi-Matthew, like his fellow *telonai*, was despised and rejected by orthodox Jewish society. Jesus himself was attacked because he was mingling with such people: 'When the Pharisees saw this, they said to his disciples, "Why does your master eat with tax collectors and sinners?"' (Matthew 9:11). Yet Levi-Matthew was a Jew himself. The disciples Andrew (Peter's brother) and Philip were Jews with entirely Greek names. But Levi-Matthew's names both indicate old and honoured Jewish origins. As Levi, he was a member of the tribes of the Levites, who had control over the conduct of Temple worship in Jerusalem. Having chosen the disreputable but profitable profession of customs official, he remained proud enough of his origins to retain the name at the moment of his calling. Later, St Matthew's Gospel, like the others, gave preference to his second name, Matthew – a name no less exalted than his first, meaning 'Gift of God' in Hebrew.

What else can we say about him? We know the name of his father, Alphaeus (Mark 2:14), who has been identified by some scholars as the father of 'James the son of Alphaeus' (Mark 3:18). Matthew seems not to have belonged to the inner circle of the disciples – the two pairs of brothers, Peter, Andrew, John and James – and his life after the Resurrection is not recorded in the New Testament. His name is mentioned for the last time in Acts 1:13, when the core group of apostles, diminished by the suicide of Judas, meets in an upper room in Jerusalem.

Some forty years after the composition of Acts, the theologian and historian Papias returned to the subject of Matthew and is the earliest surviving authority to have attributed the Gospel to him – an attribution that was never seriously questioned in the early Church.[20] But even as a Gospel author, St Matthew would have remained a helper, 'a servant of the word', as St Luke so aptly puts it at the beginning of his own Gospel, where he discussed his predecessors and fellow authors without mentioning their names (Luke 1:2). In this sense, as a 'servant', Matthew was never the subject of a cult of personality, even when his text began to spread around the Roman Empire and to overshadow St Mark's earlier Gospel. No adulatory biography of him seems to have been written and our knowledge of his later life is therefore negligible. The second-century author, Heracleon (AD 145–80), claimed to know that the apostle was not martyred but died a natural death.[21] Beyond this vague memory, all is speculation.

Sketchy as this portrait is, it includes far more sound information than is known about many classical authors. A certain amount can be said about St Matthew with confidence. But this is not a book about the apostle or the Gospel which bears his name.[22] It is a study of a particular papyrus, its origins and implications. Our purpose in this chapter has been to show that there is no overriding philological, archaeological or historical reason to dispute the proposition that the fragments of the Jesus Papyrus date from before AD 70. Nor do any scholarly rules have to be rewritten to consider this thesis with an open mind.

There have been two sides to this debate in recent times. On the one hand, there is the academic consensus in favour of later dates. This school questions the authenticity of the Gospels in a variety of ways and – in one or two cases – even suggests that the gnostic writings of the second, third and fourth centuries are more reliable than the canonical Gospels (for this, see recent books by Crossan and Lüdemann). But there have also been glimpses of progress. In 1976 John A. T. Robinson's *Redating the New Testament* generated a furore. Who, after all, would have expected the arch-liberal author of *Honest to God* to propose dates before AD 70 for all New Testament writings? An intellectual bolt from the blue, the book provoked argument among many academics in Anglo-Saxon countries.

It did not turn the tide, however. German New Testament scholars all but ignored *Redating the New Testament* and not until 1986, ten years later, did Robinson's work appear in Germany when a Catholic and an Evangelical publishing house joined forces to have it translated and put into print. The fact that the book was produced by such religious publishers merely encouraged the scholarly community to ignore it. Robinson's sequel, the posthumously published *Priority of John* (1985), based on his Oxford Bampton Lectures, has yet to find a publisher in Germany and has hardly made a major impact upon academics elsewhere. Yet the book is a minor masterpiece, especially in its first two chapters which explore the methodological problems associated with its subject. One must look for other reasons than poor scholarship to explain why it has been so neglected.[23]

New Testament scholarship suffers when it distances itself from other textual disciplines, notably classical philology and papyrology. But there are grounds for optimism in the efforts of both younger and more established scholars to question orthodoxy, incorporate sound research from other fields and offer innovative analysis. Richard Bauckham at St Andrew's University, Rainer Riesner at Tübingen and Craig L. Blomberg at Denver are three protagonists of the younger generation. Martin Hengel at Tübingen, I. Howard Marshall at Aberdeen, E. Earle Ellis at Dallas, Harald Riesenfeld at Uppsala, Klaus Haacker at Wuppertal and Klaus Berger at Heidelberg are six who have been batting for longer. Berger's latest contribution to the discussion is still proving hard for many of his colleagues to accept: developing Robinson's work, Berger argued for a date of c. AD 66 for St John's Gospel and of AD 68/69 for Revelation. He did so not in a commentary or introduction, but in a detailed and densely-argued monograph which deals with the history of early Christian theology and with the methods needed for its correct analysis.[24]

Berger's book takes issue with an orthodoxy which has dominated New Testament studies of the twentieth century. It has been aptly mocked by other writers, two of whom it is worth quoting at length. In 1952 A. H. N. Green-Armytage distinguished memorably between common sense and the academic mind-set in his book *John Who Saw*:

> There is a world – I do not say a world in which all scholars live but one at any rate into which all of them sometimes stray, and which some of them seem permanently to inhabit – which is not the world in which I live. In my world, if *The Times* and the *Telegraph* both tell one story in somewhat different terms, nobody concludes that one of them must have copied the other, nor that the variations in the story have some esoteric significance. But in that world of which I am speaking this would be taken for granted. There, no story is ever derived from facts but always from somebody else's version of the same story.

He continued:

> In my world, almost every book, except some of those produced by Govern-

ment departments, is written by one author. In that world, almost every book is produced by a committee, and some of them by a whole series of committees. In my world, if I read that Mr Churchill, in 1935, said that Europe was heading for a disastrous war, I applaud his foresight. In that world no prophecy, however vaguely worded, is ever made except after the event. In my world, we say, 'The first world war took place in 1914–1918.' In that world they say, 'The world-war narrative took shape in the third decade of the twentieth century.' In my world, men and women live for a considerable time – seventy, eighty, even a hundred years – and they are equipped with a thing called memory. In that world (it would appear), they come into being, write a book, and forthwith perish, all in a flash, and it is noted of them with astonishment that they 'preserve traces of a primitive tradition' about things which happened well within their own adult lifetime.[25]

It is hard to improve on this witty deconstruction of a certain type of modern New Testament scholarship. Six years before, Dorothy L. Sayers, who was a distinguished literary historian as well as an author of detective novels, had also poked well-aimed fun at the methods of her colleagues. Addressing St John's Gospel in 1946, she turned to the 'notorious dispute' surrounding this book of the New Testament:

Into the details of that dispute I do not propose to go. I only want to point out that the arguments used are such as no critic would ever dream of applying to a modern book of memoirs written by one real person about another. The defects imputed to St John would be virtues in Mr Jones, and the value and authenticity of Mr Jones's contribution to literature would be proved by the same arguments that are used to undermine the authenticity of St John.

Suppose, for example, Mr Bernard Shaw were now to publish a volume of reminiscences about Mr William Archer: would anybody object that the account must be received with suspicion because most of Archer's other contemporaries were dead, or because the style of G. B. S. was very unlike that of a *Times* obituary notice, or because the book contained a great many intimate conversations not recorded in previous memoirs, and left out a number of facts that could easily be ascertained by reference to the *Dictionary of National Biography*? Or if Mr Shaw (being a less vigorous octogenarian than he happily is) had dictated part of his material to a respectable clergyman, who had himself added a special note to say that Shaw was the real author and that readers might rely on the accuracy of the memoirs since, after all, Shaw was a close friend of Archer's and ought to know – should we feel that these two worthy men were thereby revealed as self-confessed liars, and dismiss their joint work as a valueless fabrication? Probably not; but then Mr Shaw is a real person, and lives, not in the Bible, but in Westminster. The time has not come to doubt him. He is already a legend, but not yet a myth; two thousand years hence, perhaps –[26]

In this elegant satire, Sayers was sniping at the form critic Rudolf Bultmann and his efforts to 'demythologize' the New Testament. Her essay poking fun at the excesses of scepticism was an early response to the scholarly trend inspired by Bultmann, which, as we shall see, remains influential in unsuspected ways. It is a warning against a particular kind of preconception, prevalent in New Testament studies even today. In the same spirit, our purpose in this chapter has been to show that there is no compelling scholarly reason to reject early dates for the Gospel texts. Our aim in the next three chapters will be to explore the contribution which papyrology can make to this debate, the controversies it has already provoked and the manner in which the Jesus Papyrus was itself redated. The scholar engaging in such research is wise to recall the advice of St Paul's first letter to the Thessalonians (5:21) 'Test everything and hold on to what is good.'

3

The Jesus Papyrus in Context: the Science of Papyrology and Christianity at Qumran

Hunt:	Petition concerning repayment of loan
	Petition complaining of ... non-payment of loan.
Grenfell:	Letter on beer tax to the *taracheutai* 'mummifiers'.
Hunt:	But *taracheutai* might mean 'salt-fish suppliers'.
Grenfell:	It might! It might! It might! It might! It might!
God:	I do wish some *literature* would come to light.

Tony Harrison, *The Trackers of Oxyrhynchus* (1990)

They were utterly and completely dumbfounded, because they had not seen what the miracle of the loaves meant; their minds were closed.

Mark 6:52

O ne thing is certain about papyri: they smell pleasant when they burn. So, at least, we are told by an antique trader who in 1778 bought a papyrus roll of AD 191/192 from some Egyptian peasants and had to look on helplessly as they set fire to fifty further scrolls, clearly enjoying the fragrance of the smoke.[1] As Charles Huleatt knew well, the ancient manuscripts which are the subject of papyrology tend to have survived the depredations of time only by chance. The papyrologist is more often the beneficiary of fortune than of the forethought of our distant ancestors. Konstantin von Tischendorf, who discovered one of the two most valuable codices of the whole Greek Bible, the Codex Sinaiticus, at St Catherine's Monastery in Sinai in 1844, found the first 129 sheets of that codex in a room full of combustible rubbish.[2]

Even in the twentieth century, the methods used to preserve papyri have left much to be desired. Kando, the famous Bethlehem shoe salesman and antique dealer, stored some of the most important of the Dead Sea Scrolls under the floorboards of his shop until he was able to sell them – or, in the case of some of the scrolls, until they were requisitioned by the Israelis after the conquest of the Jordanian-occupied territories in 1967. Sometimes, moreover, accidents befall papyri in the key moments after discovery – as in the unfortunate experience of the Qumran scholar who found a scrap of papyrus, held it against the sunlight ('Could it be a fragment from Genesis?') and then watched it crumble into dust.

After discovery, the task of the papyrologist is to preserve, identify and publish ancient manuscripts. Papyrus itself is manufactured from the stem of an aquatic plant mainly cultivated in Upper Egypt.[3] Although the texts discussed in this book are indeed on papyrus fragments, the science of papyrology incorporates the study of ancient texts written on many other materials including parchment, vellum, leather, linen, slivers of wood, wax tablets and potsherds (*ostraca*). It is thus distinguished from epigraphy, the study of inscriptions on stone and marble.

The Greek translation of the Old Testament, the so-called Septuagint of the third century BC, refers to the papyrus plant three times, in Job 8:11 and 40:16 and Isaiah 19:6. 'Can papyrus grow where there is no marsh?' asks Job 8:11 (RSV) rhetorically, referring to the special conditions required for the cultivation of the plant. Centuries later, as we have seen, Pliny the Elder (AD 23–79) described the production of papyrus sheets, opening his treatise with a celebration of them as the basis of human civilization.[4] He was scarcely exaggerating: papyrus scrolls were the most important medium for the transmission and recording of information. From the oldest-known Egyptian papyrus manuscript (P. Berlin 11301, *c.* 2700 BC), to the oldest extant Hebrew papyrus found in a cave at the Wadi Murabba'at near the Dead Sea and dated to *c.* 750 BC (P. Murabba'at 17), to New Testament times and beyond, this fragile reed plant provided the material for documents of every kind.

The production of papyrus sheets and rolls took place in Egyptian workshops, most of them clustered near the delta marshes of the Nile. The finished product was exported all over the Mediterranean basin and further north, south and east. Because of this regional monopoly and because the vast majority of papyri have been found at ancient Egyptian sites like Fayyûm or Oxyrhynchus, there is sometimes a misconception about the geographic scope of papyrology. In one recent introduction to the field, papyrology was said to be confined to texts from Egypt. At some universities it is taught in the Department of Egyptology. But as we point out in the next chapter, papyrus fragments bearing poems, epics, plays, Gospel texts and letters could have come from virtually anywhere in the Empire. The discovery of such a text in Egypt does not imply that it was written there or that a copy could not be found elsewhere in the region. In addition, there are several sites outside Egypt where Hebrew, Greek and Latin texts on papyrus, leather and wood have come to light – from the Wadi Murabba'at, the Nahal Hever, Masada and Qumran on the Dead Sea to Petra in Jordan, Dura-Europos in Syria, the Avroman Mountains in Kurdistan, Pompeii and Herculaneum in Italy, and as far north as Vindolanda on the border of Roman Britain. Papyrology should be considered as a subdivision of Egyptology only when the texts in question are composed in one of the Egyptian languages or dialects.

The textual analysis of a papyrus like the Magdalen fragments perfectly illustrates the range of methods used by the papyrologist investigating ancient manuscripts. The first step is to decide what form of literary artefact the fragments were originally a part of. Because the Jesus Papyrus has text on both sides, it seems safe to assume that it was part of a codex (the precursor of the modern book) rather than a scroll. Yet, even in this context, it is important not to jump to conclusions. A *scroll* with writing on both sides is mentioned in Ezekiel 2:9–10: 'When I looked, there was a hand stretching out to me, holding a scroll. He unrolled it in front of me; it was written on, front and back; on it was written 'Lamentations, dirges and cries of grief.' There is a slightly more ambiguous example in Revelation 5:1: 'I saw that in the right hand of the One sitting on the throne there was a scroll that was written on back and front and was sealed with seven seals.' It is ambiguous because, at the probable time of Revelation's composition, Christian scribes had already introduced the codex with text on both sides of the sheet. Might the Greek word *biblion* in Revelation 5:1 mark a break with tradition and be the first reference to such a codex book, rather than to the old-fashioned scroll? The practical significance of such a suggestion can be understood by anyone who is familiar with the modern fax machine. Just as the codex was the precursor of today's hardback book, a fax roll closely resembles the ancient scroll, especially on those machines which do not cut the pages.

As we shall see in Chapter 5, the shift from scroll to codex was an important watershed, not only for the Magdalen Papyrus but for Christian manuscripts in general. It played a vital role in the development of the canon, the official collection of New Testament writings. When Christian communities and churches adopted the codex, this was a natural opportunity to decide which texts should be handed down to posterity. Inevitably, not every text was copied from one format to the other. If present-day publishers decided to produce only paperbacks, not all the existing hardbacks would be reprinted in the new, standardized format. Instead, texts would be selected and discarded. Even today, not every hardback transfers to the mass-market paperback format. In the same way, if a particular scroll in the first-century Mediterranean world was left uncopied, it would drop out of use once that scroll had fallen apart.

This is a critical point. There are still scholars who maintain that the first Christians never used the scroll and that they began keeping records in codex form. If some papyrologists are correct in assuming that the Christian codex was introduced before the year AD 70,[5] then even Revelation 5:1 could be said to refer to this particular literary format. But does this passage allude to the first or the second stage of the transmission of Christian documents?

Revelation was certainly written at a time when the traditional scroll was still very much part of practical experience, or, at the very least, a feature of living memory. The vivid imagery of Revelation 6:14 illustrates this: 'the sky disappeared like a scroll rolling up and all the mountains and islands were shaken from their places.' If they had not seen and used scrolls themselves, this verse would have been incomprehensible to the communities who were expected to read the book of Revelation. Indeed, the scroll was of paramount importance to early Christianity. Jesus himself read from a scroll of Isaiah in the synagogue of Nazareth (Luke 4:17). Likewise, a late-second- or early-third-century fresco in the Roman Domitilla Catacombs demonstrates the continuing awareness of the scroll and its importance. This painting portrays St Paul with two *capsae* (containers of scrolls), each filled with five scrolls. These vessels are probably intended to signify the equal value of the five scrolls of the Torah – the first five books of the Old Testament – and of the five historical writings of Christendom – the four Gospels and Acts.[6] In the same catacombs, we encounter a mural of St Petronilla, depicted with a *capsa* at her feet and an opened book, a codex, at her left shoulder. The relationship between these two frescoes is more important than might at first be apparent.

A long time after the transition from scroll to codex, the artists responsible for these frescoes – and those who commissioned them – knew exactly how to distinguish between the two forms of Christian literary transmission. St Paul, who was martyred in AD 64 or 67, is shown only with scrolls. St Petronilla, who according to tradition was martyred in AD 98, has both scroll and codex beside her: the artistic representation of a time when the new format had taken over, but the old, traditional scroll was still widely remembered and may even have continued in use here and there.

Leaving aside the controversial interpretation of Revelation 5:1, the turning-point is visible in the New Testament. One of the so-called pastoral Epistles, 2 Timothy, tells the story in 4:13: 'When you come, bring the cloak I left with Carpus in Troas, and the scrolls, and especially the parchment notebooks'. Most modern translations fudge the language, but the original Greek text is unambiguous. The two decisive words in the passage are *biblia* and *membranae*. *Biblia*, literally 'books', should here be understood as a reference to 'scrolls'. This, at any rate, is the common usage of the word prior to the introduction of the codex.[7] The scrolls in question may well refer to Old Testament books in Greek translation, or indeed to the first Christian scrolls preceding 2 Timothy. The second technical term, *membranae*, is more illuminating. It is, first of all, a Latin word, transcribed into Greek. There is academic consensus that the author of 2 Timothy is talking about parchment notebooks. Commenting on this passage, Colin Roberts noted that St Paul is in fact 'the only Greek writer of the first century AD to mention the parchment note-book'.[8] It was a relatively small step from notebook to book, from *membranae* to codex. Yet the theological and sociological implications of this step were momentous.

Christians had used the scroll not merely because it was a convenient literary form. As the St Paul mural in the Domitilla Catacombs shows, the scroll was also a statement of identity. The very first Christians were Jews, or of Jewish origin. Among the Gospel authors, St Luke may have been the only exception and even this is far from certain. Until missionary work among non-Jews became the normal practice, spreading the good news was more or less confined to the Jewish community. A fair number of the canonical New Testament texts, such as the Epistle

to the Hebrews, the Epistle of James and St Matthew's Gospel itself
illustrate these profound links with Jewish thought and tradition – to
the extent, indeed, that non-Jewish readers would have found it difficult
to follow them without help.

In such circumstances, the scroll was the natural means of communication. Any other literary format would have signalled a dis-
quieting break with well-established tradition. Even the Babylonian
Talmud, (a collection of texts of post-New Testament times) polemical
and aggressive wherever it mentions Christianity, confirms this. It refers
to the existence of Christian scrolls in Jewish possession and decrees
that they shall not be saved in case of fire, even though the name of
God is mentioned in them.[9] The Talmud is a useful source in this
context precisely because it is of comparatively late date and generally
anti-Christian. It is extremely improbable that its mention of early
Christian scrolls would have been fabricated.

Scrolls and Codices: Qumran Cave 7 and the Dead Sea Scrolls

What are the implications of this argument for the Magdalen Papyrus
of St Matthew's Gospel? The codex fragments appear to be very early
indeed, older than any others surviving from the New Testament. But
they cannot be from the original Gospel manuscript or a direct facsimile
of it since this must have been a scroll. This, of course, poses the
question: What happened to all these early Christian documents? The
earliest scrolls would seem to have been transcribed on to the new
codex form as soon as they became tattered or otherwise illegible. Thus,
the last surviving scroll exemplar of St Matthew's Gospel would quickly
have disintegrated and disappeared. But what if there was a place where
Christian texts were stored before the codex became the predominant
form? And how might such a store help us in our quest to redate the
Jesus Papyrus and the New Testament?

Thanks to the accident of history, such a place exists: Cave 7 at Qumran.
This site has aroused pugnacious interest among scholars ever since José
O'Callaghan, the renowned editor of the Palau-Ribès papyrus collection
(housed at the Seminari di papirologia, Sant Cugat des Vallès near

Barcelona) suggested in 1972 that some of the papyrus fragments found in the cave were New Testament texts.[10] Among the various Qumran locations, Cave 7 is unique. As in the other caves, its eighteen fragments are all pieces of scroll (excluding a nineteenth fragment of inverted writing preserved in the form of an imprint from a lost papyrus on hardened clay). But in Cave 7 the writings are exclusively in Greek, and exclusively on papyrus. Elsewhere in Qumran there are only six other Greek texts, all of which are in Cave 4, among hundreds of Hebrew and Aramaic scrolls. Only two of the Cave 4 examples are papyri, the other four being leather fragments.

We can be sure of the latest possible date by which the Christian texts in Cave 7 would have been deposited: AD 68.[11] This was the year in which the settlement, the Khirbet, of Qumran and the nearby areas of caves were overrun by the 10th Roman Legion 'Fretensis'. The cave appears, therefore, to provide firm physical evidence that Christian scrolls were indeed in circulation before the introduction of the codex.

Two criticisms have been levelled at this general approach to the dating of Cave 7. First, it has been argued that the inhabitants of Qumran, or other people, including Christians, might have returned there *after* AD 68. Second, it is argued that these documents were first deposited more than sixty years later, during the Bar Kokhba revolt (AD 132–5). This 'second stage' notion was advanced by the Austrian scholar Kurt Schubert, convinced that the papyrus 7Q5 from that cave is a fragment of St Mark's Gospel.[12] Yet all serious archaeological investigation has discounted the idea that – unlike the caves in other Dead Sea *wadis*, such as the Wadi Murabba'at and the Nahal Hever[13] – the Qumran caves were reinhabited after AD 68. Even more importantly, the very fact that these Christian scrolls *are* scrolls – a judgment accepted by Kurt Schubert – rules out the theory that the caves were reopened after AD 68 or that the texts were deposited later, *c.* AD 132–5. In the thirties of the second century, it would obviously have been Christian codices rather than scrolls that anyone might have deposited in Cave 7. A reopening after AD 68 can be ruled out for related reasons. Had Cave 7 been reoccupied, its scrolls would have been used once more and would, at some stage of wear and tear, have been exchanged for codex copies. Since the fragments are not from codices, they cannot have been deposited after AD 68.

Finally, the palaeographic evidence argues against later dates. Long before O'Callaghan had identified fragment 7Q5, it had been ascribed by Colin Roberts to the so-called *Zierstil* (decorated style), which peaked in popularity at the turn of the century. Regarding 7Q5 as a late example of the style, one might say (with Roberts) that it could be no later than AD 50. Allowing for the possibility that the style fell out of use more slowly, one might even be prepared to add a few years – which, as we shall see in Chapter 5, is a complex matter. In this case, the archaeological end-date of AD 68 limits the scope for palaeographical speculation.

The Papyrologist at Work: how to Identify a Papyrus

But are Schubert, O'Callaghan and many others right in their conclusion that there really are Christian scroll fragments among the finds in Cave 7 at Qumran? The controversy – a vital one to the debate which is the subject of this book – has been raging ever since 1972. There quickly emerged an apparent consensus that the scrolls are not Christian, with a consequent lull in interest during the late 1970s and early 1980s. In 1984, however, the debate was reopened by Carsten Thiede with a paper in the scholarly journal *Biblica*.[14] Many publications, in German, English, French, Dutch, Italian, and Spanish, joined the fray to express opposition or support.[15] New Testament scholars convinced that St Mark's Gospel could never have reached the Essene community of Qumran at so early a date were opposed by academics who were equally sure that this was not only possible, but quite plausible. Leading papyrologists argued in favour of the Markan identification of fragment 7Q5. Even one of the Jewish members of the editorial board of the Qumran scrolls, Shemaryahu Talmon (Jerusalem), has publicly argued that Cave 7 could have been Christian.[16] In 1994 the last word on this particular identification seemed to have been uttered by one of the great papyrologists of our time, Orsolina Montevecchi, Honorary President of the International Papyrologists' Association. She summarized the results of her analysis in a single, unequivocal sentence: 'I do not think that there can be any doubt about the identification of 7Q5.'[17]

None the less, some scholars still refuse to accept that the fragment is part of St Mark's Gospel – a crucial identification which is at the heart of the new debate on the dating of the Gospel. For the most part, it is

New Testament scholars rather than papyrologists who continue to deny that 7Q5 is the only extant papyrus scroll fragment of this Gospel, written shortly or even some time before AD 68. Graham Stanton of King's College, London, dedicates a whole chapter of his latest book to the fragment – and another to the Magdalen Papyrus – in a typical effort to exclude early papyrological evidence from Gospel studies.[18] The stakes in this technical controversy are in fact extremely high. Much else depends on open-minded and detailed analysis of this particular fragment; the debate about 7Q5 is intimately intertwined with the more recent row about the Jesus Papyrus. So who is right about Cave 7?

The first major task facing the papyrologist is to make sense of the text, to reconstruct a fragmentary snippet of material in such a way that the lines yield a satisfying, acceptable whole. José O'Callaghan almost accidentally identified the tiny fragment 7Q5 – which has twenty letters, ten of them fragmentary, on five lines – as Mark 6:52–3. Working on an annotated edition of Greek Old Testament manuscripts, he came across volume III of the official series of Dead Sea Scrolls editions[19] which included the finds from Cave 7. The editors had managed to identify two of the fragments: 7Q1 as Exodus 28:4–6 and 7Q2 as Baruch 'Letter of Jeremiah' 6:43–4. Hence O'Callaghan's interest in this cave. None of the other sixteen fragments, nor the reversed imprint on clay, had been identified by the original editors. But the fifth fragment, 7Q5, offered a rare and intriguing combination of letters in line 4: *nu/nu/eta/sigma*. To the first editors, this combination had suggested the possibility of the Greek word *egennesen* and thus, possibly, a genealogical text. The difficulty with this suggestion was that such a text, reconcilable with all the other letters preserved on 7Q5, does not survive in Greek literature, biblical or non-biblical. O'Callaghan, however, thought of other Greek words with the *nu/nu/eta/sigma* sequence and, having excluded words which did not fit the context, tried the Greek name of the Galilean lake, *Gennesaret*. It was an inspired intuition.

His problems had only just begun, however. Astonishingly, there is only one passage in the whole Greek Old Testament, the Septuagint, where the name of the lake is written in such a way that the combination *nu/nu/eta/sigma* occurs: the deuterocanonical book of 1 Maccabees

11:67, in which it appears as 'Gennesar'. Elsewhere, the lake is called 'Chenereth' or 'Chenara'. However none of the other legible letters in fragment 7Q5 would fit 1 Maccabees 11:67. As part of his papyrological investigation O'Callaghan was also obliged to trawl through the New Testament in search of an alternative reading. And there, in Mark 6:52–3, was the word 'Gennesaret' in a passage which appeared to match everything else on the fragment: 'They were utterly and completely dumbfounded, because they had not seen what the miracle of the loaves meant; their minds were closed. Having made the crossing, they came to land at Gennesaret and moored there.' Herbert Hunger, the Austrian papyrus scholar, later alluded to the irony of these verses which seem to anticipate the twentieth-century reaction to O'Callaghan's discovery: 'their minds were closed'.[20]

The editors of the modern English translation quoted above, the New Jerusalem Bible, grasping that one story ends with verse 52 and another begins with verse 53, left a blank line between the two sections and added a title link: 'Cures at Gennesaret'. Ancient scribes had no such devices at their disposal. Instead they projected one letter into the left margin, as in the Magdalen Papyrus; or two, as in the Paris Papyrus, of St Luke, P4, also from Luxor; or they left a gap between the two relevant verses, a so-called *spatium*. In such cases, there would also have been a horizontal line underneath the beginning of the line, a *paragraphus*. Needless to say, this can only be detected where the beginning of the line has survived intact; in the case of 7Q5, it has not. But with or without *paragraphus*, the *spatium* indicates the beginning of a new sequence, a new paragraph. In other words, the gap in line 5 fulfils the narrative purpose of the blank line and the subtitle in the Jerusalem Bible.

Considered together with the occurrence of *Gennesaret*, this *spatium* fits St Mark 5:52–3 like a glove – all the more so as the first word after the gap, the clearly legible Greek word *kai* ('and'), is indeed the first word of St Mark 5:53. It is also worth noting that sentences beginning with 'and', so-called 'paratactical *kais*', are a typical Markan structure. Finally, the one letter just legible before the gap, although half destroyed by a tear in the papyrus, is an *eta* – a fact accepted even by O'Callaghan's detractors. And St Mark 6:52 ends with an *eta* – the last letter of the perfect passive *peporomene*: '(their hearts) were hardened' or, in the English of the New Jerusalem Bible, '(their minds) were closed'.[20]

Observation and Deduction: a Papyrus and its Context

Three significant problems remain, however. The first is related to textual reconstruction. The rebuilding of complete lines depends upon 'stichometry', which involves calculating the average number of letters per line. Every scribe and manuscript is characterized by such a 'measure' and variations are only permitted within a certain range of letters. The Jesus Papyrus, with its three fragments and text on both sides, has a total of twenty-four lines. They offer a beautifully regular number of letters per line:

Fragment 1, verso: 16 / 16 / 16 / 15
Fragment 2, verso: 16 / 16 / 15
Fragment 3, verso: 16 / 17 / 17 / 18 / 17
Fragment 3, recto: 15 / 15 / 17 / 15 / 16
Fragment 1, recto: 15 / 17 / 15 / 17
Fragment 2, recto: 16 / 16 / 15

The exact average is sixteen letters per line, with a maximum of eighteen and a minimum of fifteen. On the basis of such an average measure, it has been possible, as we shall see in the following chapter, to improve the first edition of the Jesus Papyrus. Thus, the grammatically superfluous word *humeis*, which exists in all other Greek manuscripts of Matthew 26:31, cannot have been included in this version of the text. With it, line 1 of Fragment 1, recto, would have twenty letters; without it, fifteen.

Stichometry is a vital tool in textual reconstruction. Only if the end of one fragmentary line and the beginning of the next fragmentary line 'match', and are reconcilable with the visible text in the middle, can we achieve an acceptable result (in the case of 7Q5, both ends are missing). The comparative yardstick for New Testament writing is one of the standard editions of the Greek text, with all its manifold variants. But what happens when the text of a given line does not conform to the established stichometry, or to any other known New Testament manuscript? In the case of the Magdalen Papyrus, it is easy to accept the stichometrical exclusion of *humeis*, since the identification of the three papyrus fragments as verses from Matthew, chapter 26, is undisputed.

In the case of 7Q5, however, it is the very identification which is at stake; any deviation from the standard text of the passage in question would have to be closely scrutinized. The stichometry of 7Q5 is as regular as that of the Magdalen Papyrus: 20 / 23 / 22 (including the *spatium* of the length of two letters) / 21 / 21: an average just above twenty-one, with twenty and twenty-three as the extremes. If this measure is applied to the visible letters on the fragment, there is no room for the three Greek words in Mark 6:53, *epi ten gen* ('on to the land'). They would have belonged either to line 3 or to line 4. With them, line 3 would have had thirty-one letters, or line 4 thirty. So could there have been a version of Mark 6:53 without these three words?

To answer this question, we must remember that the papyrus scroll fragments from Cave 7 must be older than AD 68. The fact that the words *epi ten gen* appear in the standard text editions of the Gospel – a version based on second-, third- and fourth-century manuscripts – is a consequence of the Jewish revolt against the Romans which resulted in the destruction of Qumran in AD 68, of Jerusalem with its Temple in AD 70, of Masada in AD 73/74 and of many other parts of the country during that period. One of the places razed by the Romans was the town of Gennesaret or Kinneret, only recently rediscovered and excavated by archaeologists in the very region identified by St Mark. This particular phrasing – *epi ten gen* ... *eis Gennesaret*: 'to the land of Gennesaret' – became necessary after the destruction of the inhabited area which had had the same name as the lake, so as to avoid confusion. Before the event, these three words would have been pure pleonasm, all the more so as Gennesaret was a place within daily range of people living at Capernaum, where Jesus and his disciples had lived and worked for some time. One can therefore turn the tables: in a papyrus written before AD 70 we might *expect* these three words to be missing. The fact that they are indeed absent from 7Q5 conforms to our knowledge of topographical history as it applies to Mark 6:53.

There is also a philological basis for this conclusion. The later addition of *epi ten gen* yielded a very awkward Greek, a 'tormented text' as one commentator described it, suggesting a makeshift change to an existing structure. The parallel passage in St Matthew's Gospel betrays this uncertainty, as do early translations like the second-/third-century Bohairic and the fifth-century Latin Vulgate. In brief, classical philologists acknowledge that the text without *epi ten gen* is not only shorter, but a better version. The stichometry of Mark 6:53, in other words, does not undermine the identification of 7Q5 with this Gospel, but actually strengthens it.[21]

The second problem facing the papyrologist is different but equally important. It concerns the first letter of the word after the *kai*, the 'and', in line 3. In Mark 6:53, this word is *diaperasantes*: '(they,) having made the crossing'. As anyone can see, it begins with the Greek letter *d-*. But it is equally obvious that on papyrus 7Q5 the first letter after the *kai* is not a *delta* but a *tau* or *t*. Several opponents of the Markan identification have concentrated on this variant. Is this a simple misspelling, or are there more systematic reasons for this apparent change? On such a small fragment, with text on a space slightly larger than a postage stamp (3.3 × 2.3 cm), every clearly legible letter counts. One cannot blithely explain away such a variation as a simple spelling error.

It is worth noting here that a genuine spelling mistake *does* occur in the Magdalen Papyrus. On the recto or back side of Fragment 2 (Matthew 26:32–3), the Greek word *galilaian* (Galilee) is spelt *galeglaian*. Here the scribe had been thinking in terms of so-called *itacism*, a spelling variant based on the identical pronunciation of different letters or combinations of letters: because, for example, *-ei-* was pronounced in the same way as *-i-*, it was quite possible and legitimate to write *-ei-* instead of *-i-*. However, instead of writing *-i-* after the *-e-* the scribe wrote *-g-*, ending up with *galeglaian* instead of the acceptable *galeilaian*. For reasons unknown, he added the horizontal bar that turns an *iota* into a *gamma*. This small error has little impact upon our overall approach to the Jesus Papyrus, the textual provenance of which is clear. But what about the apparently more significant shift from *-d-* to *-t-* in the Qumran papyrus 7Q5.

The first clue comes from Jerusalem, the home of the earliest Christian community. When Herod the Great rebuilt the Temple, he had an inscription placed on the second wall, prohibiting entry to non-Jewish strangers on pain of death. The inscription is mentioned by the first-century Jewish historian Flavius Josephus (*Jewish Antiquities*, 15, 417) and it is the background to an incident in the Acts of the Apostles, 20:27–36, where St Paul is threatened with execution after being seen entering the holy precincts of the Temple in the company of the non-Jew Trophimus. The text of the barrier stone is indeed unequivocal in its warning: 'No foreigner is to enter within the balustrade and embankment around the sanctuary. Whoever is caught will have himself to blame for his death which follows.' Two verbatim copies of this stone have been found by archaeologists, a complete one, which is now in Istanbul, and a fragment, now at the John Rockefeller Museum in Jerusalem. The spelling is striking: in line 1, the Greek word *medena* ('nobody') is spelt *methena*, and in line 3, the word *dryphakton* ('barrier stone') is written *tryphakton*. Quite obviously, the scribes disliked the soft -*d*-. In both cases, if for different reasons, they turned it into a hard -*t*- or -*th*-.

For our purposes, the change at the beginning of the word *tryphakton* is the more revealing as it corresponds to the initial change at the beginning of *d/tiaperasantes*. It cannot have been an accidental spelling mistake, given that in ancient Greek *delta* and *tau* (or *delta* and *theta*) look as dissimilar as *d* and *t* do in English. As the first editor of the complete barrier stone, Charles Clermont-Ganneau, had already noticed in 1872, the variants faithfully reflect a characteristic way of pronouncing the -*d*- in Greek-speaking, Second-Temple Jerusalem. Whatever we may think about the author of St Mark – and many think he was the Jerusalemite John Mark, writing in Rome with the authority of St Peter whose oral teaching material he used – the 'Jerusalem experience' and Jerusalem sources are undoubtedly the foundations of this Gospel. Thus the *d/t* shift in a papyrus of St Mark's Gospel – dated before AD 68 and therefore before the disappearance of the stone in AD 70 – is a compelling example of a regional spelling variation which would have been familiar, and visible, to all in the city as long as it stood.

Predictably, the discovery of this challenging inscription prompted intense debate. In 1905 the German epigrapher Wilhelm Dittenberger pointed out that even the Greek grammarian Herodianus Technicus, writing in Rome much later, towards the end of the second century, knew of this change and tried to explain it etymologically rather than phonetically. Dittenberger argued – against the explicit evidence of the contemporary historian Josephus – that the stone was not Jewish at all but erected by the Romans. Yet even if the stone had been put up by non-Jews, the masons might still have been local. In 1989 the Israeli scholar Peretz Segal settled the matter by establishing the local origins of the inscription.[22] Dittenberger may not have liked the linguistic implications of the inscription, but writing almost seventy years before O'Callaghan's identification of 7Q5 he had no theological axe to grind. More remarkable is the extent to which some academics still go to deny the significance of the inscription – nowadays, of course, in the context of the Cave 7 controversy. One German patristic scholar not only resuscitated Dittenberger's theory but made much of the fact that the discovery of the stone was 'accidental'.[23] Yet most such archaeological and papyrological discoveries are 'accidental' by definition. It is less easy in practice to dismiss unpalatable evidence on the grounds that it has come to light fortuitously.

As with the question of *epi ten gen*, the solution to the *d/t* problem hinges on more than archaeology and history. As far as papyrus evidence is concerned, there are no fewer than twenty biblical manuscripts which have such a shift of consonants. One of them is the P4 at the Bibliothèque Nationale in Paris, a codex papyrus of St Luke's Gospel which will concern us again in Chapter 5. Moreover, a text dated to AD 42 exists with *tikes* instead of *dikes*; that is, with the change of *d-* to *t-*, preceding the same vowel as in 7Q5, *-i-*.[24] In summary, it was perfectly possible to switch from *d-* to *t-* before AD 70, either by accident or because of regional custom. The inscription from the Temple shows us that the peculiar spelling of 7Q5 in Mark 6:53 is not surprising at all. Once again, this eccentricity helps to confirm the identification and very early date of the papyrus.

As far as 7Q5 is concerned, a third problem remains, one which introduces us to yet another technique of papyrology. So puzzling is it that the great papyrologist Herbert Hunger needed twenty-three pages and twenty-two illustrations to achieve the first step towards its solution.[25] In line 2 of 7Q5, the reconstructed text of Mark 6:52 reads: *all'en autōn he kardia pepero(mene)*: 'their hearts were hard(ened)'. The last letter of the Greek word *autōn*, 'their', is obviously a *nu*. But some have insisted on a different reading in the papyrus. The preceding letter, an *omega*, is clear enough. But the *nu* is said not to be a *nu* at all but a *iota*. If this is so, then the word cannot be *autōn*. It therefore follows that the passage cannot be Mark 6:52.

By coincidence, an almost identical problem occurs in the Jesus Papyrus. In 1953 Colin Roberts, the first editor of the Magdalen fragments, had read *autō* in Fragment 3, recto, line 1. Early in 1995, Thiede corrected this to read *autōn*, with far-reaching consequences for the reconstructed text, as we shall see in the following chapter. In 7Q5, the letter in question is severely damaged. There is a left vertical stroke which could be either a *iota* on its own, or the left stroke of a *nu*. To the right of this stroke, no ink is visible for a few millimetres, until a curvature appears which moves upwards into what appears to be the beginning of another fragmentary vertical stroke; then the stroke moves down again in another curve towards the lower right. What could this be? Remnants of an *alpha*, as some have suggested? The one *alpha* which does exist, in line 3, does not support this theory. Did the traces to left and right originally belong together when the papyrus was undamaged? Could they have been the lines of a *nu*? Sceptics would deny this on the grounds that the remnants of ink are simply too far apart.

Drawing on numerous examples from contemporary, earlier and later papyri, Herbert Hunger demonstrated conclusively in his afore-mentioned essay that the remaining traces of ink could be reconstructed to form a perfect *nu*, curvatures and all. He and Thiede even measured the length of comparable letters within fragment 7Q5, with a remark-able result. There are two complete *etas* in this fragment, in lines 4 and 5. Measuring their extremities in width – which is what matters in our comparative case – one notes a difference from 3.0 mm (*eta* in line 4) to 3.5 mm (*eta* line 5). The complete and undisputed *nu* in line 4 of fragment 7Q5 also measures 3.0 mm. The width of the letter in line 2, if reconstructed as a *nu*, is 3.5 mm. In other words, the allegedly impossible distance between the left vertical stroke and the strange remnants on the right are entirely consistent with a *nu*. They conform well with the small flexibility which the scribe permitted himself in drawing his *etas*. It is important not to forget that the margin of error in question is only half a millimetre.

Yet scribes may be flexible in a way that some contemporary sceptics are not. To settle the matter once and for all, in April 1992 Carsten Thiede took the 7Q5 papyrus to the Investigations Department (Division of Identification and Forensic Science) at the Israel National Police in Jerusalem, for analysis under their electronic stereo micro-scope. Here, for the first time, the remains of a diagonal line became visible, beginning at the upper end of the left vertical stroke (which some thought was an *iota*) and moving downwards to the bottom right. The line was not complete; the traces broke off after a few millimetres, but it was long enough and straight enough to be conclusive: it must be the diagonal middle line of a *nu*. O'Callaghan, Hunger and others had been vindicated: the letter is a *nu* and the word is *autōn*, as required by Mark 6:52.[26]

In an astonishing attempt to turn the visual evidence on its head, Graham Stanton's recent book *Gospel Truth?* includes a plate with a diagram, attributed to Geoffrey Jenkins, in which the undisputed *nu* from line 4 of 7Q5 has been superimposed on the damaged letter in line 2. Ignoring the difference in letter-width in this papyrus, established by Hunger and Thiede, Stanton claims that the minute discrepancy actually visible on his diagram 'shows that the letter cannot be a *nu*, thus undermining the theory that 7Q5 is part of St Mark's Gospel'. It is remarkable that a scholar of Professor Stanton's repute would treat the evidence in such a manner in order to revive a discredited claim. The incomplete drawing of the underlying letter fragment from line 2 is the first distortion; the second is the omission of the diagonal line established by the Jerusalem analysis; the third is the conclusion which contradicts even this misleading diagram: the fragment can of course be reconstructed into a *nu*, as Hunger has shown. Regrettably, his paper is neither quoted nor mentioned by Stanton.[27]

Errors and their Detection

The case of fragment 7Q5 demonstrates what can be achieved by papyrology. It also shows that there are virtually no limits to the scholarly acrobatics which some academics will perform to dismiss a thesis that does not fit their intellectual paradigm. Kurt Aland, the late grandmaster of New Testament criticism, employed the computer at his institute in Münster, Germany, to show that 7Q5 cannot be a fragment of St Mark. His case persuaded many, until another German scholar, the New Testament historian and epistemologist Ferdinand Rohrhirsch, demonstrated that Aland had committed several methodological errors and had programmed his computer in such a way that a result other than Mark 6:52–3 was inevitable.[28]

Others continue to offer alternative identifications.[29] Others still refer pointedly to the minuteness of 7Q5, as though a small fragment could not be safely identified. Certainly it is a tiny scrap – twenty letters on five lines, as we have seen, and ten of them damaged. But that does not rule out confident identification. Smaller fragments have been so analysed without the result provoking comparable objections. In the same Qumran cave, fragment 7Q2 has only one more letter – twenty-

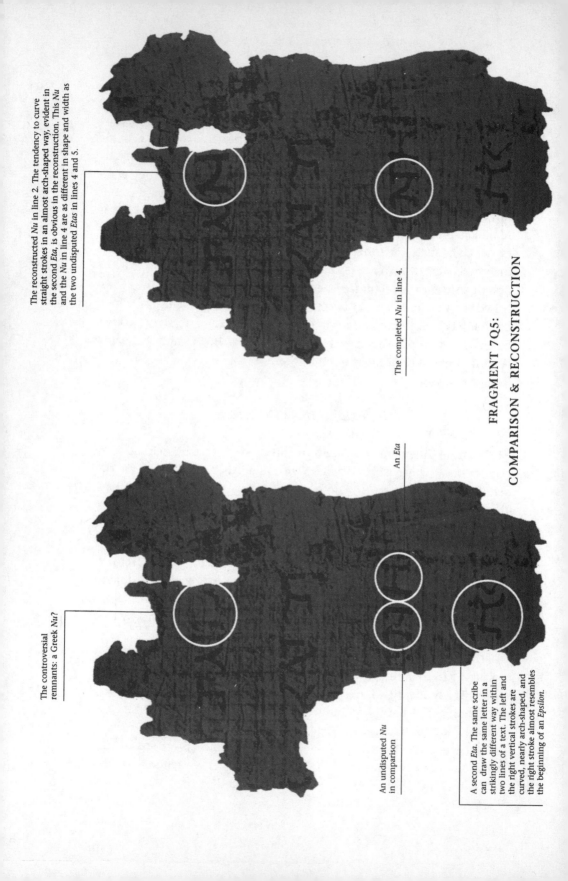

The reconstructed *Nu* in line 2. The tendency to curve straight strokes in an almost arch-shaped way, evident in the second *Eta*, is obvious in the reconstruction. This *Nu* and the *Nu* in line 4 are as different in shape and width as the two undisputed *Etas* in lines 4 and 5.

The completed *Nu* in line 4.

The controversial remnants: a Greek *Nu*?

An undisputed *Nu* in comparison

An *Eta*

A second *Eta*. The same scribe can draw the same letter in a strikingly different way within two lines of a text. The left and the right vertical strokes are curved, nearly arch-shaped, and the right stroke almost resembles the beginning of an *Epsilon*.

FRAGMENT 7Q5:
COMPARISON & RECONSTRUCTION

one on five lines. Yet its identification as Baruch (Letter of Jeremiah) 6:43–4 has never been disputed, in spite of the fact that its textual variants and deviations compared to the standard text of the Greek Old Testament are much more complex and far-reaching than are those of 7Q5 compared to the standard text of the New Testament.[30]

An equally striking parallel is the Oxyrhynchus papyrus XXXVIII 2831. This was identified as a passage from Menander's comedy *Samia*, 385–390, even though it measures only 2.4 x 3.3 cm, includes a mere nineteen letters on five lines, and is far from identical to the previously agreed text of the play. It offers, indeed, 'some additional variants'.[31] Instead of doubting its identification and rejecting its inclusion in official lists, classical philologists accepted the new papyrus, integrated it in new standard editions of the play and supplied it with its own inventory number, O 16.[32]

A third and final example, closer to Qumran, is the Masada fragment 721a, the oldest known papyrus of Virgil which was discovered on the fortress overlooking the Dead Sea and edited in 1989.[33] Dated to AD 73/74, it has only fifteen visible letters on a single line, two of which are damaged to the point of illegibility. Despite the meagre extent of the data, and the fact that it was found at Masada of all places, this fragment has been identified as Virgil's *Aeneid*, 4, 9, without controversy or quibble. Papyrus 7Q5 is Mark 6:52–3 as surely as P. Oxy. XXXVIII 2831 is from Menander's *Samia* and P. Masada 721a is from Virgil's *Aeneid* – if not more so.

The Virgil papyrus from Masada also puts paid to one of the favourite ploys of those who believe that small scroll fragments cannot be safely identified. Kurt Aland and his followers have argued that the text on the back, the verso, facilitates textual identification, and that such a verso text is necessary for confident analysis of small fragments.[34] This argument has been used as part of the case against the Markan identification of 7Q5, which has no text on the verso. Yet the Virgil papyrus shows that this is a misleading test to apply. There is indeed text on the other side of this fragment. It bears a single line, again with fifteen letters, including one complete, rare word, *titubantia* ('swaying' or 'stammering'). But this line does not belong to any known work of Virgil's, nor indeed to any extant work of Latin literature. This side of the fragment has no bearing whatsoever on the identification of the front, the recto, with *Aeneid*, 4, 9. It could not possibly do so. In short, insisting on a verso text is a pointless standard to apply.

In conclusion, it is necessary to emphasize the obvious. A papyrus fragment is exactly that – a fragment. This means that words and letters on the edges – on all four or only on some of them – are incomplete. Unlike damaged, partly illegible letters in the middle of a fragment (such as the *nu* in line 2 of 7Q5), such marks may not always be completely reconstructible. In many instances, however, the surviving material is sufficient for a safe assignment. This is the case in line 3 of 7Q5 where the half-visible letter before the gap, the *spatium*, must be an *eta*, because what is left does not allow for any other letter in the Greek alphabet. In the Magdalen Papyrus, likewise, the first five letters of the half-broken-off fourth line of Fragment 1, recto, must read *taute* (with a final *eta*), because nothing else would sensibly match what remains visible. Any reconstruction of damaged letters has to make sense; this point is as vital as it is obvious. Thus, one might conceivably imagine a *delta* or *lambda* rather than an *alpha* after the initial *tau*, and a *chi* instead of an *upsilon* after that, since the upper parts of these letters look identical. But what would we make of *tdchte* or *tlchte* rather than *taute*? Such words do not exist and would not make sense in the context of this fragment.

The same basic rule of papyrology applies to 7Q5. All that remains visible in line 1, for example, is the bottom curvature of a letter that could be an *epsilon*, an *omicron*, an *omega*, a *theta*, or a *sigma*. In the context of Mark 6:52–3, it must be an *epsilon*. It is perfectly reasonable to assume as much, and to write it with a dot underneath, signifying its reconstruction from incomplete remains. The basic rule has been observed: a letter must be reconstructed only in such a way that it makes sense within a plausible context. There is not a single letter in fragment 7Q5 which cannot be reconciled with one in the Markan passage: a remarkable degree of compatibility which no comparable attempt at identifying the fragment has achieved. In brief, the point of this painstaking analysis has been to confirm an already plausible thesis and to defend it against scholarly attack.[35]

We have come full circle in this chapter and, in the process, seen something of the papyrologist at work. There is indeed a papyrus scroll fragment of a Gospel in existence – 7Q5 from Qumran Cave 7 – which bears the text of Mark 6:52–3. It must be dated before AD 68 and could be as early as AD 50.[36] It is not from one of the early collections of Jesus's sayings, which may have preceded the complete Gospels. The Cave 7 fragment does not quote Jesus at all, in contrast to the Magdalen Papyrus which quotes him no fewer than four times. Nor is it a passage from a Passion story, versions of which, according to some scholars, circulated before the first Gospel was finished. It is a text with two connected narrative passages from the Galilean ministry of Jesus, which belongs to the final redaction of the full Gospel according to St Mark – albeit to its first, pre-AD 70 textual version. All this is crucial background to our exploration of the Jesus Papyrus, which must not be considered in isolation. The case of 7Q5 and its scholarly history tell us much about the context of the Oxford and Barcelona codex fragments, to which we turn next.

4

The Earliest Christian Book:
the Magdalen Papyrus Examined

Despite attempts by archivists to get him to use microfilms or facsimiles of documents in his research, Horatio always insisted on working with the originals. Anything else, he used to tell archivists, was like being asked to make do with photocopies of one's love letters.

Andrew Roberts, *The Aachen Memorandum* (1995)

What can we know of the religious and cultural milieu which produced the Christian codex, of which the Magdalen Papyrus is our earliest example? It made sense for the first Christians to use the scroll initially, since it was the standard Jewish format for literary works and for everyday communication. Any break with this practice would have generated unnecessary suspicion and undermined the claim of the Jewish-Christian evangelists that faith in Jesus as the Messiah was the logical fulfilment of prophecies shared by all Jews and now realized in the form of a Jew from Nazareth.

As early as AD 62, however, the ultimately unbridgeable rift between Jewish Christians and other strands of first-century Judaism was emerging. In that year, the leader of the Christian community of Jerusalem was executed by a group of Jews, acting on the orders of the High Priest Ananus. This Christian leader was none other than James, 'the Lord's brother' as he is called by St Paul (Galatians 1:19). James was known and revered as a devout Jew who continued to pray on his knees in the Temple every day so fervently that he earned the nickname 'camel knees'.[1] His execution was an illegal act. Since it took place in AD 62, outside the historical scope of the New Testament, it is not mentioned there. But we have a reliable report from the Jewish historian Flavius Josephus, in his *Jewish Antiquities*, *20*, 197–203:

The younger Ananus, who, as we have said, had been appointed to the high priesthood, was rash in his temper and unusually daring. He followed the school of the Sadducees, who are indeed more heartless than any of the other Jews, as I have already explained, when they sit in judgment. Possessed of such a character, Ananus thought that he had a favourable opportunity because Festus [the Roman procurator] was dead and Albinus [his successor] was still on the way. And so he convened the judges of the Sanhedrin and brought before them a man named James, the brother of Jesus who was called the Christ, and certain others. He accused them of having transgressed the law and delivered them up to be stoned. Those of the inhabitants of the city who were considered the most fair-minded and who were strict in observance of the law were offended at this. They therefore secretly sent to King Agrippa urging him, for this was not the first time that Ananus had acted unjustly, to order him to desist from any further such actions. Certain of them even went to meet Albinus, who was on his way from Alexandria, and informed him that Ananus had no authority to convene the Sanhedrin without his consent. Convinced by these words, Albinus angrily wrote to Ananus threatening to take vengeance upon him. King Agrippa, because of Ananus' action, deposed him from the high priesthood which he had held for three months, and replaced him with Jesus the son of Damnaeus.

For Jerusalem's Jewish community as well as for Christians, this was a dramatic sequence of events. After all, the stoning of James 'and certain others' by the Jewish court, the Sanhedrin, was a bitter signal to those Christians struggling to conduct a dialogue among Jews. Though many other Jews had taken action against Ananus and the Sanhedrin, the execution was a clear warning to end the evangelizing. By then, the mission among the Gentiles had already taken off, originally launched by St Peter, whose baptism of the Roman centurion Cornelius and his household is described in Acts 10, and vigorously continued by St Paul. The events of AD 62 would have been seen as a turning-point by those missionaries looking beyond Jewry to a wider world.

Two years later, a second catastrophe occurred, this time in Rome. On the night of 18/19 July AD 64, Rome went up in flames and ten of its fourteen boroughs were destroyed. As rumours spread that Nero himself had started the conflagration, and as they persisted in spite of his generous rebuilding programme, it became necessary to find a plausible scapegoat. For this unenviable role, the Emperor chose the city's Christian community.[2] Some Roman followers of Jesus may already have attracted the adverse attention of the authorities, not least those apocalyptics who might have been foolish enough to welcome the city's ill fortune. The burning of the decadent capital of the empire, the 'Whore of Babylon', could easily be said to be the prophesied beginning of the final cosmic clash. It seems also that there were divisions among Roman Christians over questions of attitude and interpretation. Christians denounced and betrayed other Christians when the persecution started – probably in the spring of AD 65, the climate being right by then for the cruel outdoor evening spectacles so bluntly described by the Roman historian Tacitus (AD 55–c. 120) and others. He tells us of disagreements among the followers of Jesus, as does the first-century Christian author Clement of Rome who writes that divisions and jealousy were the reasons for the capture and execution of St Peter and St Paul in the course of the persecution (1 Clement, 5:1–5). The purge seems to have lasted until Nero's death in AD 68.

All our sources suggest that Christians and Jewish Christians were by now clearly distinguished from the Jews. In the early years, Jewish Christians and Jews were often confused by outsiders. This was of benefit to Jesus's followers, who would have profited from the privileges enjoyed once more by the 50,000 Jews in Rome now that Claudius's expulsion of Jewish and Christian leaders between AD 49 and AD 54 was safely in the past.[3] But with Nero's persecution the boundaries between the two groups were no longer blurred. The authorities sought out and punished the Christians and only the Christians; Jews were not affected. A wall between the two communities was erected in the largest city of the empire and the dialogue was not resumed.

Six years later in AD 70, after nearly five years of military conflict and siege, Jerusalem fell to the Romans, the city and Temple were destroyed, and the Jews were expelled. With the destruction of the Temple, the last natural place of contact between Jews and Jewish Christians disappeared. While the Jews had to remain outside Jerusalem, the city's Christians who had not participated in the revolt against the Romans were soon allowed to return, settling once more on the south-western hill, today's Mount Zion. There, they built their first church, which is still visible in the room mistakenly called the 'Tomb of David' (David's tomb was actually in the east, on Mount Ofel). Still standing there are clear traces of a synagogal building, among them a niche for the Torah scrolls. Yet this was not a synagogue. Though the builders were evidently preserving some of the architectural traditions they had inherited, they introduced a subtle but important change. The niche is not directed towards the site of the Temple, as it should have been, but towards Golgotha and the Empty Tomb.[4] It is not quite large enough for more than the Torah scrolls and could hardly have been used to store Christian scrolls as well.

Since the Torah was still the common scriptural foundation for all Jewish Christians, this was logical enough until the five historical Christian writings came to be seen as having equal authority (a shift for which, as we have seen, the mural in Rome's Domitilla Catacombs is visual evidence). Initially, then, Christian scrolls appear to have been stored elsewhere – although it is quite conceivable that the niche was later used to house an ordinary bookcase for codices, which could have held both Old and New Testament writings. Whatever practices were adopted on Mount Zion, we can be sure that this was a period of transition and fragmentation. Forced to remain outside Jerusalem, the Jewish leadership settled in a place to the west of the city called Jamnia, some six kilometres from the Mediterranean. Otherwise known as Jabneh or Jabneel, the town still awaits excavation.

According to a story told in the Talmud, the emperor Vespasian permitted Johanaan ben Zakkai to establish an Academy or Yeshiva at Jamnia: after the destruction of Jerusalem by his son Titus in AD 70, the Sanhedrin was expelled along with the Jewish inhabitants and later moved to Jamnia. This soon became a centre of spiritual activities and reforms, and also dealt with the Christian question. After the events of AD 62, 64/65 and 70, what should be the official attitude towards the spreading denomination which claimed to embody the new, true Covenant? In AD 80 at the latest,[5] the Academy formally accepted the so-called 'Birkat ha – mînîm', the curse on the Christians from the 'Eighteen Benedictions'. The Talmudic treatise 'Berakoth' (Brachot) 28b/29a, attributing the 'Benediction' to the authority of Rabban Gamaliel and the Academy, provides the chronological framework. A version of the text was discovered at the end of the nineteenth century in the Geniza of the synagogue in Cairo:

May apostates have no hope and may the kingdom of impertinence be uprooted in our day. May *the Nozrim and Minim* (i.e., the Christians) dis-

appear in the twinkling of an eye. May they be removed from the book of
the living and not be inscribed among the just. Bless you, Lord, you who
cast down the proud.

The tract Berakoth 28b/29a from the Babylonian Talmud has this to
say:

The eighteen benedictions are in fact nineteen. Rabban Levi says: The
benediction against the 'Minim' was established at Jamnia . . . Our teachers
have taught: Simon *ha peqali* [the flax heckler] formulated the eighteen
benedictions at Jamnia in the traditional order, in the presence of Rabban
Gamaliel. Rabban Gamaliel said to the sages: 'Is there someone capable of
formulating a benediction against the "Minim"?' Then Samuel the Small
got up and did it. The following year, he forgot the benediction and had to
meditate two or three hours without being asked to come up [from the
lower place of the prayer leader]. How could it be that they did not let him
come up? Did not Raw Juda ben Ezechiel say in the name of Rabbi Abba
Areka: the one who has made a mistake in any of the other benedictions is
not asked to come up, but if it is the benediction against the 'Minim' one
asks him to come up, because it is feared that he did it on purpose being a
'Min' himself? The case of Samuel the Small was different, for it was he
who had decreed the benediction [against the 'Minim']. But one might
have feared that he had retracted.

In such a severe social context, the curse on the Christians had many
everyday consequences, not least the expulsion from the synagogues
of those Christians of Jewish origin who still went to these common
places of worship. What happened at Jamnia only completed the
process of separation which had begun in AD 62 with the execution of
James. The result was the opening of a gulf between the two communities which the Christians were unable and, by now, probably
unwilling to mend.

As early as AD 62 and certainly by AD 70, therefore, Christians were
free to abandon the scroll, the symbol of reassuring continuity, and to
convert to the codex which they themselves helped to develop from
membranae, the notebooks already used in the circle of St Paul (1
Timothy 4:13). It is probable that the change did not take place suddenly. As we saw in the previous chapter, scrolls and codices would
have co-existed for some time, until the last scrolls fell out of use and

were not replaced. The break in literary practice was encouraged by the fact that the Romans were familiar with the notebook format before their contact with the New Testament.[6] The word *membranae* in 2 Timothy 4:13 makes clear that the Romans were already experimenting with the codex at this time – a trend for which the epigrams of the Roman poet Martial (d. AD 102) are the best evidence.

All the practical advantages of the notebook and its more sophisticated descendant, the codex, could now be exploited. Since text appeared on both sides of the sheet, it made economical use of papyrus. It was small and often pocket-sized, easy to handle, to skip through for reference and to store. The codex was also a convenient means of disseminating collections of texts. Rather than five scrolls, one such book was needed for the Gospels and Acts, for example, making it easier to despatch Christian texts throughout the Roman Empire.[7] Considered in this historical light, the Magdalen Papyrus of St Matthew's Gospel could theoretically have existed in, or soon after, AD 62. Both Italo Gallo and Colin Roberts have argued that the codex was in use before AD 70, a claim which corresponds with the evidence we have about the shift from scroll to codex in early Christendom.

Comparing the *scroll* fragment 7Q5 from Qumran, the subject of Chapter 3, with the *codex* fragments of the Jesus Papyrus (P. Magdalen Greek 17 / P64) and its Barcelona counterpart (P. Barc. inv. no. 1 / P67), we should allow for the possibility that they are of similar antiquity. As already suggested, St Mark's may have been the first Gospel to be completed, preceding St Matthew's extended version by a few years. A scroll of St Mark therefore had the advantage of being distributed first and may even have had the backing of St Peter.[8] But St Matthew's Gospel soon surpassed it in general popularity. The new text was more exciting, stimulating and immediate in tone; it included more action, more and longer sayings of Jesus (the whole Sermon on the Mount, for example) and Christ's Resurrection appearances up to the moment of his great commandment to evangelize all peoples to the ends of the world.

Not surprisingly, therefore, there are many more early papyri of St Matthew's Gospel than there are of St Mark's. Even so, the evidence of Cave 7 suggests that St Matthew was beaten to Qumran by St Mark – and no scroll of St Matthew of a comparable date has come to light elsewhere. A fragment may yet be found among the unopened and unexcavated scrolls at Herculaneum, where there was a Christian community before the destruction of the town under the lava of Vesuvius in AD 79, but this is pure speculation. What is clear is the outstanding importance of the Magdalen codex scraps. The Markan scroll, 7Q5, from Qumran confirms that a literary tradition about the life of Jesus had begun in scroll form during the first generation of disciples and eyewitnesses. The Magdalen Papyrus is evidence of something even more dramatic: the institutional maturity of the early communities, the precocious development of the Church, its strategic missionary thinking, and its spirit of enterprise. The first Christian 'book', with its remarkably early date, documents a decisive moment in the recording, preservation and dissemination of the Christian message. But this is only part of its historical significance. A detailed papyrological study of the fragments reveals all manner of significant characteristics which enrich our knowledge of the dawn of Christianity.

The Magdalen Papyrus Examined

The basis for any scholarly study of the Jesus Papyrus is the first edition completed by Colin H. Roberts in 1953.[9] Surprising as it is that papyrologists waited half a century after the arrival of the fragments at Oxford to edit them, Roberts's edition is none the less useful and succinct. In only five pages he established his version of the text on all six sides and added his editorial comments. He began by noting that 'only belief that Hunt's dating in 1901 (i.e., to the fourth century) was substantially incorrect would excuse a detailed study of such minute fragments'. As we shall see in the next chapter, Roberts's intuition was justified beyond his own expectations and conclusions. He also underestimated the importance of the fragments in respects other than those connected with their date.

Roberts began with a physical description which is worth repeating:

There survive three pieces from the same leaf of a codex: frag. (a) 4.1 cm × 1.2 cm, frag. (b) 1.6 × 1.6 cm, and frag. (c) 4.1 cm × 1.3 cm. As there are two columns to a page and as verso precedes recto it follows that on the recto frag. (c) precedes frag. (a) and (b).

It also follows, we may add, that these are certainly codex fragments. Roberts then notes what is written on the fragment:

There were 15–16 letters to a line and approximately 35–36 lines to a column; the area of writing on the page would have measured roughly 10.5 x 16.8 cm; the proportions of the complete page would probably have been much the same. The double column format is noteworthy since, contrary to common opinion, in the earliest codices the single column format is much more common; it may be significant that in early Christian codices (i.e., those assigned to the second century or to the borderline between second and third centuries) the only examples hitherto known of the double column format have been those of books of the Old Testament.

The final comment is interesting. The option to choose between single and double columns per page was apparently there from the very beginning. Copying the Greek Old Testament was, of necessity, one of the initial tasks facing the first Christians, since they based their preaching on the Old Testament and its prophecies. They must have acquired some of their copying and writing expertise in this manner before the first indigenous Christian texts became available.

Roberts extrapolates:

To contain the entire Gospel of St Matthew the book must have run to about 150 pages; we may conclude that in all probability it contained nothing else. As verso precedes recto in the second half of the Gospel it is almost certain that this was not a single quire codex.

After this description of the codex format, Roberts adds a number of observations which will be discussed in Chapter 5:

Nomina sacra occur on the recto, vv 23 and 31; in neither passage is the line over the suspension now visible but there is no reason to think it was omitted. Of some interest is the projection into the left margin of the initial letter of *autois* in v. 31; this line is the first complete line of what is a new section of the text (beginning with *tóte* in the preceding line) both in the Codex Bezae and Codex Alexandrinus (the latter reading *kaí* in place of *tóte*) which mark it in the same way as does the papyrus; the Vaticanus leaves a space before *tóte*. This system of division can now be carried back a couple of centuries if our dating of the papyrus is correct.

The nature of the *nomina sacra*, holy names, is explored in Chapter 6 and briefly explained in the Glossary. As to the system of division described by Roberts, this can usefully be compared to the Qumran papyrus 7Q5 which, as we saw in the previous chapter, has a gap or *spatium* in the place where the new section begins between Matthew 6:52 and 53. This method remained popular and recurs in as late a text as the fourth-century Codex Vaticanus. The Magdalen Papyrus is the first example of the alternative method described by Roberts. Another possibility, visible in the Paris Papyrus P4 of St Luke's Gospel, was to use two projecting letters instead of only one. Scribes and their patrons had a number of options open to them for different tasks but clarity and consistency would have been their first consideration in view of the *scriptio continua* of antiquity, the uninterrupted sequence of letters without divisions between words or sentences. However, this posed problems for scribes and readers alike and would have had few attractions for the first Christians.

Roberts spends the next page and a half discussing the date of the papyrus, which will be the subject of our Chapter 5. As part of this discussion he prints his reading of the text on the six fragments, adding two explanatory footnotes. He ends his article thus:

> The papyrus contributes one unique reading in v. 22, apart from an obvious error in v. 32. It is noteworthy that here and in one other reading in this verse its text diverges from that of two other papyri, p37 and p45.

It is easy to be put off by this dry technical language. Indeed, it is hard to believe that Roberts is discussing a manuscript which, in later years, would provoke worldwide controversy. Yet the science of papyrology, for all its technicality and minute attention to detail also speaks to the layman. Esoteric as these procedures may seem, they provoke questions of a far more general nature. Let us look at the fragments again and see what can be said about these tiny letters, words and lines.

A curiosity of Roberts's article is that he does not mention that the fragments all derive from chapter 26 of St Matthew until he offers his edition proper on page 236, where the chapter is indicated twice in minuscule Roman letters: xxvi. At this point it is worth setting out the translated English text of these fragments from Matthew 26:

Fragment 1, verso (Matthew 26:7–8)
poured it on his head as he was at table. When they saw this, the disciples said indignantly

Fragment 2, verso (Matthew 26:10)
Jesus noticed this and said, 'Why are you upsetting the woman? What she has done for me

Fragment 3, verso (Matthew 26:14–15)
Then one of the Twelve, the man called Judas Iscariot, went to the chief priests and said, 'What are you prepared to give me

Fragment 3, recto (Matthew 26:22–3)
They were greatly distressed and started asking him in turn, 'Not me, Lord, surely?' He answered, 'Someone who has dipped his hand into the dish with me

Fragment 1, recto (Matthew 26:31)
Jesus said to them, 'You will all fall away from me tonight, for the scripture says

Fragment 2, recto (Matthew 26:32–3)
I shall go ahead of you to Galilee.' At this, Peter said to him

In printing this translation, we have not tried to copy the line divisions of the Greek fragments or the fragmentary character of words at the beginnings or ends of some lines; and, needless to say, the difference between Greek and English syntax means that the word order of the translated sentences does not follow that of the original. Nor were the translators of the New Jerusalem Bible – or of any other, for that matter – aware of the unusual features of the Magdalen Papyrus. But this rendering offers a basic idea of what is in these fragments: scenes from the Passion story of Jesus, at Bethany, at the Last Supper, and the negotiations of Judas with the chief priests. We have here the moment before the disciples' outcry, a quotation of Judas, a question posed by the disciples, the prelude to a saying of St Peter and no fewer than four sayings of Jesus himself: not a meagre yield from three small codex fragments.

The remarkable quantity of spoken text on the scraps has, as we have seen, prompted the suggestion that the Jesus Papyrus was not part of the completed Gospel but from a collection of Christ's sayings. This would be a convenient way of accepting a very early date for the manuscript while denying that it was part of a mature Gospel text. Though none has survived, such collections may well have existed; most scholars who believe so refer to the root source as *Logienquelle* (source of *logia*, or sayings) or simply 'Q'. But the Magdalen Papyrus fragments are not only a sequence of words attributed to Jesus; several other people are quoted and the different utterances are set within a finely structured narrative (Matthew 26:7–8: the story of the anointing of Jesus; Matthew 26:14–15: Judas Iscariot walking off to meet the priests). Others have suggested that the early date of the fragments can be explained away because all six extracts are drawn from the Passion story. As mentioned earlier, such a text may have circulated independently, before the composition of the Gospels, although this is pure speculation. The Magdalen Papyrus does nothing to advance this thesis, since its sister papyrus P67 in Barcelona (parts of Matthew 3 and 5) records events in the life of Christ that occurred long before the Passion story, such as John the Baptist meeting Jesus and the Sermon on the Mount. And there can be no doubt that the Oxford and Barcelona manuscripts were originally part of the same complete Gospel codex.

Not all of the six sides of the three fragments are equally noteworthy. The first text, Matthew 26:7–8 on Fragment 1, verso, for example, is quite unremarkable, conforming to the standard text and offering no particular palaeographical highlights. In his 1953 edition, Roberts omitted several words which could be reconstructed from the stichometry; Thiede merely completed the lines in his edition of 1995.[10] The second passage, Matthew 26:10 on Fragment 2, verso, is again fairly straightforward, until one reconstructs the complete lines, which Roberts did not do. The stichometry of line 1 strongly suggests that the Greek word *Iēsous* ('Jesus') was abbreviated to IS, evidence of a 'holy name' or *nomen sacrum*. The modern equivalent would be 'Js noticed this and said . . .'

The third text, Matthew 26:14–15 on Fragment 3, verso, is the first to make us think hard about what the scribe was trying to achieve. In line 2, he does not write the Greek word for 'twelve', *dódeka*, but the numerical symbol '$\iota\beta$' (*iota* and *beta*), comparable to a modern scribe writing the letters 'XII' for 'twelve': 'Then one of the XII, Judas Iscariot . . .'. Only the lower half of the *beta* remains visible on the fragment, but this and the stichometry of lines 1 and 2 suggest a clear identification. Roberts noticed this, but a second peculiarity escaped his attention: immediately after the 'twelve', a word is missing. It is hard to express the force of this omission in English, but suppose that instead of the literal 'Then went one of the twelve, he who was called Judas Iscariot ...' we were to read: 'Then went one of the XII called Judas Iscariot.' The Greek word missing is the article *ho* before *legómenos*.

This is the only known instance of such an omission in any papyrus of St Matthew's Gospel. Generally in the New Testament, it occurs only in connection with place-names, as in St Matthew 2:23 (Nazareth) and St John 4:5 (Sychar). Does this reflect a mere slip of the pen or a conscious decision by the scribe to keep the style of the text simple and avoid unnecessary embellishments? Was he in fact writing for an early Christian community which did not yet expect elegant prose or refined rhetoric? This is an important question, to which we shall return.

The fourth is perhaps the most important among the six sides of the Magdalen Papyrus. To resolve the questions it poses, Carsten Thiede had to make use of a new microscope: an epifluorescent confocal laser-scanning device which he and his colleague Georg Masuch, a biologist, recently developed and patented. Matthew 26:22–3 on Fragment 3, recto, had already tested Roberts's powers of deduction. Line 1, damaged and partly illegible, preserves a single letter which is sufficiently complete to allow for only one reading: it is an *omega*. Of the preceding letter, only a vertical stroke remains, resembling the elongated stroke of a complete *tau* elsewhere in the Jesus Papyrus. Following the *omega*, there appears to be a high dot and, immediately to the right of it, the beginnings of a letter which could be a *nu* or, less probably, a *mu*. As the rest of Fragment 3, recto, necessitates the identification of the passage with Matthew 26:22–3, line 1 must contain the remnants of 26:22, and the letters *tau* and *omega* would belong to the *autōn* ('of them').

Roberts was impressed by the high dot. Clearly, he thought it was a punctuation mark set before the ensuing question of the disciples – literally, 'Not me, Lord, surely?' Consequently, he had to assume that the fragmentary letter after the dot was a *mu*, not a *nu*, for the word must then be the interrogative particle *meti*, in the sense of '*surely not?*' Such a reconstruction would be unique, as Roberts himself observed. But it would also be unnecessarily awkward Greek. Indeed, this verse suffered all sorts of contortions in later manuscripts, as is clear from the extensive footnotes on page 76 of the so-called 'Nestle-Aland', *Novum Testamentum Graece*, now in its 27th revised edition. But Thiede recognized that the letter after the *omega* was a *nu* after all. Thus, the sentence was quite different, in two notable respects, not only from Roberts's reconstruction but also from the standard printed texts of the new Testament.

If the letter is indeed a *nu*, then the saying of Jesus which precedes the question of the disciples ends with *hekastos autōn* ('each of them'). It is a matter of syntax and of subtle style. The standard text, as it appears in Greek New Testament editions and which ends ... *legein auto heis hekastos*, would mean literally, 'And very saddened, every (single) one of them said to him ...' The reading of the Jesus Papyrus, however, is: 'And very saddened, each of them said ...' The exact nuance cannot be easily rendered in English. The Magdalen version emphasizes that the disciples were all joining in, all speaking at once – a realistic description of a dramatic moment. The standard text, on the other hand, would have us believe that the disciples spoke one after the other, waiting their turn in an orderly manner. The unembellished style of the Magdalen Papyrus seems to be trying to convey the excitement and tension of a crucial moment in Jesus's life, while the later variants hint at the subsequent campaign to present the disciples as mature apostles-to-be, behaving in a disciplined and stately fashion.

In the debate about Thiede's work, Roberts has had his defenders. Attention has been drawn, for example, to this apparent high dot next to the right-hand 'shoulder' of the *omega*. Had Thiede ignored this or assumed that it belonged to the *omega*, as a broken-off, decorated elongation – as appears in the *alpha, delta* and *lambda* of the Magdalen Papyrus? This was an important question. If it was meant to be a dot, a punctuation mark, then the *nu* could again, if only tenuously, be interpreted as a *mu*. On this particular textual question, we would be back to square one.

The issue was resolved once and for all in June 1995 when the Jesus Papyrus was brought to Germany by Dr Christine Ferdinand, the Fellow Librarian of Magdalen College, Oxford. In her presence, Thiede and his colleague Georg Masuch analysed the fragments under their confocal laser-scanning microscope. Unlike any other modern microscope, this state-of-the-art device is capable of differentiating between twenty separate micrometre layers of a papyrus manuscript, selecting individual

St Matthew. From a copy of the Gospels of St Matthew and St Mark, made probably at Liège early in the second half of the 11th century, perhaps for the German King Henry IV (1054—1106).

Above: Charles Huleatt (middle row, right), ordinand, Wycliffe Hall, 1887. Robert Girdlestone (second from right, back row) told his pupils: 'There is one remedy and one only for this evil state of things, namely the *Gospel*.'

Left: The only portrait of Huleatt in later life. The discoverer of the Papyrus told his wife: 'I have failed in everything.'

Luxor Hotel: Thomas Cook's finest monument and Charles Huleatt's home for a decade of winters: 'a place of delights' for British expatriates.

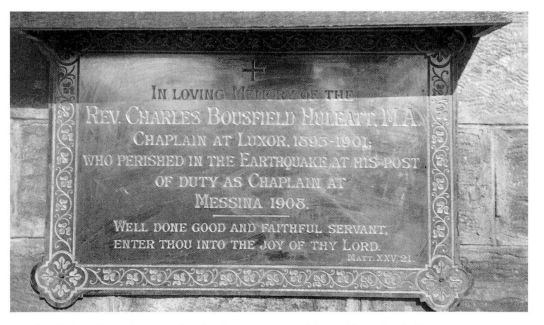

IN LOVING MEMORY OF THE
REV. CHARLES BOUSFIELD HULEATT, M.A.
CHAPLAIN AT LUXOR, 1893-1901;
WHO PERISHED IN THE EARTHQUAKE AT HIS POST
OF DUTY AS CHAPLAIN AT
MESSINA 1908.

WELL DONE GOOD AND FAITHFUL SERVANT.
ENTER THOU INTO THE JOY OF THY LORD.
MATT. XXV. 21.

The little-noticed plaque to the chaplain's memory at Luxor Hotel, funded by an appeal in *The Times* launched by Huleatt's mentor, the distinguished Egyptologist Archibald Henry Sayce.

The Magdalen Papyrus: verso (*above*); recto (*below*). The precise wording of each fragment is discussed in chapter four.

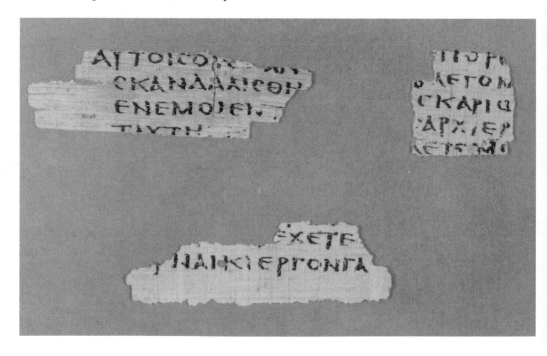

The Qumran papyrus scroll fragment 7Q5 (Mark 6: 52—3)

The Nile at Luxor (*above*). Luxor Temple (*below and right*). The ancient monument a stone's throw from Huleatt's lodgings, is said, according to a late legend, to have been visited by Jesus and the Virgin. The chaplain was fascinated by these 'relics of heathendom'.

Above: The Old Library at Magdalen where the Papyrus lay in a display case for most of this century. *Below:* Carsten Peter Thiede with Dr Christine Ferdinand, Fellow Librarian of Magdalen College with the confocal laser scanning microscope used to analyse the Magdalen Papyrus.

strata; of measuring the height and depth of ink on, and within, the papyrus sheet; of printing the result on a video printout, including topographical charts with detailed measurements, if desired; of detecting the imprint of the scribe's pen or stylus on the papyrus even where there is no ink left and determining which way an individual letter was drawn; and, finally, of collating all this information into a three-dimensional photograph, if necessary.

Looking at the high dot under this microscope, Thiede and Masuch soon established that there had never been any link with the *omega* to its left, nor indeed with the letter to its right. A punctuation mark, after all? They measured the ink of the letters and of the dot. Here, the result was clear. While the letters possess a thickness (height and depth) of 12.1 micrometres, the dot measures only 4.0. It is an accidental ink blot, and no more – a common enough feature on ancient papyri. Thus, Thiede's reconstruction was vindicated, including the *nu* after the *omega* (which was also checked). The results of this analysis were presented at the 21st Congress of the International Papyrologists' Association in Berlin on 15 August 1995 and met with unanimous approval.

The new reading of the text on line 3 of Fragment 3, recto, is identical with the reading in another early papyrus, the P45, commonly dated to the early third century, but probably considerably older, and apparently (the passage is fragmentary) with the text of the papyrus P37, of Codex D (the famous early-fifth-century Bezae Cantabrigiensis at Cambridge University Library),[11] and many other manuscripts. The P45 is our earliest extant codex of all four Gospels and Acts; part of it is now at the Chester Beatty Library, Dublin, and part at the Austrian National Library, Vienna. The P37 is an early-third- or late-second-century codex fragment of Matthew 26:19–52, held at the University of Michigan, Ann Arbor. Yet there is only one widely recognized critical edition of the Greek New Testament which treats this reading as the best and most reliable one: the Bover-O'Callaghan *Nuevo Testamento Trilingüe*,[12] a trilingual Greek–Latin–Spanish edition, first published by José Maria Bover and continued in later editions by José O'Callaghan, the papyrologist who correctly identified 7Q5.[13]

It is clear that this original reading, preferable for internal textual reasons and now corroborated by the oldest manuscript of St Matthew's Gospel, should replace the rival text in the two most widely used versions of the Greek New Testament, the United Bible Societies' *Greek*

New Testament (now in its fourth revised edition) and the Nestle-Aland *Novum Testamentum Graece*. Even so, a rearguard action is currently being mounted at the Münster Institute, which oversees the latter text, one of whose members, Klaus Wachtel, recently published an article refusing to recognize the change. It is possible that he was not aware of all the relevant evidence.[14] However, the matter is now beyond dispute.

While the Magdalen Papyrus was under their microscope, Thiede and Masuch also took a closer look at line 2 of Fragment 3, recto. This, too, is an important line, as it contains a second example of a *nomen sacrum*, a holy name. In verse 22, the disciples address Jesus as *kyrie*, 'Lord', written with only the first and last letter, 'KE'. It is as if the English translation were to read: 'Not me, Ld, surely?' The letters are severely damaged but enough is left to establish this to be the case, as Roberts did in 1953 by putting tiny dots underneath each of the letters to signify that they are damaged and only partly legible. Hardly anything looks reconstructible at the right end of the line, but Roberts tentatively suggested *de*, the second word of 26:23, a conjunctive particle which could be rendered as 'but' or 'now then . . .' but often remains untranslated. In Thiede's edition, the editorial bracket which signals the division between visible fragments of letters and the ensuing reconstruction of the line as it would have appeared when complete, was set after the *delta* and before the *epsilon* of *de*. Little depends on this difference, since the text would be the same either way. But for Thiede and Masuch the exercise offered a welcome chance to find out what their microscope was capable of establishing.

Under a twentyfold objective, a minute fibre of papyrus with specks of ink at the far end became visible. The two researchers took a computerized measurement of the maximum length from the clearly visible horizontal stroke at the left to the last of these specks and compared it to the length of a complete *epsilon* on another of the three fragments (Fragment 1, recto, line 3). The two measurements were identical. But why is there no complete horizontal stroke, a necessary part of an *epsilon*? Thiede and Masuch produced a three-dimensional image and the answer become obvious. Precisely along the line where that horizontal stroke once was, there is a papyrus fibre from which ink had flaked off – and continues to flake off.

If this letter is an *epsilon*, then the letter to its left must be *delta*. Yet it does not resemble a *delta* – rather more a low and smallish *omikron*.

The microscope detected three tiny spots, thick enough to be integral parts of a former letter, above the apparent *omikron* circle. A complete *delta*, from Fragment 1, recto, line 2, was set underneath, and the computer drew white lines into the inner triangle. This triangle was then transferred to the traces of the apparent *omikron* and the dots above it. It fitted. The letter to the left of the reconstructed *epsilon* is indeed a *delta*, unlikely as this seemed at first. Thus, the last legible combination of letters, the last word on line 2 of this fragment, is a *de* after all. The extraordinary potential of this new technology in manuscript analysis had been demonstrated once again.

The fifth side of the Magdalen Papyrus, Fragment 1, recto, Matthew 26:31, has three notable characteristics. As Roberts had noticed, and as quoted earlier in this chapter, the initial letter, the *alpha* of the first word, *autois* ('to them'), is projected into the left margin. As in the sister papyrus, P67, at Barcelona, where it occurs in Matthew 5:21 and 5:27, this signifies the first complete line of a new section which began in the preceding line. Furthermore, here in line 1 we have our third instance of a *nomen sacrum*, a holy name. *Iēsous* ('Jesus') is written IS, as if the modern English Bible said 'Then Js said to them ...' There is a third peculiarity in this line, one which was not noticed by Roberts. After *pantes* ('all'), every edition of the standard Greek text prints *humeis* ('of you'). But there is no room for this word in this line of the Magdalen Papyrus. As noted in the previous chapter, with the superfluous word *humeis* it would have twenty rather than fifteen letters, four above the average for this papyrus. Here, such an excessive length would be particularly irregular, as the line already has a surplus letter to the left, the *alpha* projected into the left margin. One might of course consider this a petty or pedantic matter. The importance of this omission is that it provides further evidence of the Greek style used by the Jesus Papyrus scribe: correct, simple and unembellished.

We come, finally, to the last side of these scraps: Fragment 2, recto (Matthew 26:32–3). For Christians, this is of especial significance because it contains the earliest manuscript evidence for the name of St Peter (*petros* in line 3). Otherwise its only notable aspect is the spelling mistake already mentioned in the context of the *d/t* shift in 7Q5: in line 2 the word for Galilee, *galeilaian*, is misspelt *galeglaian*. Examination of the scrap under the confocal laser-scanning microscope confirmed that the horizontal stroke on top and to the right of what should have been a *iota* is neither an optical illusion nor an accident. The scribe did indeed draw that line, turning the *iota* into a *gamma*. He was, it seems, as fallible as any modern calligrapher.

Taking all these detailed observations into consideration, the Magdalen Papyrus is a remarkable contribution to our understanding of early Christian scribes, the Jesus tradition and its literary origins. In Chapter 6, we shall return to the question of the *nomina sacra*. Here, we conclude by considering the close relationship of the Magdalen Papyrus, P64, and the two fragments kept at the Fundación San Lucas Evangelista in Barcelona, numbered P67 in the Gregory-Aland list of New Testament papyri.

The Barcelona Papyrus and the Paris Codex

In 1962, nine years after his first edition of the Magdalen Papyrus, Colin Roberts published a 'Complementary Note' to Ramón Roca-Puig's second edition of the Barcelona Papyrus.[15] He wrote:

> When in 1956 Professor Ramón Roca-Puig published a booklet entitled *Un Papiro Griego del Evangelio de San Mateo*, with an edition of the papyrus in the possession of the Fundación San Lucas Evangelista. I suspected that the hand in which the two papyri were written was one and the same, and correspondence with Professor Roca-Puig confirmed this beyond doubt. The Barcelona fragments are part of two leaves covering in part Chapters III and V of the Gospel. It is unlikely that either leaf was conjoint with the Magdalen College leaf, and it therefore remains uncertain whether the codex was a single quire codex or not. The whole gospel would have occupied some 90 pages.

Roberts proceeded to advance his reasons for a second-century date for both papyri, P64 and P67, citing a number of manuscripts, not a single one of which is itself precisely dated. None the less, he acknowledged that 'the hand in which the text is written is a carefully written book hand that may be regarded as a *precursor* [our italics] of the style commonly known as Biblical Uncial'.

The palaeographical characteristics of the Jesus Papyrus and the two Barcelona fragments are indeed so strikingly similar that no one seriously disputed their common provenance. But it is the Magdalen scraps which offer the more intriguing evidence about early Christian scribal traditions. The Barcelona manuscript, for instance, does not have a single *nomen sacrum* or significant stylistic variant.[16] Nor do the fragments include any narrative elements: John the Baptist is speaking, Jesus is replying, and there is also a fragment from the Sermon on the Mount. Even so, the Barcelona texts should not be ignored. They include the oldest papyrus evidence for a saying of the Baptist and the oldest known passage from the Sermon on the Mount. Here are the English translations from the New Jerusalem Bible, disregarding the fragmentary beginnings and ends of the papyrus:

Fragment 1, verso (Matthew 3:9)

and do not presume to tell yourselves, 'We have Abraham as our father,' because, I tell you, God can

Fragment 1, recto (Matthew 3:15)

Jesus replied, 'Leave it like this for the time being; it is fitting that we should, in this way

Fragment 2, recto (Matthew 5:20–2)

if your uprightness does not surpass that of the scribes and Pharisees, you will never get into the kingdom of Heaven. You have heard how it was said to our ancestors, 'You shall not kill'; and if anyone does kill he must answer for it before the court. But I say this to you, anyone who is angry with a brother

Fragment 2, verso (Matthew 5:25–8)

he may hand you over to the judge and the judge to the officer, and you will be thrown into prison. In truth I tell you, you will not get out till you have paid the last penny. You have heard how it was said, 'You shall not commit adultery'. But I say this to you, if a man looks at a woman lustfully

We conclude our brief discussion of the Barcelona Papyrus with Ramón Roca-Puig's note on a remarkable photographic error.[17] In Fragment 2, verso, line 9 (part of Matthew 5:27), two dots had been discovered next to the Greek word *hoti* ('for that', 'that'). Hubert Greeven of Kiel University had interpreted these as a diairesis, a separating mark to signify independent syllables or single vowels as opposed to diphthongs. In principle, this claim might have made sense, since there is indeed a word after *hoti* which begins with a vowel *erréthe*. But Roca-Puig, after a fresh analysis of the papyrus carried out *à la luz de sol* ('in the light of the sun'), realized that the two dots are not made by ink but tiny scratches on the damaged papyrus. He warned that future papyrologists should be wary of trusting photographs alone.

In so doing, Roca-Puig drew attention to a fundamental rule of his craft: photographs are a poor substitute for the original papyrus. Carsten Thiede had an illuminating experience in this context, when working on the critical first edition of the Papyrus 'Bodmer L' from the Biblioteca Bodmeriana (Fondation Martin Bodmer) at Cologny near Geneva.[18] A photograph of the papyrus provided by the library clearly showed a horizontal stroke under parts of line 2 of the recto. The mark might have had important implications for Thiede's edition. At Cologny, however, Thiede discovered that there is no such horizontal stroke on the papyrus itself and that the phantom mark was merely a blemish on the photographic plate. Such experiences are commonplace among papyrologists who have had to make do with photographs – often the only practical means of studying a manuscript in an archive thousands of miles away. For definitive results, however, it is essential to examine the original.

Seeking links between fragments which may be spread across libraries around the world is one of the most difficult and important tasks facing papyrologists. A recent example is the edition of the second-century papyrus of the *Acts of Martyrs*, the *Acta Alexandrinorum* at Yale, the P. Yale 1385, which belongs to a papyrus of the same work, the PbuG 46, at Giessen University Library on the other side of the Atlantic.[19]

In conclusion, we turn to a related question which has attracted scholarly attention since the link between the Oxford and Barcelona fragments was established. Are there other papyri which might have belonged to the same codex? One candidate immediately suggested was the codex P4, or P. Supplementum Graecum 1120, at the Bibliothèque Nationale in Paris. Close similarities between the Magdalen and Bar-celona papyri and the much larger codex fragments in Paris were first noticed by Peter Weigandt who passed on his observation to Kurt Aland. Aland wrote about these similarities in a paper published in 1966,[20] since when it has been widely assumed that he and Weigandt were correct. Among others, van Haelst, Roberts and Skeat contributed to the popularity of this view.[21]

The Paris papyrus, P4, of St Luke's Gospel not only appeared to add a second Gospel to this old codex. With four leaves containing more text than any of the Oxford and Barcelona fragments, and passages from the first six chapters of St Luke, it seemed likely to offer valuable additional information about the techniques used by the scribe who had allegedly worked on the three different manuscripts. As early as 1967, however, Aland began to express doubts about the relationship between P4 and P64/67.[22] In 1981, he changed his mind completely, differentiating between the Magdalen and Barcelona papyri, on the one hand, whose text he described as *fester Text* (firm or stable text) and the Paris P4, on the other, described as *Normaltext* (normal text). Ruling out any formal unity of the papyri on textual grounds, he underlined the difference by dating P64/67 'ca 200' and P4 'III'.[23] Although both dates are far too late, as we shall see, the point is that Aland had become convinced that they were written at different times. In brief, he himself provided three compelling reasons to suppose that P4 and P64/67 are not from the same codex: the different reconstructed format, the different text type and the different dates.

There are indeed palaeographical similarities between the three, though more so in photographs than on the original papyri. Unaware of Aland's change of mind, in 1983 Roberts and Skeat reasserted their belief in the connection without advancing new reasons; the American scholar Philip W. Comfort did the same in 1992, in an introduction to textual criticism, 'The Quest for the Original Text of the New Testament'.[24] It was not until early 1995 that simultaneous analyses by Thiede and Comfort, prompted by the former's re-edition of the Magdalen Papyrus, settled the matter: P64 and P67 did once belong together, but P4 did not. None the less, P4, the Paris codex, may well have come from the same scribal school or centre, commissioned by a different patron and only slightly later in date. Comfort published his results in the same journal as Thiede's report on an investigation of the original sheets in February 1995.[25]

The reasons for the new position are clear. First, the separate fragments of a title page preserved with the other papyri in box 5 of the Supplementum Graecum 1120: 'EYAGGELION KATA MATHTHAION' (Gospel according to Matthew), which encouraged some scholars to believe that the Oxford and Barcelona papyri of St Matthew may have belonged to the same codex, is written in a hand distinctly different from all three papyri. In particular, it is broader and wider, with a flat *nu* and markedly longer elongated upper horizontal strokes in the two *gammas*.

Second, there can be no doubt that the material of the papyrus in P4 is different from that in P64/67. The dark brown of the Paris fragments, in contrast to the light hue of the Oxford and Barcelona fragments, is organic and cannot be ascribed to different means of preservation and conservation. This observation alone seems to rule out the possibility that the Paris fragment originally belonged to the same codex as the other two.

Third, one of the most striking features of P64/67, the projection of a letter into the left margin in order to signify the first complete line of a new section which begins in the preceding line, is executed differently in the Paris papyrus. Its scribe always used two letters, rather than one, for this purpose. The photographs supplied in the first edition of P4 are not very useful for serious analysis, being of a deplorable quality. But even here one can see the unambiguous examples of *ar/chomenos* in Fragment B, verso, first column – Luke 3:23 (Plate IV), and of *el/egen* in Fragment D, verso, first column – Luke 5:36 (Plate VI).[26] While this would not in itself rule out the possibility that the same scribe was at work – after all, any scribe might change his or her stylistic traits from time to time, not least if asked to do so by a customer – such variation would not occur in one and the same book.

Fourth, the differences between the letters of P64/67 and P4 are less apparent but no less significant than the similarities. The scribe of P4 has a tendency to raise *omega* and *omikron* above the bottom line, for instance, but to keep his *rho* right on the line. This, in fact, is much like his *tau*, which in P64/67 extends underneath the bottom line in the same way as the *upsilon*, and which always has a straight top bar in P4, but not always in P64/67.[27] Fragment A, recto, of P4 offers the most distinct examples, visible even on the photograph.

Considered together with the reasons for Kurt Aland's change of mind and Philip Comfort's argument that the pen strokes are finer and thinner in P4 than in P64/67, these observations would seem to seal the issue. How, then, to explain the clear similarities? As Comfort notes, the Paris Papyrus and the Magdalen fragments were both acquired at Luxor, albeit at different times and by different people. It is possible that the same scribe produced all three papyri at different periods. A more probable explanation is that the manuscripts emerged from the same scribal centre and thus share certain basic characteristics.

In the course of this analysis, Thiede has come to a new view about the date of the Paris Papyrus. In his re-edition of the Magdalen fragments, he accepted the scholarly consensus on this point. But fresh research has shown that the Paris Papyrus of St Luke's Gospel is not much later than P64/67. Comfort, who had not seen the additional comparative material for the new dating of the Magdalen Papyrus when he wrote his article,[28] tentatively adopted a more conservative position suggesting an early-second-century date for the Paris Papyrus. Even so, it is now recognized as the earliest extant manuscript of St Luke's Gospel – an example of the redating process which is the subject of the next chapter.

5

The Jesus Papyrus Redated

If accepted, this date would revolutionize our understanding of the origin
of the Gospels and just about every other aspect of earliest Christianity.

Graham Stanton, *Gospel Truth?* (1995)

It is clear that a papyrological nemesis awaits those who, without good
reason, throw away explicit ancient testimony.

E. G. Turner, *Greek Papyri. An Introduction* (1968)

In the research mentioned in the last chapter, the American scholar
Philip Comfort reached a highly significant conclusion. In spite of
the difficulties, he wrote in 1992, many manuscripts were being
assigned earlier dates than before. 'For example, the Pauline codex P46
has been redated by Young-Kyu Kim to *ca*. AD 85. To this day, Kim's
early dating of P46 to the later part of the first century[1] *has not been
challenged on palaeographical grounds* [our italics]. And the Johannine
codex P66 has been dated to *ca*. 125 by the papyrologist Herbert
Hunger.[2] Other manuscripts have been pushed back from the third
century to the second century – namely, P32 (*ca*. 175), P45 (*ca*. 150),
P77 (*ca*. 150), P87 (*ca*. 125), P90 (*ca*. 150).'[3]

The redating of the Jesus Papyrus is the most spectacular example of
the process observed by Comfort. But why is this such a complex
question at all? Since Carsten Thiede's work on the manuscript was first
published, many have asked why the fragments cannot be subjected to
radiocarbon dating, thus settling the controversy once and for all. Early
in 1995 Dr Christine Ferdinand, the Fellow Librarian of Magdalen
College, took the three fragments to the famous Oxford laboratory
where the Turin Shroud and many other remarkable artefacts have been
radiocarbon dated. The fragments proved too small and too light for
such a procedure. Even the new technology of Accelerator Mass Spec-

trometry requires a minimum weight of 20–25 mg, which is destroyed in the course of the analysis. The three Oxford fragments weigh 45, 25 and 21 mg respectively. It would be an act of scholarly vandalism, therefore, to subject them to such a test, particularly as there are letters right to the very edges of the scraps: not even the tiniest sample could be spared for analysis.

The Barcelona fragments are almost equally small. Although Fragment 2 is larger than the largest Magdalen fragment – 5.0 × 5.5 cm compared to 4.1 × 1.3 cm – more than a third, all bearing text, would be lost for ever under radiocarbon testing. Only scrolls or papyri with large, blank margins are suitable for such dating methods. Nor should it be assumed that radiocarbon dating is infallibly reliable, or even more reliable than the methods it is sometimes thought to have superseded. The date achieved by this modern process is accurate only within a margin of +/– 50 years. It dates the material on which the handwriting appears rather than the handwriting itself. Nor does it necessarily improve upon the results achieved by the traditional method of comparative palaeography. When several of the Dead Sea Scrolls were radiocarbon dated in 1991, the date achieved was identical to that already put forward by papyrologists.[4] It is wrong to think that radiocarbon dating is an irreproachable technique; or that comparative palaeography is hopelessly speculative. Rigorous analysis of script and scribal practice is the surest method to use when dating a manuscript such as the Jesus Papyrus.

'It would be a very brave man who would deny that such a text, or any text, might be susceptible to further improvement' – a wise observation made by a renowned academic, the papyrologist Herbert C. Youtie.[5] This remark – buried, unfortunately, in a collection of specialist lectures – deserves to be heeded by all scholars in the field. Yet the ongoing improvement of existing texts and editions is not a task which many papyrologists relish. There are always new papyri which desperately need to be identified and published – several thousand in Berlin* alone, which should be more than enough to keep the next generation or two

* At the Ägyptisches Museum, which now, following German reunification, holds the complete Berlin papyrus collection, one of the largest in the world.

of scholars busy. There are few incentives, therefore, to look afresh at a text published more than forty years ago.

There are now about a hundred New Testament papyri at museums and libraries all over the world. Some were found and published in the nineteenth century, others only in the last few years. A number are still awaiting detailed analysis by a scholar. There are even some fragments which may or may not be part of the New Testament at all – small scraps whose very nature is disputed among papyrologists. The oldest among these papyri are the very first remnants of the texts of the Gospels, of St Paul's letters, or indeed of any of the twenty-seven writings collected in the New Testament. Considered as a widely dispersed archive, these manuscripts are a priceless part of mankind's heritage, the most valuable literary treasures of Christendom. As such, they demand the most careful (and continuous) scrutiny, the relentless analysis of the historian and the papyrologist. Nor is the science of papyrology static: new insights, improved analytical techniques and the most up-to-date microscopes have ensured constant progress in the field. It is always legitimate, therefore, to ask whether the arguments of fifty and one hundred years ago stand up to debate today.

When Charles Huleatt acquired the St Matthew fragments in Luxor and sent them to his old college, he knew they contained phrases from St Matthew's Gospel. He had some impression of their age, but was content to leave a more definitive assessment to scholars at his old university. As we have seen, two of the greatest papyrus experts of the time were Oxford men: Arthur Hunt was associated with Huleatt's undergraduate college, while Bernard Grenfell was a Fellow of The Queen's College a short distance up the High. In 1898 Grenfell and Hunt had begun their co-editing of the Oxyrhynchus papyri: Greek, Latin and Coptic texts found by themselves and others in Upper Egypt. So vast was the number of papyri discovered that even now, a century later, not all have been published.

For papyrology, the implications of this find were momentous. For the first time, a cache of papyri had come to light which included hundreds of letters, documents, contracts, applications, poems, dramas and New Testament texts. Here at last was a vast sample of writings which could be compared to each other, dated and analysed as a group. The Oxyrhynchan finds also covered several centuries and were witnesses of a culture in transition from Hellenistic times, when the town was a Greek colony, to its later status as a Roman provincial capital and, finally, a Christian bishopric. Slowly, comparative patterns emerged which matured into a framework of scholarly yardsticks and categories. Faced by thousands of fragments, Grenfell and Hunt had to develop a system of fixed coordinates in order to organize the extraordinary quantity of evidence. One such precept – a crucial one for our purposes – applied to the dating of codex fragments.

In classical antiquity, as we have seen, the scroll was the common format, bearing text on its inner side only (with a very few exceptions, one of which is mentioned in Revelation 5:1). Rolled up, it protected the writing inside. The length of the scroll was decided by the patron's requirement. Sheet after sheet of papyrus, parchment or leather was attached to the next until the required length was reached. With practice, the finished product was easy to handle; it was also aesthetically attractive, which doubtless explains the enduring appeal of the scroll for formal and ceremonial purposes to the present day. The codex, on the other hand, was practical but comparatively untidy. Sheets of papyrus were folded once, twice or more often to achieve the required size, a technique still used in modern book production. Although this was economical in that both sides of a page could be used for writing, it meant that scribes had to use both surfaces (recto and verso) rather than the smooth, stylus-friendly inner surface of the scroll. This could cause problems. When the papyrus fibre was awkward to write upon, letters could become irregular and less elegant, and the ink would tend to flake off later.

When the Magdalen Papyrus came to light at the end of the last century, it was widely assumed by papyrologists that the codex was invented and introduced by the Christians and produced *en masse* at scribal centres under the benevolent eye of the imperial authorities. This assumption persisted for much of the twentieth century. In particular, it was believed that the shift in practice was initiated during the second half of the third century when there was a lull in the persecution of the Church following the murder of the Emperor Decius, and pursued with renewed vigour under the first Christian emperor, Constantine, after the famous toleration edict of Milan in AD 313. On this basis, there was no reason to assume that the codex preceded the later third century. The implications for the dating of fragments such as the Magdalen Papyrus were clear enough. It could be taken for granted that such manuscripts were not produced before the late third or early fourth century.

Yet the persistent idea that the codex was a late Christian invention reflected presumption rather than fact. One of the first principles of dating is to look for reliable data about related historical events. Hence, a document discovered a century from now which referred to the Berlin Wall as an existing structure could be assumed to have been written between 1961 and 1989. Archaeologists are sometimes able to provide a terminus date, after which a manuscript could not have been produced, such as the destruction of Pompeii and Herculaneum by Vesuvius in AD 79. By definition, the tablets and papyri discovered there must be older than this. In the case of the codex, a similar date exists: the years in which the Roman poet Martial wrote his epigrams.

Born in Spain, Martial spent most of his active life in Rome. Of his fifteen books of poems, most are short, trenchant satires, mercilessly attacking the decadence of Roman society. But Martial, like his fellow satirist Juvenal, often made accurate observations about the social world in which he lived, alongside his less factually reliable witticisms. One of his more eccentric pursuits was the encouragement of what we would call paperback editions of classical authors such as Homer, Virgil, Cicero, Livy, Ovid and others. In *Epigram* I, 2, he praises the enterprise in eloquent phrases:

> If you want to take my books with you, wherever you go,
> So that they may accompany you on long journeys,
> Go and buy those small-size paperback editions,
> Others fill your bookshelves, but mine are handy.
> However, do not be ignorant and do not look in vain
> All over Rome. I tell you where to go and find them:
> Go straight to Secundus who once served under the learned
> > Lucensis.
> You will find him behind the Temple of Pax, at the
> > Palladian market.

This epigram belongs to Martial's middle period, AD 84–6. The Latin words used to describe these manuscripts clearly refer to the codex format. In other words, there was clear proof of the existence of the codex in the eighties of the first century even before the first physical evidence for that format was unearthed by archaeologists. In view of

Martial's testimony, it was always wrong to assume that codex fragments should be dated, by definition, to the late third or early fourth century.

However, this is precisely what happened. In 1898 Grenfell and Hunt published a vellum codex fragment, found at Oxyrhynchus.[6] It is a fascinating text, containing parts of a lost 'history of the Macedonian Wars'. Their analysis of the handwriting suggested a very early date in the first century, perhaps even before AD 79. Even so, they proceeded to assign the manuscript to the late third or even fourth century for the simple reason that it was from a *codex*. We now know that Hunt made a mistake when he examined the Jesus Papyrus in 1901 and declared that it must be dated to the third but 'with more probability to the fourth century'.[7] Yet the scholarly assumptions which led him to this conclusion are still current.

When Carsten Thiede suggested that the Magdalen manuscript and its sister fragments in Barcelona could be dated to the mid-first century – AD 70 or even earlier – three principal lines of criticism emerged. First, it was argued that there was no Gospel according to St Matthew at such an early time and that the dating was therefore a logical impossibility. Second, it was claimed that the author had overlooked a crucial monograph on Biblical Uncial (see Glossary) by the Italian scholar Guglielmo Cavallo who proposes that this particular style was a late development. Third, it was suggested that Thiede had based his redating upon comparative material from areas of the Roman Empire which bore no relation to the Magdalen Papyrus. Since Charles Huleatt had acquired the fragments at Luxor, it was alleged that they must be of Egyptian origin and that Thiede's redating was unacceptable on the grounds that there were no Christian scribal centres in first-century Egypt.

The last objection is clearly facile. It is akin to suggesting that one could not buy a bottle of Chianti in London in 1996 since this wine is produced in Italy rather than in Britain. As we have seen, it is quite wrong to assume that a papyrus found in Luxor must have been written there or even in Egypt. Such a manuscript could have been produced almost anywhere in the Roman Empire (or beyond), imported, used, stored, forgotten or thrown away, rediscovered almost two thousand years later and sold to a curious chaplain.

By the same token, the idea of thriving Christian scribal centres in first-century Egypt should not be dismissed out of hand. We know, for instance, that there were followers of Jesus in Alexandria, a focal point of Mediterranean Judaism. One of its synagogues was so vast that the collective 'Amen' had to be signalled by flags. Increasingly, the Jews of this city had become Greek-speakers – so much so, in fact, that by the third century BC the Bible had to be translated into Greek for them. This was the practical purpose behind the production of the Greek Old Testament, the Septuagint, which soon spread all over the Roman Empire. By New Testament times, even in Palestine there were those who preferred to quote from the Greek translation rather than the Hebrew original. Thus, many of the Old Testament citations in New Testament texts are taken from the Septuagint. Likewise, the synagogal community of Alexandrian Jews in Jerusalem – mentioned in Acts 6:9 – was clearly Greek-speaking.

But Alexandria was more than a centre of translators and scribes. Elaborate philosophical works were also produced there, such as the Book of Wisdom which is still included in the Apocrypha to the Old Testament. Among Alexandria's finest intellects was Philo (15 BC–AD 50), a Jewish theologian and philosopher and an exact contemporary of the earliest Christians. His works, written exclusively in Greek, combined Greek philosophy and cosmology with Jewish piety and influenced many Christian thinkers. Indeed, we encounter one such Christian contemporary in the pages of the New Testament: Apollos, the brilliant preacher and missionary who is described as 'an eloquent man, well versed in the scriptures' (Acts 18:24, RSV) and who later continued St Paul's work in Corinth (Acts 18:27–19:1), was a Jew from Alexandria. Tradition has it that St Mark lived in Alexandria for a long time and that his Gospel, written in Rome, was received there with particular warmth, copied, and then distributed to other places of Christian worship. In the second century, furthermore, one of the most eminent Christian authors was Clement of Alexandria. Born in Athens, he studied and taught in the great Egyptian city – a shift of location which well illustrates its intellectual renown and cultural importance.

Against such a background, it is implausible to argue that Christians could not have written, copied and distributed papyrus documents in first-century Egypt. To rule out an early date for the Magdalen Papyrus because it was found in Egypt is quite misconceived. For even if no such scriptoriums existed in its towns and cities, such a manuscript might easily have reached Egypt from Rome, Corinth or elsewhere in the literate Mediterranean world.

It is important to see the Magdalen Papyrus as the product of its social world, a real historical context of scribal centres, copying, distribution, patrons and readers. St Luke, for one, made excellent use of this system: he dedicated both his Gospel and its sequel, the book of Acts, to a high-ranking Roman civil servant, 'his Excellency' Theophilus (Luke 1:3, Acts 1:1). In those times, the dedicatee of a book was obliged to pay for its copying and distribution. Thus, an impoverished poet would look for a wealthy paymaster in the hope that a combination of flattery and talent would lead to his work being widely circulated. In St Luke's case, Theophilus himself was apparently eager to obtain the book – and the author provided him with a detailed account so that he 'may know the truth concerning the things of which you have been informed'. A Roman of Theophilus's stature had easy access to the scriptoria of the imperial administration, to individual scribes awaiting his commissions and, most importantly, to the so-called *tabellarii*, the highly efficient postmen of the Empire. Using an irregular but reliable network of couriers, everybody could send mail even to distant destinations. But it was the privilege of the nobility and of those in public service to use the imperial mail which could cover vast distances in a short time. Both systems were capable of remarkable feats: Corinth (Greece) to Puteoli (Italy) in five days was a normal delivery-time and in favourable weather conditions it was possible to send a letter from Rome to Alexandria in only three days. Documents sent from Thessaloniki in north-east Greece routinely reached Ascalon in Palestine within twelve days. These delivery-times surpass even today's postal services. Who in 1996 could hope for a letter posted in Rome to reach Alexandria three days later?

The outstanding efficiency of communications in New Testament times is an important consideration in our investigation. The communities, tribes and towns of this era were not cultural islands, insulated from outside influence. Until recently, however, scholars assumed that the Dead Sea Scrolls were written and stored by an exclusivist Jewish sect of anti-establishment fundamentalists. These people, the Essenes, had supposedly rejected the liberalism of the Jerusalem Temple and retreated to a monastic community in the Judaean desert, where they led an austere and highly disciplined life. This community was said to have produced hundreds of scrolls with Old Testament texts, intricate commentaries and their own distinctive theological works, which they then stored in caves.

According to such an interpretation, Essene teaching then reached the early Christians, perhaps via John the Baptist, and a variety of Qumranic elements eventually found their way into Christian faith and liturgical practice. This romantic conception, still current in many textbooks, has had to give way to a much more realistic and complex assessment. There is also a lunatic fringe of Qumran publications – books which claim that Jesus was crucified beside the Dead Sea and buried alive in Cave 7, or that the scrolls contain coded information about St Paul as a Roman secret agent and James the Just as Teacher of Righteousness, or that Qumran itself was a fortress manned by heavily armed zealots. None the less, more respectable work has revealed a great deal about Qumran, its inhabitants, caves and relationship to the broader social world.

The people of Qumran took an active part in the cultural market-place of information and textual exchange. They imported scrolls from Jerusalem, from Damascus and even from Rome: in Cave 7, a jar was found which carried the Hebrew inscription 'Roma' twice on its neck, indicating the provenance of its contents. Only recently, in 1995, further inscribed jar fragments were found on Masada, Herod's palace and fortress, which was conquered by the Romans in AD 73. These jars contained wine rather than scrolls, Herod having ordered his favourite vintage from Italy – the renowned Falernian wines from Campagna perhaps. The sender indicated in Latin – a language well understood by at least some of Masada's inhabitants – what kind of wine it was, where it came from and where it was destined to go. These shards are the only contemporary documents which mention Herod's name in Latin. They also have much to tell us about contemporary communications. Even on a mountain fortress in the desert, overlooking the lifeless Dead Sea, a buyer could procure vintage wine direct from his favourite vineyard in Italy within a couple of weeks.

In view of this first-century 'internet', it should not surprise us that Christian papyri were found at Qumran, or that a Roman officer left behind at Masada a papyrus sheet with the earliest extant quotation from Virgil;[8] or that there are, among hundreds of Hebrew and Aramaic texts discovered at Qumran, twenty-five Greek documents, six in Cave 4, nineteen in Cave 7 – a reflection of the multicultural, multilingual society of which this community was a part. Nor should we be surprised that the nationalist defenders of Masada, in their last stand against the Roman

10th Legion, were as happy to read Greek as Hebrew and Aramaic. The papyri, potsherds with Greek inscriptions and the Greek letter of Abascantos, sent to his friend Judas at the oasis of Ein Gedi, are all evidence of the ease and fluency with which Greek – the cultural language of the Roman oppressor – could be integrated into everyday life. Even Latin, as Herod's jars suggest, was familiar to the natives of Palestine.

St Matthew's Gospel and the Jesus Papyrus must be considered in such a setting. The social arrangements and technology of the first century not only permitted extremely fast connections between people but also the equally fast development of texts. Let us assume, as most scholars do, that this particular Gospel was written somewhere in the Syrian province of the Roman Empire, perhaps in Antioch. Now known as Antakia, this city in south-eastern Turkey is about 500 km north of Jerusalem. Christians and non-Christians alike were regular travellers on the road between the two places. It was a routine journey for ordinary citizens as well as merchants or postal services to take. A Gospel or any other book written in Antioch and meant to be read in Jerusalem could easily have reached its destination within a week. Sent to Rome, or to Alexandria, the parcel would have gone by sea mail whenever possible. Even allowing for detours, it would have been in the hands of its new owners before long. Where a Gospel came from, in other words, would have had little effect upon the time it took to reach its readers. Conceivably, a papyrus of St Matthew could have reached Luxor a few weeks after the composition of the Evangelist's original was complete. A scroll of St Mark's Gospel might have reached Qumran from Rome within a fortnight, via Jerusalem or direct from the port of Yafo or Caesarea Maritima where the ship would have berthed.

The earliest Christians took these speedy communications for granted; St Paul, for instance, told the recipients of his Letter to the Colossians: 'After this letter has been read among you, send it on to be read in the church of the Laodiceans; and get the letter from Laodicea for you to read yourselves' (Colossians 4:16). Those whom he was addressing clearly knew exactly how to copy the letter and would doubtless have preserved the original as a treasure. The reproduction would have been sent to Laodicea, by messenger or through the postal service, with a covering letter telling the new recipients to dispatch their own epistle, as instructed.

Further evidence for such practices is recorded by Eusebius of Caesarea, the famous church historian, librarian and Bishop of Caesarea
Maritima who lived from *c*. AD 260–340. Quoting a source from Rome,
where St Mark's Gospel was written after the departure of St Peter from
the city,[9] Eusebius writes: 'And they [the Romans] say that the Apostle,
knowing by the revelation of the spirit to him what had been done,
was pleased at their zeal and ratified the scripture for study in the
churches.'[10] Again, this would have posed no logistic difficulty. Copies
of this short Gospel – dozens, perhaps, or more – could have been
swiftly produced by amateur or professional scribes and despatched to
the communities, north, west, east or south, from Athens to Corinth,
Jerusalem to Alexandria. When the manuscripts reached their destinations, they would be copied once again by local scribes and disseminated rapidly to other groups.

Applying the Tools of the Trade

Having seen how quickly and efficiently documents could be distributed
and copied throughout the Roman Empire, we can now turn to the key
question of the comparative material which may be used for the dating
of the Magdalen Papyrus. Confronted with a manuscript of unknown
date, as we have seen, the first step is to examine its handwriting – its
palaeographical traits – and the characteristics which distinguish the
writer. These can include the general appearance of the script, the
average length and height of the lines, punctuation marks, individual
letters, their formation and the manner in which they are linked or
separated.

The next step, comparison with other papyri, is more complex. The
first danger lies in the selection and quantity of material to be used. In
1994 Carsten Thiede argued that manuscripts from three different
places – Qumran, the Nahal Hever and Herculaneum – would suggest a
date during the second half of the first century for the Magdalen
Papyrus. The key point is that the latest possible date for any documents
found at Qumran is AD 68 and for Herculaneum AD 79. Thiede was
immediately accused of assuming that 'all scribes of the Jewish diaspora
wrote in the same script'.[11] In response, it is worth quoting an observation made by Peter Parsons of Oxford University, one of the most

eminent figures in international papyrology, who was asked in 1991 to
date the inscription preserved on a vase discovered in Italy, at a site
called 'Mola di Monte Gelato'. Parsons wrote:

> Palaeographers debate whether different areas practised different sorts of
> script. For documentary hands there is indeed some evidence of local
> peculiarities ... For literary hands, the evidence itself ... is minimal. The
> Monte Gelato text adds interestingly to that evidence, and speaks for
> uniformity: I can see nothing in the script that would be surprising in
> Greco-Egyptian manuscripts of the same period.[12]

Thus, the obvious conclusion was to look not only for comparative
material from central Italy but also for 'parallels from the other side of
the Mediterranean'.[13] These were precisely the methods used by Thiede
when redating the Magdalen Papyrus.

The second danger in choosing material for comparison stems from
the fact that every good papyrologist knows hundreds, if not thousands,
of papyri to which he or others have assigned dates. These manuscripts
tend to be neatly categorized – one such category being the Biblical
Uncial already mentioned. The papyrologist often accepts this scholarly
framework uncritically, uses the categories he has inherited, and assigns
manuscripts to them without keeping an open mind about the categories themselves.

The label 'Biblical Uncial' is an attractive one to apply to the Jesus
Papyrus. Nobody questions that the fragments are from a biblical text
or that the letters are indeed uncial in form, capital letters, distinguished
by curves, occasional ligatures and so on. Those critics who drew attention to this style, and to Guglielmo Cavallo's textbook on the subject,
seemed to have a point.[14] Yet it was clear that certain key assumptions
had persisted out of respect for tradition rather than because they were
logically defensible.[15]

When the British papyrologist Colin Roberts published the first
edition of the Magdalen Papyrus in 1953, he was aware of two previous,
informal datings: Huleatt himself had suggested a date some time in
the third century, while in 1901 Hunt had added up to a century to
this estimate. As we have seen, the latter's argument was based on the
faulty principle that manuscripts written in codex form could not be
earlier than the third or even the fourth century. Roberts was aware

of this error and soon realized that the Magdalen fragments were considerably older.

He deduced as much from their comparison with other papyri from the Berlin and Oxyrhynchus collections. A good example of this procedure is his statement that 'in the Magdalen fragments the minute *omikron* and the flat *omega*, common in third-century hands, are absent'.[16] Though Roberts's analysis corrected Hunt's error, it suffered from the problem of relativism: the comparative papyri which Roberts used are neither precisely dated nor clearly datable. Where it is possible to estimate a possible period, as in the case of Oxyrhynchus papyrus 661 (from the *Iambi* of Callimachus), a late-second-century date emerges. Yet this manuscript, for instance, is visibly later in style than the Magdalen Papyrus. So the question is not resolved.

With the late-second-century date proposed by Roberts, the papyrus had none the less acquired a new significance. It was now the oldest known papyrus of St Matthew's Gospel, though not the oldest text of any gospel. Roberts himself had published the oldest known papyrus fragment of St John's Gospel in 1935, assigning it to the first quarter of the second century. Ever since, the St John Papyrus, P52 (or John Rylands Greek 457 after its inventory number at the John Rylands University Library, Manchester), has been considered by far the oldest surviving New Testament manuscript. Roberts's redating of the Magdalen Papyrus, though remarkable, did not challenge this assumption. Three years later, in 1956, Ramón Roca-Puig published the Barcelona Papyrus and the two scholars agreed that the five fragments belonged to the later second century.[17] The two most popular editions followed this lead. 'About 200' is the date given in the *Greek New Testament* of the United Bible Societies and '*c*. 200' is that in the Nestle-Aland *Novum Testamentum Graece*.

Thiede's new edition of the Jesus Papyrus was not primarily concerned with dating. He was more interested in improving the text of the fragments. But the question had to be asked: was Roberts right? Had techniques improved or had the samples of papyri available changed sufficiently to challenge his claim? Clearly the most fascinating group of new manuscripts to have emerged in recent decades are the Dead Sea Scrolls. Discovered between 1947 and 1955, the scrolls and fragments from the Qumran caves have been subjected to countless investigations. But the Greek fragments among them had not been used for comparative purposes in the dating of other Greek literature, in spite of the fact that their latest possible date was indisputable: AD 68.[18] The Qumran texts thus fulfilled one of the criteria of reliable comparative palaeography: they were datable and therefore an ideal starting-point for a reassessment of the date of the Magdalen Papyrus.

For a papyrus to be 'datable' is not especially unusual. Certain indications of date are necessary, either from the archaeology of the site where the text was found, or a clue from the text itself. In the same way that Qumran manuscripts must precede the year AD 68 and texts found at Herculaneum and Pompeii can be no younger than AD 79, so a reference to the reign of Emperor Domitian would restrict a papyrus to AD 81–96. Such a manuscript, the 'P. London 2078', a private letter, had been used by Colin Roberts in his search for the earliest end of the range in his dating of the St John Papyrus, at Manchester, the P52. Although the date in this case could not be narrowed down to a specific year, there was at least a precise range – an earliest and a latest possible year.

Such a papyrus would be called 'datable' rather than precisely 'dated'. Literary texts such as novels, poems, plays and historical writings rarely include precise information about the year in which they are written. The earliest Greek New Testament manuscript with a date is the minuscle number 461 at St Petersburg, a Gospel codex of AD 835. The earliest dated manuscript of any biblical text is a Syriac 'Peshitta' translation of Genesis and Exodus on vellum, dated to the year 775 of the Greek era, which is AD 463/64 in modern chronology. But much older non-biblical dated manuscripts have survived, even from the first-century AD, and can be used for comparative purposes.

Our starting-point must be the date previously assigned to the Magdalen Papyrus: late second century. It was a date arrived at by addressing all the arguments which might be mustered in favour of a later date. Any survey of third- and fourth-century texts will confirm that Roberts and Roca-Puig were right in one respect: however early these fragments are, they are certainly no later than the late second century. So what about the second century itself? There are indeed a number of similarities with second-century hands in the Magdalen fragments but these are somewhat tenuous, more probably reflecting the partial survival into the second century of much older stylistic traits. More importantly, those second-century manuscripts which at first appear most comparable are themselves only indirectly dated; they are papyri for which there is no related archaeological or internal chronological information. This might suggest a sort of scholarly stalemate in which it is best to accept Robert's uncontentious conclusion. Yet it was Roberts himself who provided the incentive to pursue the redating.

As we have seen, the *nomina sacra* or holy names – abbreviations of the Greek words for 'Lord' (*kyrios*) and 'Jesus' (*Iēsous*) – are one of the most striking features of the Magdalen Papyrus. They became popular in early Christianity and were soon used as shorthand for other words like 'God' (*theos*), '(Holy) Ghost' (*pneuma*) and further terms related to the Holy Trinity. Usually, the first and last letters would be used, KS for *kyrios*, IS for *Iēsous* and so forth.

The sudden and general adoption of this new system seems to have been a conscious attempt to emulate the Jewish custom of abbreviating the name of God. It was a momentous decision for – as we shall see – it implied a dramatic theological claim about the nature and role of Jesus.

As early as 1979, Colin Roberts was convinced that such a system could not have been the spontaneous decision of an individual scribe. 'The system was too complex for the ordinary scribe to operate without rules or an authoritative exemplar,' he wrote.[19] He suggested that it was developed and introduced by one of the two early Christian communities which possessed such authority, the Jerusalem Church or the Church at Antioch where the followers of Jesus were first called 'Christians' (Acts 11:26). Roberts tends towards Jerusalem as the likely origin of the new scribal practice because of the city's traditional authority as the community of St Peter and St James. Of necessity – and crucially – he then suggested that this development took place before AD 70, the year in which the city and the Temple were destroyed. In fact, as the Christians left Jerusalem at the beginning of the Jewish revolt against the Romans in AD 66,[20] this is the more probable 'final date' for any directives from Jerusalem.

The appearance of *nomina sacra* in the Magdalen fragments is not the only reason to investigate the possibility of a much earlier date than the late second century. That they are codex fragments does not, as we have seen, in any sense rule out an early date. As the Italian papyrologist Italo Gallo has written, the codex as a format was in common Christian use during the first century, 'not later than 70 AD'.[21] There is a clear case for examining first-century comparative material to see where this leads us.

The Qumran caves have provided us with Greek texts which may be older than the first century BC but cannot be later than AD 68. Of the six sizeable texts found in Cave 4, one of the leather scrolls and one of the papyri are especially useful for comparison with the Magdalen fragments.[22] Both preserve passages from Leviticus (their catalogue names are 4QLXXLev[a] and Pap4QLXXLev[b]). The papyrus consists of no fewer than ninety-five fragments and is written in a far from uniform script (as Peter Parsons noted when he commented on its date on behalf of its editors[23]) but could be dated to the mid-first century AD. In general appearance, the manuscript bears certain similarities to the Magdalen Papyrus, especially on the more uniform Fragments 24 and 25 (Leviticus 5:8–10). More particularly, some of the individual letters, such as the *alpha*, *beta*, *gamma*, *epsilon*, and *omikron*, are closer to the script of the Jesus Papyrus than others. This is an interesting starting-point but not quite enough for a reliable dating reference.

The leather manuscript of Leviticus, however, offers remarkable affinities. To highlight their characteristics, Peter Parsons provided drawings of letters from the Qumran fragment which – though he cannot have been aware of it – emphasize the likeness between the Qumran text and the Magdalen Papyrus. If anything, the leather manuscript is the more archaic, as though it belongs to a somewhat earlier period of the same style. For example, the letters touch, or nearly touch, each other more regularly than in the Magdalen Papyrus and its Barcelona counterpart. In the three small Magdalen fragments, this scribal practice – which was almost completely abandoned in second- and third-century Bible manuscripts – can be observed surprisingly often. It is visible between *epsilon* and *tau* (Fragment 2, verso, line 2), *upsilon* and *tau* (Fragment 1, recto, line 4), *nu* and *tau* (Fragment 1, recto, line 3, and verso, line 3), *alpha* and *iota* (Fragment 2, recto, line 2) and between *nu* and *alpha* (Fragment 2, verso, line 3). This may not be one of the most obvious characteristics of the Jesus Papyrus but it is a significant one in this context.

A further similarity should be noted between the Oxford and Barcelona fragments of St Matthew's Gospel, on the one hand, and the Leviticus leather text, on the other. In marked contrast to typical examples of the second-, third- or fourth-century Biblical Uncials, the letters on the two papyri are drawn in an even manner, the horizontal and vertical strokes being equally thick. The leather scroll from Qumran is also characterized by a style of lettering which predates the Biblical Uncials. Peter Parsons suggested a date in the late first century BC for the leather scroll, which would make it some fifty years older than the papyrus scroll of Leviticus found near by. We know that the earliest possible date that could be considered for the Magdalen Papyrus is the year of the last events recounted in the Gospel: the death, Resurrection and Ascension of Christ which most scholars would place in AD 30.[24] The leather fragment from Cave 4 helps narrow the field further, providing us with a useful preliminary example of a Greek hand that suggests a first-century date for the Jesus Papyrus.

In Cave 7, just beneath Cave 4, overlooking the Wadi Qumran, eighteen Greek papyrus fragments were discovered in 1955 and one reversed imprint of a Greek papyrus on hardened soil.[25] The importance of the *texts* from this cave was discussed in Chapter 3; it is the *handwriting* on the fragments which is of interest in the context of redating the Magdalen Papyrus. Similar styles are visible on Fragment 7Q6[1], for example, and, to a lesser degree, on Fragments 7Q1 and 7Q2. But these two caves are not the only such sites where Greek texts have been found. A sensational discovery was made in August 1952 at the Nahal Hever, south of Qumran, when Bedouins came upon a cave with a Greek scroll of the 'Minor Prophets'. In later years, Israeli archaeologists identified this as the 'Cave of Horrors' and found nine further fragments of the same scroll.

Two different scribes with distinctive approaches had been employed to write this scroll. Scribe A's hand more closely resembles the style of the Magdalen Papyrus, in general appearance as much as individual letters. But scribe B also offers some similarities, particularly and interestingly in the letters *eta* and *mu*, where the affinities between scribe A and the Oxford fragments are less marked. From time to time, both scribes use characteristics of the so-called *Zierstil* (decorated style) or *Häkchenstil* (hooked style), ornaments with little dots and hooks added, or elongations which were popular in the first centuries BC and AD. Although less frequently, these also occur in the Magdalen Papyrus, on the letters *alpha*, *gamma*, *delta* and *lambda*, for instance. Scribe B, furthermore, brings to mind a style which has been named 'Herculanean', as most of the examples of it were discovered during the excavation of Herculaneum. All texts from Herculaneum must, as we know, predate AD 79. Quite without reference to this site, the Nahal Hever scroll of the 'Minor Prophets' was indeed dated to the mid-first century AD.[26]

Summarizing the evidence from the Dead Sea Scrolls, we can be satisfied that these Greek texts are closer to the Magdalen fragments than alternative second- or third-century papyri. This evidence is sufficiently compelling to suggest a first-century date, a date towards AD 70 or earlier, for the Jesus Papyrus. It is worth reiterating that the Greek comparative material from Qumran had not otherwise been used to date Greek manuscripts. We should also remember that the Dead Sea community who collected these scrolls played an active part in the Greek-speaking world, which embraced such distant places as Rome, Herculaneum, Alexandria and Luxor. However monastic their way of life, they were not culturally isolated and their manuscripts now play a helpful role in the dating of early New Testament papyri.

Nor should Masada be neglected. Many Jews from Qumran found refuge there until the fortress was overcome by the Romans in AD 73/74, taking with them scrolls such as the *Sabbath Songs* and contributing to Masada's multilingual culture. A fair number of Greek documents were found among the many Hebrew and Aramaic texts, including letters and notes with information about the supply of food and water. As so often in antiquity, potsherds or *ostraca* were also used for a variety of purposes, to record whole poems or for the briefest of communications. Among the Greek *ostraca* from Masada, there are several examples which resemble the style of the Magdalen Papyrus. An astonishingly close match is the fragmentary *ostracon* No. 784, bearing the personal names 'Lea' and 'Amm(ias)'. We know that this potsherd must be older than AD 73/74.[27]

Critics of such comparative work – particularly those who are inexperienced in palaeography[28] – continue to argue that reference material from the Dead Sea Scrolls is inadequate when considering a papyrus found in Upper Egypt. Yet, as we know, the Greek Dead Sea Scrolls and the Jesus Papyrus could have come from practically anywhere in the Roman Empire and even, in principle, from the same place – somewhere like Alexandria, where both Jews and Christians were busy writing. None the less, it is still useful to examine Greek papyri found or acquired in Egypt, the major source of all Greek manuscripts that have survived from antiquity.

First-century papyri are common enough at Oxyrhynchus and a perusal of the published finds soon yields a strikingly useful text: the oldest known papyrus of a work by the Greek comedian Aristophanes (*c.* 448–*c.* 380 BC), *Equites* (*The Knights*). It is written in a careful, round hand, with medium to small letters and distinctly bilinear (that is, the letters are kept between two imagined lines), with the exception of the two letters with extensions *phi* and *psi*. This manuscript matches the Magdalen Papyrus in technical detail as much as in its general appearance and individual letters. Just one example of many: in the Magdalen Papyrus, there are also two letters that do not keep within the lines: *rho* and *tau*. The date assigned to this unique Aristophanes papyrus is 'late first century BC or early first century AD' and it does, in many respects, look like an older sister to the Oxford fragments.

But whereas the Qumran texts are clearly datable at one end of the spectrum, neither the leather scroll of the 'Minor Prophets' nor the Aristophanes papyrus are dated or datable at the other end; their dates have had to be assigned by comparative methods. This is one of the problems in the dating process. By depending exclusively on such manuscripts, the papyrologist finds himself basing his work on a fragile logical structure of loose data kept upright only because the pieces of evidence happen to be supporting each other. In the words of the theologian Austin Farrer, commenting not on papyri, but on the dating of New Testament writings: 'The datings of all these books are like a line of tipsy revellers walking home arm-in-arm; each is kept in position by the others and none is firmly grounded. The whole series can lurch five years this way or that, and still not collide with a solid obstacle.'[29] Equally, the papyrologist who relies on the range of dates associated with a particular style – Biblical Uncial, 'decorated', or some other – is in a scholarly straitjacket which prevents him from looking at individual cases on their own merits. Any attempt at reasonably precise dating depends on open-mindedness and flexibility of approach; being prepared for the exception rather than a vindication of the rule.

In a comment on the nature of textual criticism, the great Cambridge latinist and poet A. E. Housman laid down a scholarly precept which applies equally well to palaeography:

Textual criticism is ... not susceptible of hard-and-fast rules. It would be much easier if it were; and that is why people try to pretend that it is, or at least behave as if they thought so. Of course you can have hard-and-fast rules if you like, but then you will have false rules, and they will lead you wrong; because their simplicity will render them inapplicable to problems which are not simple, but complicated by the play of personality. A textual critic engaged upon his business is not at all like Newton investigating the motions of the planets; he is much more like a dog hunting for fleas. If a dog hunted for fleas on mathematical principles, basing his researches on statistics of area and population, he would never catch a flea except by accident. They require to be treated as individuals; and every problem which presents itself to the textual critic must be regarded as possibly unique.[30]

Having come thus far, what is needed is a precisely dated and possibly unique manuscript which corroborates what we have already concluded about the Magdalen Papyrus. Such a manuscript – a dated papyrus resembling it almost like a twin – does indeed exist. It comes from Oxyrhynchus and was published in the second volume of the Oxyrhynchus papyri in 1899. Only two years before Huleatt's gift reached Oxford, the one dated papyrus that can help to pinpoint the age of the Magdalen fragments was edited by Hunt and Grenfell for the Egypt Exploration Fund in London.[31] This papyrus is an intriguing document in its own right: it is a letter, written by (or on behalf of) the Egyptian farmer Harmiysis to the civil servant Papiskos and his colleagues at Oxyrhynchus. He tells the appropriate authorities, in remarkably clear, careful, uncial handwriting, that he had twelve lambs some time ago and now wants to add seven new lambs to that number. Three officials signed the letter with their attestations, in their own distinctive, hurried, cursive styles. All four, the farmer and the three officials at Oxyrhynchus, dated the document. In the florid style of the time, Harmiysis writes:

> I declared, in the present 12th year of the Nero Klaudios Kaisar Sebastos Germanikos the Autokrator, at the above-mentioned [town of] Phthochis, that I have twelve lambs from my stock of animals.

Translated into modern chronology, this twelfth year of Nero's reign is the period AD 65/66. The three officials, in their attestation, are more bureaucratically precise and confirm the seven new lambs with the date 'In the year 12 of Nero the Lord, Epeiph 30': that is, 24 July, AD 66.

This manuscript therefore provides us with an exact date. (It also, by coincidence, refers to Nero as 'lord', *kyrios*, a word applied to Jesus on Fragment 3 of the Magdalen Papyrus.)

Thus, our examination of the various indirectly dated, datable and precisely dated papyri from the period suggested by the researches of Colin Roberts and Italo Gallo indicates a conclusive result. The comparable material yields a date of *c.* AD 66 for the Magdalen Papyrus, with a distinct tendency towards a slightly earlier date in the mid-first century. Conversely there is no equally conclusive comparable material from later periods. Thus, the usual palaeographical 'margin of error' would allow for an earlier, but not for a later date. The fragments at Oxford and Barcelona belong to a particular type of uncial writing that flourished in the mid-first century AD, with precursors at the beginning of the century. Since the text on the fragments is from a complete Gospel, rather than an earlier collection of Jesus's sayings or Passion stories, we can be sure that the manuscript cannot be older than AD 30. As we noticed in the comparison with the Qumran leather scroll and the Aristophanes papyrus, the St Matthew fragments represent the later phase of this particular type of handwriting.

Remaining Challenges

The Oxford and Barcelona fragments, P64 and P67, come from a Christian codex which, as we have seen, presupposes earlier scrolls. Necessarily, St Matthew's original, the lost 'first scroll' so to speak, must predate the Jesus Papyrus by a number of years. This is an unpalatable conclusion for New Testament scholars convinced that St Matthew's Gospel is a later, community creation, describing Jesus as a miracle-worker, theological thinker and prophet in a way which would meet the liturgical needs of the eighties of the first century. To some academics and many ordinary Christians however already convinced that the Gospels consist of authentic eyewitness material from apostolic times, the result has come as no surprise.

The papyrologist can only offer his forensic findings. Papyrological analysis, the editing and dating of ancient manuscripts, must be conducted without scholarly preconception and free from the constraints of a particular doctrinal agenda. Equally, it is legitimate to point out where the findings of papyrology and palaeography might lead. The worldwide controversy caused by the redating of the Magdalen Papyrus has repercussions for a broad range of orthodoxies about the early Church, the historic Jesus and the origins of the Gospel. In our final chapters, we examine these.

It is important that the papyrological quest does not end with the three fragments in the Old Library of Magdalen College. Two papyri of St Matthew's gospel, one of St Luke and – following the datings suggested by Herbert Hunger and Young-Kyu Kim – one papyrus codex each of St John and of the Pauline Epistles have already been redated to the first and early second centuries. The process of re-evaluation must continue. Since, as we have seen, the Biblical Uncial category has been mislabelled, is it not worth asking whether other early papyri may also be much older than has been assumed?

Plenty of candidates suggest themselves. There is the P77 from Oxyrhynchus (P. Oxy. 2683), a small papyrus codex fragment preserving St Matthew 23:30–39. Its editors, among them John Rea and Peter Parsons, dated it to the late second or early third century; Philip W. Comfort suggested c. AD 150.[32] It is certainly later than the Jesus Papyrus, less carefully written but clearly in the same category as, say, the St John Papyrus at Manchester, the P52, which has been dated to the first quarter of the second century but could be older. Another example from St Matthew's Gospel – in fact, the manuscript which heads the list of all New Testament papyri – is P1 or P. Oxy. 2, now at the University of Pennsylvania in Philadelphia, which includes Matthew 1:1–9, 12 and 14–20. It is a magnificent example of a precise, somewhat elaborate hand, and the third-century date commonly ascribed to it is certainly incorrect. One could not compare it to the Magdalen fragments, or even to the Paris St Luke, but it is not that much later.[33]

Other Gospel fragments also strongly suggest earlier dates. The manuscript P5 or P. Oxy. 208 with passages from John 1, 16 and 20, now at the British Library, is commonly assigned to the third century, a date as widely accepted as it is deceptive.[34] The papyrus P69 or P. Oxy. 2383 at the Ashmolean Museum in Oxford bears Luke 22:41, 45–48 and 58–61 and has been dated as late as the third century. When Edgar Lobel, Colin Roberts and others first edited the latter in 1957,[35] the scholarly orthodoxy of their time enabled Roberts to see that Arthur Hunt's fourth-century dating was wrong but it prohibited him from probing more deeply – as he was eventually to do in his work on the origins of the codex. A thorough reassessment of P69, unburdened by the old preoccupation with Biblical Uncial, might well show its closeness to the Lukan papyrus P4 at the Bibliothèque Nationale, with its new date in the early second century or even late first century.

The inventory of papyri ripe for redating does not end here. There is the P70 or P. Oxy. 2384 which is partly at the Ashmolean and partly at the Papyrological Institute G. Vitelli in Florence. These fragments are from Matthew 2, 3, 11, 12 and 24 and have been dated to the third century. Again, however, there is reason to consider this estimate too late. In a recent edition of a New Testament papyrus, T. C. Skeat dated the codex fragment P90 or P. Oxy. 3523 (John 18:36–19:7), now at the Ashmolean, to the (late) second century.[36] He was attacked for his courage but is certainly right, if a little too cautious. A mid- to early-second-century date appears more likely, given the new range of comparative options we have been discussing. Skeat, at any rate, has shown that progress is possible even within the traditional paradigm, of which he is undoubtedly one of the great proponents. Though less bold in other areas, he has here provided further incentive to pursue this process of palaeographical re-evaluation. One thing is certain: if the P90 belongs to the second century, the Magdalen Papyrus – which has demonstrably older palaeography – has been correctly redated to an even earlier period.

It should be clear that the controversy spawned by the redating of the Jesus Papyrus is not an end but a beginning in terms of the re-evaluation of New Testament papyri. This single claim is the most striking example of a new paradigm in biblical scholarship which deserves broad attention. In our final two chapters, we examine some of its implications for our understanding of early Christianity and of the relevance of St Matthew's Gospel in our own times.

6

Scribes, Gospel Readers and
the Dawn of Christianity

What happy application, what praiseworthy industry, to preach to men by means of the hand, to untie the tongue by means of the fingers, to bring quiet salvation to mortals, and to fight the devil's insidious wiles with pen and ink! For every word of the Lord written by the scribe is a wound inflicted on Satan. And so, though seated in one spot, the scribe traverses diverse lands through the dissemination of what he has written.

Cassiodorus, *Institutiones, c.* AD 356

Despite a widely held opinion to the contrary, classical studies make rapid advances.

L. D. Reynolds and N. G. Wilson, *Scribes and Scholars. A Guide to the Transmission of Greek & Latin Literature,* 3rd edn., (1991)

What can we know about the men and women who first used the Magdalen Papyrus more than 1,000 years ago? How educated and cultured might they have been? And what do these tiny fragments tell us about the doctrinal development of early Christianity? We have seen what detailed textual analysis reveals about the technical aspects of this extraordinary manuscript. But it is also a window into a lost world: the spiritual and intellectual milieu of the very first Christians.

As we have already observed, Jewish society in first-century Palestine was trilingual: Hebrew was the language of the synagogue and Temple; Aramaic was the language of the everyday; and Greek had been the cultural language of the eastern Mediterranean since its conquest. Some, particularly those dealing with the Roman administration, would also have acquired a working knowledge of Latin. That the Romans used their native tongue in Palestine, in spite of general fluency in Greek, is obvious from the Latin 'Pontius Pilate inscription' found at Caesarea

Maritima. The only surviving inscription bearing Pilate's name, this is part of his dedication of a *Tiberieum*, a building in honour of Emperor Tiberius. It is also obvious from John 19:20, where the inscription which Pontius Pilate had fixed to the cross of Jesus is described: 'This notice was read by many of the Jews, because the place where Jesus was crucified was near the city, and the writing was in Hebrew, Latin and Greek.'

Needless to say, the gift of multilingualism was unevenly distributed. Even an otherwise cultivated man like the Jewish historian Flavius Josephus admitted that he found it difficult to attain fluency in Greek and to lose his accent (although some of this modesty may be a *captatio benevolentiae*, a rhetorical attempt to elicit a flattering contradiction from the person addressed). Yet the New Testament is full of instances where a keen awareness of the Greek language and Hellenistic culture is vividly apparent. Bethsaida, the town where Simon (later Peter) and his brother Andrew grew up, belonged to the realm of the Tetrarch Philippus who had done much to 'Hellenize' the area. Personal names suggest the extent to which this policy took root: Andrew is a Greek name and Simon is bicultural: it first occurs in literature not in a Hebrew text but in a Greek play written in 423 BC, Aristophanes' comedy *The Clouds*, v. 351. A third disciple from Bethsaida (John 1:44) also had a Greek name: Philip. This site, rediscovered by the Benedictine monk and archaeologist Bargil Pixner, was recently described by the American theologian Elizabeth McNamer as, from a Christian perspective, 'the most important town after Jerusalem'.[1] Among the discoveries at Bethsaida have been a fisherman's house with anchors, fishing hooks and a needle for mending nets. Also found were a wine cellar, an oven and two basalt slabs on top of one another, used for grinding grain. McNamer explained what happened after this discovery: 'One of my students tried to push the upper stone and she couldn't. Then I had two of them push it. And of course, Jesus said, "Two women will be grinding at the mill" [Matthew 24:41, RSV], and it does take two to do this.'

Jesus himself was brought up in Nazareth, only six kilometres or one and a half hours' walking distance from Sepphoris which was being rebuilt as the capital of Galilee during his youth. Some scholars maintain that Jesus and Joseph, both builders by profession, played an active part in the construction of this place: the Greek word *tecton* in Matthew

13:55 does not mean 'carpenter', as most Bibles mistranslate it, but 'builder'. Its etymological traces can still be recognized in the modern word 'architect'. Sepphoris, again, was a profoundly Hellenized place, as is clear from contemporary inscriptions and the magnificent theatre which was built while Jesus was a young man. Even in Palestine, plays were performed in Greek for a population remarkably familiar with that tongue. In Sepphoris, a town of 25,000 inhabitants, it is striking that the theatre was capable of seating an audience of 5,000. This suggests that a command of the language sufficient to understand Greek drama was not confined to the upper echelons of first-century Galilean society.

Turning to the New Testament itself, no one doubts that Jesus's first language was Aramaic and that he was able to read Hebrew. Luke 4:16–30, where he unrolls a scroll of Isaiah, reads from it and interprets the text, provides evidence of this. But there is also reason to suppose that Jesus spoke Greek: Mark 7:24–30 refers to his meeting with the Syro–Phoenician woman in the 'territory of Tyre'. St Mark seems to have been more intrigued by linguistic subtlety than the other Gospel authors and from time to time used Latin, Greek and Aramaic technical terms, always with translation. In 7:26, he writes: *He de gyne en Hellenís*, which means 'The woman was Greek-speaking.'[2] Thus, almost incidentally, St Mark tells us that the conversation with Jesus was conducted in Greek. A similar incident is recorded in Mark 12:13–17, where Jesus and the Pharisees debate the tribute to Caesar – in Greek, as demonstrated by the German archaeologist and New Testament scholar Benedikt Schwank.[3]

Between 37 BC and AD 67, not a single coin with a Hebrew or Aramaic inscription was allowed into Palestine or minted there. The text on all coins was Greek or occasionally, if the money had come via Lyons, for example, in Latin. In the following passage from St Mark, all depends upon the text on the coin, including Jesus's final declaration (which cannot be readily translated into Aramaic): 'Pay to Caesar what belongs to Caesar – and God what belongs to God.' Such a coin, bearing a portrait of the Emperor Tiberius, would have been anathema to orthodox Jews. While the portrait itself contravened the second commandment, the inscription included the title of Caesar as the son of *Divus Augustus*, the God or Deified Augustus. Though the inscription was in Greek, this was still outrageous blasphemy – as would have been fully understood by those who handled such coins. Once again, this passage illustrates the extent to which Greek played a part in the social world of early Christianity.

In parenthesis, it is worth noting that in the same incident Jesus uses a term borrowed from the language of the Greek theatre. The word *hypokrisis* ('hypocrisy') appears in Mark 12:15, while Jesus addresses the Pharisees directly in Matthew 22:18 as *hypokritai* ('hypocrites'). The Greek word means actors and thus, by extension, those who pretend, who act a role. We might even speculate that Jesus picked up this word, rarely used in its figurative sense before his time, as a member of the audience at Sepphoris.

There are other events described in the Gospels where Jesus seems to have spoken in this cultural lingua franca, such as his interrogation by Pilate, and the scene in the garden after the Resurrection where the risen Christ meets Mary Magdalene and she mistakes him for a gardener (John 20:11–18). The latter conversation appears to have been conducted in Greek until Jesus addressed Mary by name. Only then did Mary turn round to face him and say in Aramaic, '*Rabbuni*' or 'Master': a sudden, conscious change of language.

Although St John's delightfully precise depiction of this scene tells us a great deal about the use of languages in first-century Palestine, this passage remains a matter for debate. A less contentious illustration of the multilingual, multicultural society to which the first Christians belonged can be found in Acts. St Paul, a well-educated Jew of Pharisaic origins, capable of quoting Greek authors at whim (Aratus in Acts 17:28, Menander in 1 Corinthians 15:33, Epimenides in Titus 1:12, to name but three) experienced his conversion on the way to Damascus. In that 'light from heaven', he encountered Jesus and became his follower. St Luke considered this event so pivotal that he recounted it three times, at critical moments in his book. The first version is his own (Acts 9:1–9), a straightforward narrative account told at the chronologically appropriate moment. The second version is St Paul's; in Acts 22:5–21, he addresses the Jews of Jerusalem, having been given protective custody by the Romans. The background to the story is interesting in its own right. Arrested, Paul surprises the officers – who had mistaken him for an Egyptian – by addressing them in Greek ('You speak Greek, then?', Acts 21:37), and is then permitted to speak to the Jews, which he does in Aramaic. They respond with bemused fascination ('When they heard him speak to them in Aramaic, they became very quiet',

Acts 22:2, NIV). Paul's version of the Damascus experience is geared towards a Jewish audience, its idiom and the explanations he employs founded on 'the Law of our ancestors' (22:3).

In Acts 26:12–23, St Paul tells the story a second time. The setting is a court appearance before the authorities at Caesarea Maritima where, once more, he is in Roman custody. Both his interrogators – King Herod Agrippa II and the recently arrived Roman procurator Festus – had been brought up in the Roman educational system and would have been familiar with the literature, philosophy and languages of the Empire. As a well-educated Roman citizen, St Paul naturally addresses them in Greek. He also tailors his story to his audience, making no allusion on this occasion to 'the Law of our ancestors'. Here, he adds a saying of Jesus himself: 'Saul, Saul, why are you persecuting me? It is hard for you, kicking against the goad' (Acts 26:14). Jesus, as Paul points out, spoke in Aramaic, while he translates his words into Greek for Festus and Agrippa. The Greek rendering should have sounded familiar to them: *sklerón soi pròs kéntra laktízein*. This was an unmistakable allusion to one of the most popular cycles of Greek tragedy, the Oresteian trilogy by Aeschylus which is still frequently performed today. In the first of the three tragedies, *Agamemnon*, Aegisthus says to the Chorus (vv. 1623–4): 'Does not this sight bid you reflect? then do not kick / Against the goad, lest you should strike out, and be hurt.'

The central part of this passage, the kicking against the goad (*pròs kéntra me láktize*), occurs in a less recognizable context elsewhere in Aeschylus's writing, in his tragedy *Prometheus* (v. 235). It was also used in a similar form, though in a quite different context, by Euripides in *Bacchae* (v. 795). Even a Latin comedian, Terentius, employs it in his play *Phormio* (vv. 77–8): 'The word came to my mind: For what stupidity it is if you kick against the goad' (*Nam quae inscitia est? Advorsum stimulum calces*).

In short, therefore, these words on the lips of Jesus, quoted by St Paul, should have struck a cultural chord with his interrogators. The reference to *Agamemnon*, v. 1624, may have seemed particularly obvious. What is clear is that Agrippa and Festus would have acknowledged a shared frame of reference. They would have understood Paul's insinuation that Jesus of Nazareth, the crucified Galilean, had been familiar with the Hellenistic culture and that his apostle could quote him in Greek without awkwardness.

This was the rich linguistic soil from which sprang texts like the

Magdalen Papyrus. Jesus, his apostles and the first Christians were not uneducated simpletons. If the situation required it, they could speak eloquently in more than one language. Christianity's early mission was meant to be equally accessible to the Jewish masses at the Temple, to a Hellenized Jewish king and to a Roman procurator. Agrippa's response in Acts 26:27 indicates the force of this versatile strategy: 'A little more, and your arguments would make a Christian of me.'[4] The Magdalen fragments must be seen as the minuscule physical remnants of this formidable and dynamic strategy – a strategy which emerged not long after the events described in the papyrus itself.

We have already seen how even the nationalist defenders of Masada in their last stand against the Romans thought nothing of using Greek; how Greek documents reached the allegedly isolated community at Qumran; how St Luke used the services of a high-ranking Roman to have his Gospel copied and distributed; and how St Paul's circle of friends were accustomed to notebooks with a Latin name, the *membranae*. What can be said about the scribes who were the pivot of this remarkable system of patronage and multicultural communication?

Like the Greeks and Romans, the Christian authors and their scribes employed secretaries or *amanuenses*, trusted helpers who were well-versed in literary techniques and scribal methods. Some of them are mentioned by name in the New Testament, and St Luke refers to them generally at the beginning of his Gospel: 'Seeing that many others have undertaken to draw up accounts of the events that have reached their fulfilment among us, as these were handed down to us by those who from the outset were eyewitnesses and ministers of the word . . .' (Luke 1:1–2). Notable is the importance he attributes to the eyewitnesses behind the written records, including those preceding his own. The 'ministers of the word' are the *hyperetai*, the helpers. In New Testament times, the word was often used to denote attendants or servants in the synagogues, or attendants of kings and magistrates. In this case, it clearly refers to those who helped spread the good news about Jesus in writing.

The word occurs again in the sequel to St Luke's Gospel, Acts, 13:5. The New Testament scholar R. O. P. Taylor was the first to notice that John Mark, traditionally identified as the author of the oldest Gospel, is referred to as a *hyperetes* and member of the missionary team organized by Paul and Barnabas in about AD 46. He is so described not to indicate that he was an assistant to either of these men but apparently to declare a title or qualification. Could this refer to the fact that, by this time, he had already composed his Gospel, or at least a first version of it, and that he was therefore entitled to be called a true 'servant of the word'?[5]

Highly qualified assistants are mentioned elsewhere in the New Testament.[6] Thus 1 Peter 5:12: 'I write these few words to you through Silvanus, who is a trustworthy brother, to encourage you and attest that this is the true grace of God. Stand firm in it!' St Paul's Letter to the Romans 16:22 reads: 'I, Tertius, who am writing this letter, greet you in the Lord' ('*Ego Tertios ho grápsas ten epistolen*'). On the strength of this declaration, the American New Testament scholar Gary Burge entitled a recent article on Tertius 'The Real Writer of Romans'.[7] Men like Tertius and Silvanus (or Silas as he is also called) were more than ordinary scribes. No one would have doubted, in those days, that St Paul was the true author of Romans (see chapter 1:1) or that St Peter was responsible for his first letter (chapter 1:1). But the role of secretaries could be very important in the authorial process. It seems likely that the contrast between the rather polished Greek of 1 Peter and the gritty, Hebraic style of 2 Peter was due to Silvanus, an experienced secretary who had already proved his worth in 1 and 2 Thessalonians.

In the writing of Romans, likewise, Tertius was more than a mindless stenographer. St Paul must have valued his influence upon the finished product to allow him his rhetorical flourish, 'I, Tertius, who am writing this letter.' Secretaries often composed whole letters on the basis of notes or draft paragraphs; yet the authority of the person whose thoughts or teachings had to be conveyed was never in question. The role of the modern-day political speechwriter is broadly similar. St Paul, in any case, well understood the need to provide a guarantee of authenticity at the end of a completed text. There were those who would doubt – as they doubt today – that he really was the author, given the obvious differences of style and vocabulary in his various letters. To assuage any doubts, he occasionally added his personal signature: 'This greeting is in my own hand – Paul' (1 Corinthians 16:21); 'Look how big the letters are, now that I am writing to you in my own hand' (Galatians 6:11, REV); 'I add this greeting in my own hand – Paul' (Colossians 4:18, REV); 'This greeting is in my own handwriting; all genuine letters of mine bear the same signature – Paul' (2 Thessalonians 3:17, REV); 'Here is my signature: Paul' (Philemon 19, REV).

Paul's secretary Tertius might have had another qualification not uncommon among Christian professionals working in this part of the Graeco–Roman world. He may have been a shorthand writer, or, to use the technical term, a *tachygráphos*.[8] Shorthand writing was a more or less obligatory skill for a trained scribe. Otherwise unmentioned among St Paul's circle, Tertius may well have been chosen for this exceptional role because of his capacity to record and edit the apostle's somewhat verbose oral communications. (An example of St Paul's verbosity is described in Acts 20:7–9: 'Paul was due to leave the next day, and he preached a sermon that went on till the middle of the night ... and as Paul went on and on, a young man called Eutychus who was sitting on the window-sill grew drowsy and was overcome by sleep and fell to the ground three floors below.')

Among the disciples of Jesus, Levi-Matthew, the former customs official, would probably have had a working knowledge of *tachygraphy*. In consequence, scholars have suggested that he would have been able to transcribe the long Sermon on the Mount verbatim, much as Tertius would have been able to write down St Paul's more striking utterances. Needless to say, this notion – that we have a more or less authentic transcript of the Sermon on the Mount – infuriates those New Testament scholars who are convinced that St Matthew never wrote the Gospel and that this particular sermon is a late and unreliable compilation of scattered sayings drawn up by Christian communities. What should be appreciated is that there is no logistic, technical or logical reason why such an authentic text should not have been produced by Levi-Matthew or another witness. The possibility must be addressed with an open mind.[9]

Our knowledge of shorthand writing in New Testament times is bracketed, so to speak, by a biblical reference in the third century BC and a leather manuscript of the early second century AD. The Greek translation of the Hebrew Bible, the Septuagint, is a reasonably free rendering of the Hebrew text. It takes into account what Greek-speaking readers would understand and what they would expect to hear. Modern translations of the Bible do the same thing. In Psalm 45:1, the 'expert scribe' (NJV, REV), the 'skilful writer' (NIV), the 'ready writer' (KJV) is an *oxygráphos*, a synonym for *tachygráphos*, the shorthand writer.[10] The translator of this verse from Hebrew into Greek knew what he was doing when he chose this Greek technical term for the Hebrew *sofer macher*; in Ezra 7:6, he preferred *grammatéus tachys* to describe the qualifications of Ezra (an 'expert' scribe, the Revised English Bible once again translates, and the King James Bible again offers 'ready scribe'). The technical term *oxygráphos* must have been common enough among Greek-speaking Jews in the third century BC for its use in such a translation to have any purpose.

Secondly, there is the text on leather found in a cave in the Wadi Murabba'at near the Dead Sea, with the inventory and Plate number 164.[11] It has not been properly analysed since its first editors recognized that it was in Greek shorthand, without being able to decipher it, and it is in desperate need of restoration.[12] Because of the archaeological context in which it was found, the leather fragments must be dated to the early second century at the very latest. P. Murabba'at 164 is probably a Christian text: whatever a comprehensive decoding may yield, clearly visible in the middle of the larger of the two fragments is a 'chi-rho', the monogram of Christ, consisting of the first two letters of his name in Greek, *Christos*. They are joined into one symbol by placing the *rho*, which resembles a *P*, on top of the *chi* which looks like an *X*.[13]

Shorthand writing, in other words, was an everyday feature of the social world which spawned the New Testament and, more specifically, the Jesus Papyrus. The fragments began life in a culture in which unembellished Greek was spoken and written not only by the affluent and the intelligentsia but also by ordinary people. It was written by scribes among whom Greek shorthand was a standard skill – a skill, indeed, which St Matthew himself may well have possessed. But what do these ancient scraps of papyrus tell us about the beliefs of the earliest Christians? To answer this question, we must return to a literary feature of the fragments which reflect a conscious and dramatic doctrinal innovation: the *nomina sacra* or 'holy names'.

'Shorthand' for holy names

As we have already seen, there are two fragmentary examples of holy names, *nomina sacra*, in the Magdalen Papyrus, one on Fragment 3, recto, line 2 (KE for *kyrie*, 'Lord', in St Matthew 26:22) and the other on Fragment 1, recto, line 1 (IS for *Iēsous*, 'Jesus', in Matthew 26:31). The horizontal line above the abbreviated word, denoting a *nomen sacrum*, is missing throughout although it must have been there originally. A third instance can also be reconstructed from the stichometry of Fragment 2, verso, line 1: IS for *Iēsous*, 'Jesus', in Matthew 26:10. Even before the redating of the Magdalen Papyrus, the first two cases were considered the earliest examples of these 'holy names'.[14] The oldest text of St John, P52, traditionally dated to *c.* AD 120 and, until recently, believed to be the oldest New Testament papyrus, has no visible *nomina sacra* (although it is plausible that *Iēsou*, *Iēsoun* and *Iēsous* were abbreviated IU, IN and IS in recto, line 2 (John 18:32), recto, line 5 (John 18:33) and recto, line 7 (John 18:34)).

Clearly visible *nomina sacra* do occur in the almost complete codex P66 of St John's Gospel, commonly dated to *c.* AD 200 but probably some seventy-five years older.[15] They can also be seen in a controversial text of unknown origins, the so-called Papyrus Egerton 2 at the British Library, a combination of Gospel material and other traditions and sayings which has been dated to *c.* AD 110–30.[16] (This manuscript might be seen as vindication of John 21:25: 'There was much else that Jesus did; if it were written down in detail, I do not suppose the world itself would hold all the books that would be written'). The Egerton Papyrus is particularly significant because it illustrates the widespread use of these distinctive abbreviations in early Christianity, beyond the group of texts which were to be declared canonical.

Why are these holy names so important? Firstly, they are clearly deliberate. Their use was regular and systematic from the start. In general, abbreviation was a more common practice in antiquity than it is today. The Greeks and Romans had a precise system for the abbreviation of numbers: in the Magdalen Papyrus, Fragment 3, verso (Matthew 26:14), for example, the Greek for 'twelve', *dodeka*, is shortened to $\iota\beta$. Even now, we might use the Roman abbreviation 'XXVI' to represent, as Colin Roberts did, the chapter number twenty-six. Popular personal names or titles, the names of months and other well-established terms could also be abbreviated in manuscripts and inscriptions.[17] The use of traditional abbreviated forms and the adoption of new ones was part of the scribe's craft. In the case of *nomina sacra*, however, a remarkable innovation was involved.

As the Magdalen Papyrus shows, not long after the events in the

Gospel a highly significant system of abbreviations was introduced associated with Jesus, God and the Holy Spirit, beginning with these very words. 'Jesus', *Iēsous*, became JS / IS: *iota* and *sigma* in Greek. 'God', *theos*, became GD / THS: *theta* and *sigma*. 'The (Holy) Spirit', *pneuma*, became SPT / PNA: *pi*, *nu* and *alpha*. Associated words acquired their sacred status by the act of abbreviation. The word 'Lord', *kyrios*, for instance, could be applied to persons far removed from the Holy Trinity, as we have seen it was to Nero. Written as KS, however, it became a divine name, referring to Jesus. The Magdalen Papyrus provides us with the first example: *kyrie*, 'Lord', in Matthew 26:22, is spelt KE.

The term *nomina sacra* was coined by the German scholar Ludwig Traube,[18] who established that there were perhaps fifteen words entitled to be so abbreviated. Not all were contracted in this manner all the time, but when they were, the following system applied. Five were abbreviated by writing the first and last letter only: THEOS, 'God'; IĒSOUS, 'Jesus'; CHRISTOS, 'Christ'; KYRIOS, 'Lord'; and HYIOS, 'Son', when it referred to the Son of God. The other ten could be abbreviated by using either the first two and the last letters, or the first and the last two letters: PNEUMA, 'Spirit'; DAVID, (in his capacity as the royal ancestor of Jesus); STAUROS, 'cross'; SOTĒR, 'saviour'; PATĒR, 'father' (referring to the father of Jesus); MĒTĒR, 'mother' (referring to the mother of Jesus); ANTHROPOS, 'man' (as in Son of Man and similar references to Jesus); ISRAĒL, 'Israel'; IĒROUSALEM, 'Jerusalem'; OURANOS, 'heaven' (as, for example, in 'the Kingdom of Heaven').

The scribes did not import the Graeco–Roman and Jewish custom of abbreviation into the written records of early Christianity for idle reasons or simply to save space on a sheet of papyrus. The crucial point is that these holy names reflected a theological position. Since the Jesus Papyrus is the earliest example of this practice in Christian literature, we may be sure that it was introduced before AD 70.

The fragments are from a codex rather than a scroll. As we have seen, the Qumran scroll papyrus 7Q5, which bears St Mark 6:52–3, contains no *nomina sacra*. Another papyrus scroll fragment from Cave 7, 7Q4, has been identified by José O'Callaghan as I Timothy 3:16–4:3 – a claim which has proved resilient.[19] Indeed, even scholars who are unpersuaded by the Markan identification of 7Q5 accept that 7Q4 has verses from I Timothy.[20] For papyrologists, the fact that the first of the two fragments of papyrus 7Q4 is preserved with its right margin – which means that we know precisely how the lines ended – is extremely useful. Coming from Cave 7, this scroll had the same end-date as all the other Qumran manuscripts: it cannot have been deposited after AD 68 and must have been written before that date. Palaeographically, it belongs to the same period as 7Q5. Intriguingly, 7Q4 appears to preserve two instances of a word that would qualify as a *nomen sacrum*, but is not abbreviated.

Looking first at the stichometry, O'Callaghan's counting of letters per line appears to rule out an abbreviated *pneuma* in line 2 of the larger of the two fragments (I Timothy 4:1: 'The Spirit has explicitly said that …').[21] The gap or *spatium* preceding 4:1 already has a reconstructed length of nine letters; with an abbreviated *pneuma* (PNA) it would be twelve letters long – unlikely, if not impossible. Fragment 2 of 7Q4 is a tiny scrap of two lines with remnants of ink in line 1 and only three clearly legible letters in line 2: *omikron / theta / epsilon*. If O'Callaghan is correct, then this is I Timothy 4:3: '(… foods which) God created'. The first two letters of 'God', *theta* and *epsilon*, could be seen as conclusive evidence that this is not an abbreviated *nomen sacrum* – which, in this case, would consist of *theta* and *sigma*, the first and last letter of the word.

Unfortunately, the case is not conclusive either way. It is conceivable that the smaller fragment may belong to a later passage of I Timothy where this combination of letters may appear. None the less, there is no section other than chapter 4:3 which combines these letters and matches the stichometry. Thus, a tentative conclusion may be drawn from the only surviving New Testament scroll fragment which includes unabbreviated *nomina sacra*: the 'holy names' tradition was not introduced while the scroll was the prevalent literary format among Christians. The adoption of this practice seems to have coincided with the introduction of the codex. What doctrinal change did this scribal innovation reflect?

Most first-century Jews – and non-Jews for that matter – read the Old Testament in Greek rather than Hebrew. In these Jewish Scriptures, the name of God was considered to be so holy that it was taboo to pronounce it; in writing, therefore, God's name was abbreviated. In Hebrew manuscripts, this taboo was undetectable because classical Hebrew was written without vowel signs or points, whether or not the words were sacred. God's name was spelt as YHWH – the so-called Tetragrammaton. Since no one was supposed to know which vowels had to be added between the consonants to make the divine name intelligible, other words were usually substituted when such a text was read aloud, such as *Adonai* ('Lord'). Although scholars now believe that the correct pronunciation of YHWH should be 'Yahweh', readers devised all sorts of vowel combinations, notably one pronunciation which has endured, 'Jehova'. In the first Greek manuscripts of the Old Testament, the Hebrew letters YHWH were conspicuous as an abbreviation – initially because the Hebrew consonants were inserted into the Greek text wherever the word 'God' appeared.

The use of Greek rather than Hebrew letters to abbreviate God's name is illustrated by a document from Qumran dating from the period just before the emergence of the first Christian texts. In the fragmentary Greek papyrus scroll discovered in Cave 4 – Pap4QLXXLev[b], with parts of Leviticus – 'God' is written neither as *theos*, nor the Greek translation of *Adonai*, *kyrios*, but is represented by the vowels *iota* / *alpha* / *omega* to sound something like 'Yaoh' or 'Yaho'.[22] By the time the Christians began writing their own Greek manuscripts, rather than copying Old Testament texts, they were already accustomed to the contraction of the name and title of God. Unfortunately there is no manuscript evidence to suggest whether *kyrios* was already abbreviated at this early stage, when scrolls were still the dominant literary format: it might have been represented by the Greek consonants KS, the Greek vowels IAO or the Hebrew Tetragrammaton. Yet if 7Q4, the Cave 7 fragments of I Timothy are any guide, the word *theos*, God, was apparently not contracted. The very first Jewish–Christian scribes do not seem to have tinkered with traditional practice.

When the codex was introduced, however, this caution gave way to theological daring. As we have already seen, this was a period when Jews and Christians became estranged following the killing of James, Jesus's brother, in AD 62. It was an apt moment for a dramatic statement of faith, a theological parting of the ways. It was no longer necessary to appease Jewish sensitivities; Christian texts could declare the divinity of Jesus unequivocally. After spreading the Word through oral preaching and scroll manuscripts, it was time to write in the new codices that Jesus the Christ is Lord and God.

'In other words,' writes the American New Testament scholar and

Egyptologist Schuyler Brown, 'the four nouns which are universally accorded special treatment in the early papyri of the New Testament are not simply *nomina sacra* but *nomina divina*.'[23] The written words *theos*, 'God', *kyrios*, 'Lord', *Iēsous*, 'Jesus', and *Christos*, 'Christ', thus became the verbal core of early Christian identity. The Magdalen codex included two – *kyrios* and *Iēsous* – and doubtless others which have not survived. This usage is confirmed by the Paris papyrus of St Luke's Gospel, the P. Supplementum Graecum 1120/5: in this manuscript, *theta* + *sigma* and *theta* + *upsilon* represent *theos* and *theou* (Luke 1:68, 3:38, 4:34, 6:4, 12), *chi* + *sigma* represent *Christos* (Luke 3:15) and PNA represents *pneuma* (Luke 3:22; *pneumatos* = PNOS in 1:67; *pneumati* = PNI in 1:80).[24]

Colin Roberts was the first papyrologist to grasp that such a momentous change could not have been the decision of a single scribe. The new practice was emulated too quickly and widely to have been a mere literary eccentricity. As Roberts put it in 1979, 'The system was too complex for the ordinary scribe to operate without rules or an authoritative exemplar.'[25] He argued that the *nomina sacra* were first introduced by the Jerusalem community before the Jewish revolt which began in AD 66. The holy names were, as Roberts aptly described them, 'the embryonic Creed of the first Church'.[26]

This prototypical Creed soon became better established. One of the oldest surviving papyri of Acts (26:7–8 and 26:20), the early-third- or late-second-century P29 (P. Oxy. 1597) at the Bodleian Library, includes two instances of a *nomen sacrum*. In each case, it is the word *theos* which is abbreviated, once on the front, the recto, line 5, where *theos* becomes *theta* + *sigma*, and once on the back, the verso, line 4, where *theon* becomes *theta* + *nu*. Oddly, the *theta* does not resemble the Greek letter at all; it is a triangle with a horizontal bar rather than a nicely rounded or oval shapes with a horizontal stroke in the middle. Since the same form occurs on both sides of the papyrus, this was evidently not a mistake. Could the scribe have been a Roman who, thinking of the Latin *Deus* instead of *theos*, wrote a Greek *delta* which resembled a triangle? This seems improbable. The more likely explanation is that the triangle was used for the first letter of the 'holy name' of God as a trinitarian symbol.[27]

To whom would these subtle signals have been comprehensible? The fact that texts were so often read aloud to groups – a tradition still observed by Benedictine monks at meal-times – had more to do with the scarcity of scrolls and codices than with illiteracy among the people. Reading out loud from manuscripts such as the Jesus Papyrus required a certain amount of practice and familiarity with scribal shorthand. The person chosen to carry out this important task would have to be familiar with such technicalities as the *nomina sacra*, which were signposted by a horizontal line above the abbreviated word. Likewise, the reader had to alter the level of his voice for a chapter ending which was indicated by a horizontal bar underneath the beginning of the line or, as in the case in the Oxford and Barcelona papyri, by one letter projecting into the margin of the following line. There are many examples of such signals to the reader, none of which could have required great learning to be understood.

The sheer number of New Testament references to people reading or reciting suggests much about the literacy and worship practices of the earliest Christians. Jesus himself provides an example in St Luke 4:16–19 where he unrolls a scroll of Isaiah and reads chapter 61:1–2. Interestingly, this is a text where the Tetragrammaton for the holy name of God would have occurred twice: 'The Spirit of YHWH is on me, for he has anointed me' and '. . . to proclaim a year of favour from YHWH'. As in many surviving Hebrew manuscripts, these four letters may well have been singled out by their ancient, palaeo-Hebrew script. What is revealing is that Jesus assumes that those who listen to him have read the Torah and the Prophets: 'Have you not read what David did . . .' he asks the Pharisees (Matthew 12:3); 'Or again, have you not read in the Law . . .' (12:5 and many more times throughout the Gospel). In John 19:20, we are told of the notice affixed to the cross of Jesus that it was 'read by many of the Jews'. The Ethiopian chief treasurer, returning from a trip to Jerusalem, is seen 'reading the prophet Isaiah' (Acts 8:28). It is also clear that the Ethiopian was reading aloud; when apostle Philip met him near Gaza, 'he heard him reading', and asked him, 'Do you understand what you are reading?' (Acts 8:30). The Ethiopian's answer, that he did not understand, reflected not poor literacy but a failure to grasp the text's implications: 'How could I, unless I have someone to guide me?' (Acts 8:31). The Isaiah scroll – in the hands of the chief treasurer from a land that did not even belong to the Roman Empire – was probably written in Greek rather than Hebrew. But he and Philip were evidently at ease reading and discussing the text in a common language.

There are other examples: 'The party left and went down to Antioch, where they summoned the whole community and delivered the letter. The community read it and were delighted with the encouragement it gave them' (Acts 15:30–31). 'In our writing, there is nothing that you cannot read clearly and understand' (2 Corinthians 1:13). Indeed, 'Blessed is anyone who reads the words of this prophecy' (Revelation 1:3). St Paul's preaching was checked against the old documents by careful reading: 'Every day [the Jews at Beroea] studied the scriptures to check whether it was true' (Acts 17:11). St Paul even borrowed the image of reading as a metaphor: 'You yourselves are our letter, written in our hearts, that everyone can read and understand; and it is plain that you are a letter from Christ, entrusted in our care, written not with ink but with the Spirit of the living God; not on stone tablets but on the tablets of human hearts' (2 Corinthians 3:1–3).

The ability to write is also treated as a commonplace skill in the New Testament. On one occasion, Jesus 'bent down and started writing on the ground with his finger ... Then he bent down and continued writing on the ground' (John 8:6, 8).[28] In Luke 1:63, Zechariah, the temporarily mute father of John, the future Baptist, asks for a writing tablet and writes 'His name is John.' The postscript to St John's Gospel says: 'This disciple is the one who vouches for these things and has written them down' (John 21:24).[29] John is commanded by a voice 'like the sound of a trumpet' to write, with his own stylus, ink and scroll, the seven letters to the churches of Asia (Revelation 1:9–13). We have already noted the possibility that St Matthew was a shorthand writer and seen that St Paul authenticated his letters by writing final words of greeting and his name in his own hand. In other words, even without professional scribes and secretaries like Tertius or Silvanus, and without the help of the Roman distribution network provided by Theophilus, members of the inner circle of disciples and apostles were certainly able to read and write and to advance the recording, copying and spreading of the good news in literary form.

In summary, the early community of Jerusalem, and perhaps also of Antioch, seems to have developed and authorized the transition from scroll to codex and the introduction of the holy names no later than the sixties of the first century. This was a momentous doctrinal step, a critical event in the development of the Church: the Magdalen Papyrus is the earliest Christian book and the earliest surviving document to assert the divinity of Jesus. How was it used by those for whom it was written?

At such a distance, it is difficult to say. But one can look for clues in later sources such as *The Acts of St Peter*, a historical novel about St Peter written towards AD 180 by an unknown author probably living in Rome. Only parts of the text survive, some in Greek, some in Latin and other translations. But in these sections, we read about St Peter's stay in Rome, his miracles, his conflict with Simon the Magician, his encounter with Christ on the Appian Way, and his death. (The book also inspired Henryk Sienkiewicz's *Quo Vadis?* of 1896 and the film of the same name.) In chapter 35:6, St Peter is fleeing from Rome, having been persuaded by the church in the city to escape certain death. Outside the city walls, on the Appian Way, Christ appears to him. '*Kyrie, pou hóde?*' ('Lord, where are you going?') St Peter asks him; in Latin, '*Domine, quo vadis?*' Jesus replies: 'I am going to Rome, to be crucified once more.' The apostle understands and returns to the city to face his own martyrdom.[30] A little church stands on the site of this encounter and the imprint of Jesus's feet is preserved within. One wonders if it has ever been compared to the imprint at the Chapel of the Mount of Olives in Jerusalem. Such visual 'traces' seem to have appealed to people in previous ages. Likewise, the scene in *The Acts of St Peter* where the apostle prays for the downfall of his opponent Simon the Magician is immortalized by the imprint of his knees on a stone which can be seen affixed to a wall in the church of Santa Francesca Romana.

The Acts of St Peter remains an intriguing source because of its wealth of information. In genre, it is a blend of suspense, amusement and devotion. The text's original readers were meant to be entertained by such incidents as Simon's bout of one-upmanship with St Peter – in which he tries to prove that he can fly and breaks his leg – and moved by moments such as St Peter's encounter with Christ. Yet the exuberant inventiveness of the book is matched by an enthusiasm for verifiable detail: the fact that St Peter *was* in Rome, the fact that he was crucified in the city, place-names and so on. One such scene, illuminated by recent research, occurs in Chapter 20 of the novel in which St Peter visits the home of a Roman senator, Marcellus.[31] In a separate room of the house, a service is taking place: an image confirmed by archaeological finds which have revealed that, in the first three centuries, Christians tended to gather in rooms in private houses rather than in separate buildings dedicated to worship. The apostle opens the door and realizes that the lesson – the Gospel – is being read (*videt evangelium legi*). He enters the room, takes the scroll from the person appointed as reader, rolls it up and begins his own sermon (*involvens eum dixit*). He explains to the assembled congregation how the 'Holy Scripture of our Lord' should be proclaimed (*qualiter debeat Sancta Scriptura Domini nostri pronuntiari*). He refers to the authority behind this scripture in the plural: 'what we have written in His grace' (*quae gratia ipsius quod coepimus scripsimus*) and quotes the passage that was being read when he entered the room: the story of the Transfiguration of Jesus (Mark 9:2–13; 2 Peter 1:16–19).

The cameo is full of useful information. It tells us that oral tradition took precedence over literary tradition when the former was available; that St Mark's Gospel existed while St Peter was alive; that it existed in scroll form; and that the apostle was the authority behind this Gospel of St Mark: 'We . . .'. There may even be an indirect reference to St Peter's second letter: the use of the first person plural ('what we have written') could be understood as an allusion to the one incident mentioned both in the Gospel and in this letter – the moment of the Transfiguration.[32]

This vividly described scene, written more than a century after the events it recalls, may be the closest we can get to the bible study practices of the men and women who first handled the Jesus Papyrus. The writer recalls a time when the Gospel could still be read aloud and explained to listeners by men who had seen the events it described. He remembers the years when the first Christians assembled in homes to read the good news from the earliest scrolls. In time, they read from codices of which the Magdalen fragments are the oldest examples. We can only guess at the awe and spiritual response of those who gathered to hear such recollections. No amount of textual analysis or papyrology can tell us what they felt. That mystery – the mystery of feelings sensed across the centuries – is perhaps the strangest legacy of this extraordinary manuscript.

7

Fragments of the Truth?:
the Jesus Papyrus in Our Times

Then one of the Twelve, the man called Judas Iscariot, went to the chief
priests and said, 'What will you give me to betray him to you?'

Matthew 26, 14–15, REV

> We shall not cease from exploration
> And the end of all our exploring
> Will be to arrive where we started
> And know the place for the first time.
> T. S. Eliot, *Little Gidding*

According to many chronologies, 1996 – the year of this book's
publication – is the 2,000th anniversary of the birth of Jesus. By
any standards, Christianity has been a phenomenal success in the first
two millennia since its founder was born in Bethlehem. There are 1.8
billion Christians in the world today. More than six billion copies of
the Bible are thought to have been sold since the turn of the nineteenth
century. The New Testament Scriptures, of which the Magdalen Papyrus
is the earliest physical evidence on codex, have been translated into
2,000 languages and dialects.

Needless to say, the scholarly battle to identify the nature and origin
of the Gospels is as pitched as ever. But the first Christian texts also
continue to play an absolutely central role in the moral life of the West.
The issues which divide biblical scholars in seminars and libraries are
still of fundamental importance to millions of ordinary people in their
daily lives.

In this final chapter, we assess the Magdalen Papyrus in the context
of our own time and consider the broader implications of Carsten
Thiede's research for scholars and ordinary readers. We look at the role
played by the Gospels in the scholarship, culture and history of the

twentieth century, and the ways in which the redating process may unsettle the orthodox view of how these books were written and what they are. We also look at the possible significance of this 'new paradigm' for deeper questions of faith which affect everyone born in our culture.

Christianity, wrote T. S. Eliot, is always adapting itself into something that can be believed. But it has found the process of adapting itself to the post-modern world of doubt and cultural relativism particularly traumatic. It might be said, indeed, that the most successful faith in history has become unsure of its own historic certainties. A bishop today is as likely to deny the reality of the Resurrection as to proclaim it. When Bishop John Spong wrote in 1992 that 'a literalized myth is a doomed myth' and attacked those who clung to a 'feeble religious security system', he spoke for more senior churchmen than might be expected. In the Church of England, David Jenkins, the former Bishop of Durham, is only the most prominent critic of traditional Christian beliefs.

Why has Christianity suffered from this attack of nerves in the twentieth century? Its nightmare is Albert Camus's Meursault, the murderer who, in the final pages of *The Outsider*, realizes as he awaits execution that he can indeed find happiness in a godless world. As a final act of spiritual defiance, he lays his heart 'open to the benign indifference of the universe'. To meet this challenge – the absolute scepticism and diffident atheism of our times – Christianity has made many compromises. Our purpose in this concluding chapter is not to judge these compromises but to examine the impact of modernity upon biblical scholarship and to consider the place of the Jesus Papyrus in the context of this cultural conflict.

The Gospels – Objects of Suspicion?

Many books have changed the history of the West: Darwin's *Origin of Species*, Marx's *Das Kapital* and Freud's *Letters* are three of the most important of recent centuries. Yet the Gospels are the very building blocks of our civilization. Without them, Giotto would not have painted his frescoes at Arena; Dante would not have written the *Divine Comedy*; Mozart would not have composed his *Requiem*; and Wren would not have built St Paul's Cathedral. The story and message of these four books – along with the Judaic tradition of the Old Testament – pervade not only the moral conventions of the West but also our systems of social organization, nomenclature, architecture, literature and education and the rituals of birth, marriage and death which shape our lives. Though Christian belief has become a matter of personal choice, the key text which underpins it remains a handbook to the way we live, Christian and non-Christian alike. To ask how old the Gospels are, and why they were written, is to plumb the deepest wells of the social system which we inhabit. These questions are not the preserve of the theologian.

In spite of this extraordinary influence – or perhaps because of it – the New Testament has become an object of cultural suspicion. The instinct to undermine the Gospels has overtaken the pre-modern instinct to take their truth for granted. Today, indeed, some scholars and writers will go to almost any lengths to avoid the charge of credulity, just as their distant predecessors would have taken almost any action to avoid the opposite charge of scepticism. The post-Enlightenment world has no stakes at which it burns the heretics who dare to question its orthodoxy. It has instead the pressures of the academy, of media opinion and of a disapproving cultural elite, all of which can effectively be brought to bear on a scholar who breaks ranks. The New Testament is indeed worthy of objective analysis. Yet that is not the same thing as the instinctive distrust which it has come to inspire in many quarters.

In its most extreme form, this distrust can be absurd. In the early Church, a group of heretics known as Docetists denied that Christ ever had a real body or a narrowly 'historical' existence. The Docetists have found their modern counterparts in the handful of scholars who have pursued doubt to its logical conclusions and presented the New Testament as defiantly unhistorical. In a series of books such as *The Jesus of the Early Christians* (1971) and *Did Jesus Exist?* (1975), the author G. A. Wells argued that the Christ of history was an invention of the second century AD. Until then, he claimed, Christians worshipped only a mythical Messiah or Saviour-figure. Quite apart from the obvious complaint that this puts the cart of history before the horse of faith, Wells's hypotheses simply do not match the evidence. His argument that the Gospels were not written until AD 100 is no longer tenable; nor, as we have seen, is his suggestion that they were invented in a distinctively 'Hellenistic' setting. There was no sharp distinction between Jewish and Hellenistic culture. It is wrong to assume that what is Hellenistic is necessarily of a late date.

Most biblical scholars would agree that this approach takes scepticism too far. By seeking to deny whatever is in its path, it makes the exercise of doubt a quasi-religious responsibility. Few level-headed academics would endorse such a distortive approach to the problems of religious history. None the less, it is interesting to note that the campaign to eradicate key Christian figures from the history book remains intellectually respectable. More recently than Wells, Herman Detering has argued in *Der gefälschte Paulus* that not a single allegedly Pauline letter is the work of St Paul, that they were written by the heretic Marcion in the mid-second century, and that the New Testament's St Paul is an invention of early Catholicism. Thus, by academic sleight of hand, perhaps the most powerful human personality in the history of the Church disappears in a puff of sceptical smoke.

In a more general sense, the tendency of twentieth-century popular culture has been to present the historical Jesus as the victim of the Gospels' distortions as much as the subject of their narrative. In much popular art, literature and populist writing on Jesus, it has been insinuated that the Gospels are guilty of a form of treachery: that they disguise the real Jesus and mislead those who seek the truth about him. So deceptive is the New Testament, some allege, that the imagination is a better guide to the truth about Jesus. One writer mused recently that it was time to turn to poetry and fiction in search of the real Christ; he imagined a 'quest for the post-historical Jesus' and admitted to a 'secret hope' that his subject 'might turn out to be a gentle left-wing revolutionary, correct on women and the environment'.[1]

Fiction has played a vital role in reconditioning modern attitudes to the Gospels, often with impressive literary results. In his powerful novel, *The Last Temptation* (English translation, 1961), Nikos Kazantzakēs presented Jesus as a hesitant and troubled figure, far less the charismatic healer and spiritual leader of the New Testament than a tortured product of the post-Freudian world. He wondered what might have happened if Christ 'had taken the smooth, easy road of men. He had married and fathered children. People loved and respected him. Now, an old man, he sat on the threshold of his house and smiled with satisfaction as he recalled the longings of his youth. How splendidly, how sensibly he had acted in choosing the road of men! What insanity to have wanted to save the world! What joy to have escaped the privations, the tortures, and the Cross!' By his own admission, Kazantzakēs's purpose was to experiment, to turn sacred scripture into (often dazzling) literature. 'This book is not a biography,' he wrote, 'it is the confession of every man who struggles. 'Later – and with even more controversial results – the movie director Martin Scorsese was to attempt the same transformation of holy text into psychoanalysis on film.

In a more recent book, *Live from Golgotha* (1992), Gore Vidal imagined a computer hacker eliminating the Gospels from human memory, visits by time travellers to the early Christian era and the possibility that Judas rather than Jesus died on the Cross. The story told in the New Testament and its principal characters becomes putty in the hands of computer operators and twentieth-century television executives. The novel ends with an outrageous parody of the Crucifixion, televised from Golgotha, in which Jesus is plucked from the Cross by a Japanese sun-goddess – a sacrifice of doctrine to the tastes of modern television audiences.

Vidal's mischievous and sometimes entertaining book is merely the latest in a well-established science-fiction genre exploring the use of advanced technology – usually time travel – to reclaim the real Jesus from the alleged myths of the New Testament, or indeed to reinvent him completely. What these books share is the cultural assumption that the Gospels are an essentially suspect source. This they have in common with much populist history of recent years. In their highly successful book, *The Holy Blood and the Holy Grail* (1982), Michael Baigent, Richard Leigh and Henry Lincoln claimed that Jesus did not die on the Cross but lived to found a royal dynasty whose secrets have been protected for centuries by a Europe-wide conspiracy. The elusive holy grail of legend was in fact the holy blood of this sacred family.

Likewise, in *Jesus the Man: A New Interpretation from the Dead Sea Scrolls* (1992), Barbara Thiering argued that Jesus was married to Mary Magdalene, that they had three children, and that they were divorced prior to Jesus's remarriage. Making highly dubious use of a form of code allegedly found in the Dead Sea Scrolls, Thiering argued that the Gospels can only be truly understood if systematically deciphered. In so doing, she claimed to have discovered that Jesus was the 'Wicked Priest' of the Essene sect referred to in the scrolls; that he was crucified not in

Jerusalem but at Qumran; and – least plausibly – that Pontius Pilate journeyed to the Dead Sea especially to supervise Jesus's execution. Christianity, in other words, was an unlikely by-product of battles within the Essene community.

These fanciful claims are not, in fact, particularly novel. George Moore caused a greater scandal in 1916 with *The Brook Kerith* which portrayed Jesus as the product of Essene ideas who – having survived the Crucifixion – settled in an Essene community. What is most striking about Thiering's book, apart from its sensationalism, is the confidence with which it asserts that the Gospels are not all they seem. They speak in tongues. Their message can only be understood with help of a literary code-breaker. And if not the Dead Sea Scrolls as a code-breaker, then why not Indian scriptures? By comparing Jesus's sayings to such texts, Elmar R. Gruber and Holger Kersten have recently argued in a book called *The Original Jesus* (1995) that Christ's teachings are rooted in Buddhism. He received, the authors allege, a Buddhist education from a sect of contemplatives called the Therapeutae in Alexandria while the Holy Family was in exile. Again, the vital premise of their work is that the Gospels can only be understood with the help of a quite separate navigation device. As it stands (it is suggested) the New Testament is profoundly unreliable.

The connections between culture and scholarship are complex. But it is our belief that the profound mistrust of the Gospels detectable in some forms of popular culture has parallels in the world of serious scholarship. We believe, furthermore, that the redating of the Magdalen Papyrus and forthcoming work on other papyri have important implications for the future direction of biblical research; and that the forensic evidence of papyrology has a major contribution to make to a debate that has too often been governed by emotion. It is to this argument that we now turn.

The Gospels and Scholarship

There was a time when to question the literal truth of the Bible was to court death. In 1697 a young Scottish student called Thomas Aikenhead was hanged in Edinburgh for repeating Benedict Spinoza's rebellious claim that the author of the Pentateuch was not Moses but Ezra who lived almost a thousand years later. Thomas Paine's denial of the Bible's truthfulness in the late eighteenth century led to the imprisonment of his English publisher. In the pre-modern West, the authenticity and truthfulness of scripture – its 'verbal inerrancy' – were taken for granted.[2]

Slowly, however, the doctrine of verbal inerrancy was eroded by time and the triumph of the Enlightenment world-view. Partly, this was a matter of gut distaste, the revulsion which many scholars felt for the Evangelicals who inspired Charles Huleatt: Herbert Marsh (1757–1830), Professor of Divinity at Cambridge, drew up eighty-seven questions as 'a trap to catch Calvinists'. In a broader sense, the new, more sceptical approach to scripture reflected the development of the modern critical methods which characterize today's scholarship.[3] Following the Göttingen academic, Johann David Michaelis (1717–91), scholars began to confront seriously the possibility that there might be contradictions within scripture. They also dared to ask whether the Jesus of history was quite the same as the Christ of orthodox faith.

One of the first to pose this question was Hermann Samuel Reimarus (1694–1768), a professor at Hamburg. His ground-breaking book on the aims of Jesus and his disciples questioned Christ's divinity. It remained secret until the author's death but eventually launched the long historical quest. Perhaps the most influential of the seekers who followed Reimarus was David Friedrich Strauss whose two-volume Life of Christ advanced the theory that the supernatural events described are mythical – a theory which, as we have seen, outraged Evangelicals such as Charles Huleatt.

In 1860 the English publication of the collection *Essays and Reviews* by seven scholars (mostly from Oxford) sounded the death-knell of the old approach to scripture. Legal proceedings were started against the book; ten thousand Anglican clergymen signed a petition condemning it. Yet the critical methods of scholarly investigation which the collection endorsed were here to stay. The inerrancy of the Bible as a product of divine inspiration could no longer be taken for granted. A new era of religious history and scholarship had begun.

This victory is one of the greatest in the history of Western ideas. In a sense, it completed the project begun by the Renaissance humanists, the first Protestant reformers and the earliest printers to release the

Word of God from the control of the Church. The next phase, carried out by the thinkers of the Enlightenment and their successors, was to ask what the Word of God actually was; to question whether it was, indeed, divinely inspired; and to suggest what its textual history might have been. The great building blocks of our civilization were at last to be analysed, their structure scrutinized, the identity and intentions of the builders questioned.

The legacy of this great leap forward has been troubled, however. The twentieth century's most influential biblical scholar was Rudolf Bultmann (1884–1976) who transformed the modern approach to the Gospels. 'I am of the opinion,' he wrote, 'that we can know practically nothing about Jesus' life and personality, since the Christian sources had no interest in such matters.' Bultmann and other scholars of the form criticism school argued that the Gospels are not historical narratives but intensely stylized collections of traditional 'forms'. These collections had arisen over time, evolving from the life, worship and oral traditions of early Christian communities. They reflected the needs of the post-Easter Church – preaching, instruction and prayer – rather than the historical reality of the pre-Easter Jesus. They proclaimed a *kerygma*, or theological truth, rather than a series of historical reminiscences.[4] Rejecting the view of Justin Martyr in the second century AD that these books were 'memoirs of the apostles', Bultmann believed that the authors of the Gospels were so far removed from the historical Jesus that they could only hear the faintest whisper of his voice.

Bultmann's work encouraged the view that the Gospels were written later rather than earlier and that they were to be understood as primitive ecclesiastical manuals rather than biographies or eyewitness accounts. It focused attention upon the Christ of faith rather than the Jesus of history. From Bultmann's enormously influential perspective the 'thatness' of Jesus mattered more than the 'whatness': the fact that he existed, rather than what he did and how he lived. Why, then, continue the search for the historical Jesus?

The school of form criticism focused much-needed attention upon the theological and early ecclesiastical role of the Gospels. None the less, it has been strongly challenged since the Second World War. In particular, every respectable scholar and theologian who has rejected the claim that the quest for the historical Jesus is pointless has been comprehensively rejected. In the 1950s a 'second quest' was under way, led by that generation's best minds – Ernst Kaseman, Gunther Bornkamm and James Robinson – with inconclusive results. A 'third quest' gathered pace in the late 1970s and 1980s in the work of scholars such as E. P. Sanders, Burton Mack, Marcus J. Borg and – perhaps most obviously – John Dominic Crossan's Jesus Seminar. The seminar put the search for the historical Jesus back into the news and Crossan vaulted into the bestseller lists in 1994 with his short book, *Jesus: A Revolutionary Biography*.[5] The tendency of this new wave of scholarship has been to present Jesus as a teacher of subversive wisdom whose message would have had profound implications for the social world in which he lived, as well as for the souls of those he preached to. The view of many earlier historians – led by Albert Schweitzer – that Jesus was an apocalyptic prophet declaring the imminent end of the world, has tended to fade away, although it has not died entirely.

This is a healthy and inclusive debate, of significance to anyone with the remotest interest in Christianity's origins. The search for the historical truth about Jesus – his 'whatness' – survived the onslaught of form criticism and still has much to tell us about the world in which Christ ministered and the possible significance which his ideas may have had for his contemporaries. Yet Bultmann's influence has persisted surreptitiously in ways that are not necessarily positive; in a lucid survey of Jesus scholarship, one scholar wrote recently – and aptly – of the 'post-Bultmannian anguish' which continues to grip the academy.[6]

It is still assumed, for example, that a thick veil of tradition stood between the men who wandered through Galilee and the communities that later worshipped him. They could not see him clearly as a flesh-and-blood human being; nor did they necessarily wish to. According to this analysis, the Gospels were not an attempt to describe an awesome series of events which occurred in Palestine during the first part of the first century AD but an expression of a religious tradition that had already evolved over many years before it was written down. It has recently been described as a 'foundational claim' of the modern quest that 'Jesus of Nazareth was quite different from how he is portrayed in the gospels and creeds of the church'.[7]

The clearest proof that this is indeed the consensus among academics is the work of the Jesus Seminar. This loose-knit group of about a hundred scholars, mostly from North America, first met in 1985 at the Pacific School of Religion in Berkeley, California. Organized by the Jesus scholar Robert Funk, the seminar sought to establish, by a complex voting procedure, which of the many sayings attributed to Christ reflect his authentic voice. Each saying was put before the assembled experts who collectively judged the likelihood that it represented the real Jesus – his *ipsissima vox* (very own voice). The findings of this curious electoral college were published in 1993 as *The Five Gospels: The Search for the Authentic Words of Jesus* amid great media excitement. As a snapshot of academic opinion, the book revealed dramatically how untrustworthy most scholars consider the New Testament to be. By the reckoning of the seminar, only 20 per cent of the sayings in the Gospels are authentic or near approximations. Almost all of St John is inauthentic. Jesus never spoke of himself as 'son of God'. Nor, in fact, did he regard his own death as the purpose of his life. Rarely has there been a more comprehensive rejection of the Gospels as historical sources.

One consequence of this, as we have already noted in this chapter, has been the tyranny of theory and interpretation. If the Gospels are assumed to be unreliable, then the theorist becomes our only guide to the life of Jesus. It follows from this that almost anything can be – and has been – said about Jesus. If Jesus was not an Essene, then he was a Buddhist; or a proto-feminist and worshipper of the goddess 'Sophia'; or a Marxist revolutionary; or a politically correct left-winger who would feel at home on a university campus. It does not take much imagination to realize that excessive use of theory makes us see Jesus as we want to see him, not as he was.

Some academics, such as the American Catholic biblical scholar John P. Meier, have resisted this orthodoxy bravely – arguing, for instance, that the miracle tradition was not a fabrication of the early Church but should be traced back to the historic Jesus himself.[8] In his monumental study of the life of Christ, Meier is commendably wary of grand theory and reductionism; he makes intelligent use of the Gospel sources. Too often, however, scholars who question the above consensus in their approach to the Gospels are accused of fundamentalism. We no longer – thankfully – inhabit a world in which the literal sense of the Gospels is taken for granted. In our post-Enlightenment civilization, to argue that the Gospels are meant to be taken (at least in part) literally is a conscious intellectual decision. Paul Tillich described this transition evocatively as the shift from the 'natural literalism' of the old world to the 'conscious literalism'[9] of the modern era. The trouble is that 'conscious literalism' is no longer regarded as intellectually respectable. To suggest that the Evangelists meant what they said in anything like a literal sense is to court the charge of fundamentalism or unthinking conservatism.

A good illustration of this tendency is Bishop John Shelby Spong's best-selling book, *Rescuing the Bible from Fundamentalism* (1992). In many ways, this short study is an honourable attempt to reclaim the Bible from bigots who sometimes turn it to socially oppressive ends. Yet the language Bishop Spong uses is revealing in a more general sense. For him, literalism is *ipso facto* 'mindless'; it appeals to 'deeply insecure and fearful people'. Those who show an interest in the literal sense of the Gospel are 'anti-intellectual'. They have consigned the Bible to the 'Babylonian captivity of the fundamentalists'. Bishop Spong is richly entitled to his views on the nature and origins of the Bible. Less acceptable is the contemptuous language he reserves for scholars and believers who hold a different opinion.

We have encountered similar resistance ourselves in the visceral anger which Carsten Thiede's thesis about the Magdalen fragments has prompted among many in the academy. The vehement response to the front-page exclusive in *The Times* of 24 December 1994 was quickly apparent in the letters column of the newspaper and elsewhere. The story seemed to have struck any number of nerves. As the months passed, more and more scholars who had first been hostile became intrigued and then increasingly sympathetic as they grasped the dispassionate rigour with which the new claim was being made. Yet it was clear that many found the mere suggestion that Matthew had been written so early in the first century unsettling to their own academic and theological convictions. The battle-lines between 'conservative' and 'liberal' remain stark in the world of biblical scholarship. Indeed, many academics have found their progress up the academic ladder thwarted because of their conservative views; in some extreme cases, such scholars have been barred from the more senior professorships. For many academics, the redating of the Jesus Papyrus has become a symbol of the squabbles between conservatives and the liberal establishment.

We believe that the coming debate on the redating of the New Testament using papyrological research is badly needed and will draw some of the poison from the argument. In 1976 John Robinson was struck by 'how little evidence there is for dating *any* of the New Testament writings ... there are no fresh facts – like the introduction of carbon-14 datings into archaeology – which have clearly changed the picture'.[10] It is a shame that Robinson, whose instincts were so sound, was unable to incorporate papyrus research into his work. The whole business of dating the Gospels is, as he readily acknowledged, fraught with difficulty. The external and internal evidence is limited. Speculation tends to follow inclination. Sceptics will look for later dates; theological conservatives will do the opposite.

This is why forensic evidence is so important. There is a desperate need for an open-minded scholarly debate on the dating of the New Testament based on papyrological data rather than conjecture rooted in bias. We hope that this book is only the first shot in that debate.

The Importance of the Redating

Where might such a debate lead? As we have seen, the argument that St Matthew's Gospel was written before AD 70 would be powerful even without the evidence of the Magdalen fragments. With this new information included in the analysis, the case is extremely strong. Crossan, for instance, suggests that the Matthean source known as 'Q', some sayings of Jesus, and a few other minor sources first circulated between AD 30 and 60. That may be so. But it now appears that the finished Gospel according to St Matthew was also circulating in codex form at this time. It could conceivably have been read and handled by an eyewitness to the Crucifixion.

This suggests a great deal about the precocious development of the early Church before the destruction of the Temple. The men and women who founded the first Christian communities did so with remarkable speed and organizational skill, driven no doubt by a sense of apocalyptic mission and absolute spiritual responsibility. It also enables us to speculate in a different way about the nature of the Gospels, their character and their purpose. Many criteria have been proposed as ways of establishing the authenticity of statements in the New Testament, such as the 'criterion of multiple attestation' – material repeated in different Gospels is more reliable – or the 'criterion of dissimilarity' – sayings which are clearly alien to Judaism are more trustworthy. The objections are obvious. Since the Gospels are interdependent, the fact that a saying appears in more than one does not prove its authenticity. Likewise, the idea that only non-Judaic utterances can be reliably attributed to Jesus arbitrarily ignores the fact of his Jewishness. As a man who lived and died a Jew, why should he not draw extensively upon Jewish wisdom? Indeed, how could he not?

No completely satisfactory criterion or set of criteria has been established. But surely a simpler criterion – the 'criterion of antiquity' – has been overlooked? If material is older, it is *prima facie* more likely to be a reliable account of what happened. A diary written on the day of an event is – in most cases – better evidence than a memoir written forty years later. That does not mean the diary entry should be read any less critically or thoughtfully than the memoir. But it must be treated in a different way, as a document written in the heat of the moment rather than in the cool light of hindsight. In the same way, a religious text written twenty years after the events it describes is radically different from one written forty years after. There is, as Robinson notes, 'less likelihood of distortion the shorter the interval'.[11]

If the so-called 'tunnel' separating the life of Jesus from the work of the Evangelists was short – perhaps years rather than decades – then we need not assume that their recollections were faulty or fabricated. This does not mean that the Gospels are biographies or historical accounts in the twentieth-century sense. To claim as much would be a grotesque anachronism. Nor does the redating of St Matthew's Gospel invalidate the argument that its structure reflects the practical liturgical needs of an early 'Matthean' community. But the redating does strengthen the view that, in the words of one biblical scholar, 'the Gospels are not a doctrinal speculation but the attestation of a fact'.[12]

And what more practical need could the early communities have felt than the need for authentic information about their Lord and Saviour? It is odd that the question of accurate witness has been accorded so little significance by recent scholars, given that it was clearly so important to the New Testament authors themselves. The Lucan Evangelist says that his history was handed to him 'by those who from the beginning were eyewitnesses and ministers of the word' (Luke 1:2, REV). The author of St John, likewise, stresses that his account of the soldier piercing Jesus's side when he was on the Cross is based on eyewitness evidence: 'He who saw it has borne witness – his testimony is true, and he knows that he tells the truth – that you also may believe' (John 19:35, REV). Later the Evangelist is identified as 'the disciple who is bearing witness to these things, and who has written these things; and we know that his testimony is true' (John 21:24, REV). This suggests, like John 1:14, that the author also included many of his *readers* among the eyewitnesses of Jesus's life and resurrection.

This, it might be said, is merely a literary device to establish the credentials of the Evangelist. Yet, at the very least, the use of this particular device indicates that the communities for whom the Gospels were written valued accurate testimony. To be a witness to Christ was to be part of a spiritual elite. In Acts 10:41, Jesus is said to have appeared 'not to all the people but to us who were chosen by God as witnesses' (REV). It was not a claim made lightly or simply for show.

The question of reliable witness was evidently one of deadly seriousness. In a series of influential books, the textual scholar Birger Gerhardsson – following his mentor Harald Riesenfeld – has shown how important the accurate transmission and learning by heart of holy tradition were in the Jewish milieu of the first century AD. Diligent memorization of important texts and sayings, he argues, was a sacred task. Paul speaks often of a tradition which was handed over and received between Christians.[13] So does Matthew in chapter 15 of his Gospel. The transmission of the good news from witness to witness, from witness to convert, from convert to scribe, was probably 'conscious, deliberate, and programmatic'.[14] This, as Gerhardsson is the first to point out, does not mean that the Gospels were a stenographer's account of the life and work of Jesus. Equally, however, 'there is no reason to suppose that any believer in the early church could create traditions about Jesus and expect that his word would be accepted.'[15]

Gerhardsson's work has not been unreservedly accepted. Yet it still has much to tell us about the formal relationship between memory and text in the first decades of Christianity.[16] The redating of the Jesus Papyrus should be considered in this context. If St Matthew was written before the destruction of the Temple – perhaps many years before – it was written for men and women who would look upon the events it described as recent reality rather than generations-old folklore. Some of them would have had direct experience of Jesus's ministry; many more would know those who claimed to have seen the miracles, the raising of the dead, even the risen Christ.[17] Their faith was a tradition in the sense that it was a shared, recent experience rather than a body of folklore that had taken decades to evolve.

Even if the Gospel according to St Matthew was not written by an eyewitness it was almost certainly written for – and using the testimony of – people who were. Why should we assume *a priori* that the description of Jesus's visit to Bethany in the Magdalen fragments does not describe a real event which might be recalled by believers to whom these verses were later read out? To suggest as much is of course conjecture. But it is not inherently impossible.

Nor should we dismiss the biographical function of the Gospels. They do not resemble modern biography at all. Indeed, their authors and readers would have found the idea of a book exploring the depths of an individual's psychology, motives and character development from birth to death, *wie es eigentlich gewesen* (as it really was), quite mystifying. The sentimental Lives of Jesus which proliferated in the nineteenth century were based upon a complete misassumption about their biblical sources. That does not mean, however, that the Gospels are not, in a strictly defined sense, biographical texts. The belief of the form critics that these books were merely 'unliterary writings' – *Kleinliteratur* – and 'folk books' drawn from the ether of oral tradition has been seriously undermined.

Recently, scholars have begun to explore once more the idea that the Gospels *were* biographies in the Graeco–Roman sense and to observe their similarities with that particular, extremely stylized genre as it expresses itself in works such as Suetonius's lives of the Caesars and Tacitus's *Agricola*.[18] This process of reassessment is shedding light on the way in which the Evangelists might have mingled the real and the conventional, the naturalistic and the stereotyped, in an attempt to recall actual events in an ordered and polemical fashion. It also illustrates the extent to which Jewish and Hellenistic cultures may have intermingled. This new approach does not pretend that the Gospels were diaries or memoirs in the modern sense; nor, however, does it rule out the likelihood that they were meant to relate factual information about the life of a real man.[19] The fact that they were written in a particular literary style does not mean that they are utterly unreliable as historical sources.

The modern mind gets confused when it tries to understand what literal truth meant to the people of first-century Palestine. There peasants and townsmen believed in demons, miracles and charismatic healing. They saw the numinous, the divine and the supernatural at work in their daily lives; the 'open door' to heaven of Revelation 4 was always ajar. Reality was permanently subject to moments of petty transfiguration when the difference between the natural and the supernatural would appear blurred.

Their writings and what they said reflected this belief; they spoke and wrote in a language steeped in metaphor, allusion and reference to the supernatural. They were used to speaking in a way that allowed the possibility of magic and divine intervention. The purpose, indeed, of scripture was to explain the relationship between the two worlds. John Donne understood this better than we do. 'The literall sense is not alwayes that, which the very Letter and Grammar of the place presents,' he wrote, 'as where it is literally said *That Christ is a Vine*, and literally *That his flesh is bread*, ... in many places of Scripture, a figurative sense is the literall sense.'[20] All scriptural writing was literal in the sense that it spoke of real experience.

In the writing of the Gospels, this mixture of myth and empirical information was probably taken for granted. The modern partition between natural and supernatural was not respected: the authors did not think it odd to juxtapose the figurative with the actual, the spiritual with the down-to-earth.[21] Only recently have we started to expect our historical writings to be entirely objective, free of genre and free of mythic language. We need to read the Gospels as descriptions of the world as it seemed to their writers and to understand that these books describe a form of reality, however alien or confused it may appear to the modern rationalist reader.[22]

Whether or not one believes these events happened is entirely a matter of personal faith. What should not be doubted is that the authors of the Gospels considered them of overwhelming and perhaps even terrifying significance. We need to imagine people breathless with history, overcome by the impulse to record a quite exceptional occurrence. They felt a divinely inspired obligation to tell the world and posterity that God had been made flesh. If we lose sight of this elemental truth about the origin of the Gospels – if we become too far drawn into questions of theory and genre and forget their sheer *urgency* – we lose sight of what these extraordinary books really are. In so doing, we forget what we behold: the ancient building blocks beneath our very feet.

CONCLUSION

The Magdalen Papyrus and Faith

We have tried to sketch out the beginnings of a new paradigm in New Testament scholarship: its essence is a renewed attention to the date of the Gospels, rooted in the forensic evidence of papyrology, and an open-mindedness to the potential implications of redating for our understanding of the Gospels' origins. Our approach does not answer the question 'What is a Gospel?' None the less, it makes some answers more plausible than others. It is our hope that this will stimulate a long and productive academic debate, and also inspire a more general interest in these themes outside the academic world. The possibilities are endless and the journey has only just begun.

Thus far we can go as scholar and journalist, observers and interpreters of fact with no axe to grind. Yet – as observers of people rather than of papyri – we cannot ignore the powerful emotions and arguments which have already been triggered by our redating of P64 among ordinary believers and non-believers with no prior interest in papyrus research or Jesus scholarship.

Bultmann was wrong: the authors of the Gospels could hear far more than the faintest whisper of Jesus's voice. Indeed, the first readers of St Matthew may have heard the very words which the Nazarene preacher spoke during his ministry; may have listened to the parables when they were first delivered to the present crowd; may even have asked the wise man questions and waited respectfully for answers. The voice they heard was not a whisper but the passionate oratory of a real man of humble origins whose teaching would change the world.

To say as much has implications beyond the scope of biblical scholarship, wide as that is. Indeed, the redating of the Magdalen Papyrus speaks to those who have never heard of, or cared about, the centuries-old academic rows over the historic Jesus or the textual development of the Gospels. In the course of everyday conversation and correspondence, we have come to realize the extent to which this new claim is directly relevant to the fundamental questions of faith which all people, Christian and non-Christian, atheist and agnostic, must ask themselves. The redating of the St Matthew fragments, in other words, has a life beyond the confines of the academy.

Where will this lead? We live in an age consumed by doubt but desperate for certainty. In the West, there is a new faltering search across the political spectrum for new 'values', or ways of reinstating traditional Judaeo-Christian morality. There is a general weariness with secularism and its aversion to clear morality. There is a corresponding hunger for ideas and policies which will assert some sort of moral framework. In the memorable words of an editorial in the *Wall Street Journal*, there is a desire for 'guard-rails', the certainties which protect us from moral anarchy. The key questions asked by ordinary people today – about family values and permissiveness, crime and punishment, duty and freedoms – are not so very different from the questions asked of Jesus more than nineteen centuries ago. The New Testament remains a fundamental text for those seeking answers to these basic problems of the human experience.

In this context, the redating of the Gospel – a process which is only now beginning in earnest – may seem an enterprise appropriate to its times, to the mood of the millennium's end. There is now good reason to suppose that the Gospel according to St Matthew, with its detailed accounts of the Sermon on the Mount and the Great Commission, was written not long after the Crucifixion and certainly before the destruction of the Temple in AD 70; that the Gospel according to St Mark was distributed early enough to reach Qumran; that the Gospel according to St Luke belonged to the very first generation of Christian codices; and that internal evidence suggests a date before AD 70 even for the non-synoptic Gospel according to St John (as the highly respected German academic Klaus Berger argued in 1994[1]). These are the first stirrings of a major process of scholarly reappraisal. It concerns all of the Gospels. It affects everyone who has read them or will read them.

Two thousand years after the birth of Jesus, the books that tell of his life are being analysed once more – not by priests, theologians or literary critics but by scientists. For centuries, science has quarrelled with faith. Galileo was condemned by the Church as a heretic; Darwin's evolutionary theory made a nonsense of the Creation myth; and Freud's research into the inner promptings of the human psyche undermined the Christian belief in personal moral responsibility. For Huleatt's generation, the science of Darwinism and the science of textual criticism (as epitomized by Renan and Strauss) were unequivocally hostile forces. Yet, in the case which is this book's subject, empirical science may prove to be the handmaiden of faith rather than its arch-enemy.

This process of re-evaluation is an opportunity for ordinary people to look afresh at the New Testament and its relevance to their lives. No scientist can say that the Gospels are true. But he or she can form a judgment as to whether they are *authentic*. Responding to such claims, some people will say that evidence – the empirical findings of a science like papyrology – has nothing to do with faith and morality. Like Charles Huleatt, they do not need shrouds, miracles or even the sources of history to buttress their belief. Others may take the opposite point of view and find their beliefs profoundly affected by the redating. They may see in the redating process an unexpected convergence of faith and history; a filling-in of what Gotthold Lessing called the 'ugly ditch' between the two.

For if the Gospels are more authentic than we thought, then perhaps the gap between the Jesus of history and the Christ of faith is not as great as academics have claimed and Christians feared. These extraordinary books stand before us bathed in a new light of understanding. Jesus's voice seems anything but a whisper. In this sense, the Magdalen Papyrus speaks not only to the minds of scholars but to the hearts of all people.

'When you read God's word,' wrote the philosopher Søren Kierkegaard, 'you must constantly be saying to yourself, "It is talking to me, and about me."' Nobody who pursues this subject for long can fail to be moved and challenged by it. Our research has taken us all over the world: from Germany to America, to Egypt and Israel, and across Europe. These travels are not yet done. Yet the story of the Jesus Papyrus must end where it began, at Magdalen, the college which has been home to these precious fragments for most of this century. For it is this 500-year-old institution – founded 1400 years after the papyrus was written – that stands at the centre of the tale: that sent Charles Huleatt forth, that inspired the devotion which drove him to send the papyrus back a few years before his death. And it was to Magdalen that Carsten Thiede would later come to redate the fragments.

Today, the college is thriving. It has lost none of its medieval majesty. Indeed, it has been lovingly restored in recent years so that future generations may continue to enjoy its unique beauty. Huleatt's old mentor, Herbert Warren, would be proud of what Magdalen has become. As in his day, few experiences in Oxford compare with an afternoon walk from the High Street through the Porter's Lodge, past the President's Lodgings and the Chapel, where the *Last Supper* now hangs, through the ancient cloisters and out towards the Deer Park. It is a place to enjoy the fruits of intellect and the mason's skill and to consider what has been accomplished there.

Standing in the Old Library, amid the books and manuscripts and carved wooden gargoyles, one can only guess what tricks of fortune saved the papyrus from destruction. Looking out of the window to the splendour of the Magdalen New Buildings – as Gibbon did two centuries ago – it is odd to reflect that the three fragments of papyrus ever reached this place at all. What would the scribes have thought if they had known that their work would one day be brought here? Labouring in the blazing sun of the Near East, committing their story to fragile paper, they would have been amazed to learn that it would travel so far and mean so much.

GLOSSARY

Amanuensis

A Latin term for an assistant who takes a dictation or helps in the composition of a text, from *a manu*, someone who is at hand. Thus, Tertius (Romans 16:22) was the amanuensis of St Paul, Silvanus (1 Peter 5:12) that of St Peter. The term is still in modern use. For example, the 1995 Examination Decrees and Regulations of the University of Oxford make provisions for the use of an amanuensis 'for special and urgent reasons' (pp. 1036–7).

Babylonian Talmud

The Talmud or 'teaching' consists of the 'Mishna' ('repetition'), the body of Jewish law, and rabbinical comments ('Gemara') which often take the form of stories and folklore. The codification of the Mishnah happened in the second century AD, but its sources are much older. The Gemara was collected during the following two or three centuries. There are two Talmuds: the Jerusalem or Palestinian Talmud ('Talmud Yerushalmi') and the Babylonian Talmud ('Talmud Bavli'). The latter became the authoritative version. It contains thirty-six tractates of about two and a half million words. After centuries of attempts by the Church to suppress or destroy the Babylonian Talmud, the first complete edition was printed by the Christian publisher Daniel Bomberg at Venice, in the 1520s.

Biblical Uncial

A technical term used to describe a certain type of handwriting with capital letters ('uncials'), current in biblical manuscripts traditionally dated to the third to ninth centuries. G. Cavallo and his followers prefer the variant term 'Biblical Majuscule'. While this style acquired a certain fixity after the famous fourth-century codices Sinaiticus and Vaticanus, it is useless for a description of the many-faceted manuscripts that predate these official editions. The Magdalen Papyrus is, in any case, a precursor of this style of handwriting.

Capsa

The Latin technical term for a transportable, bucket-like container of scrolls, often cylindrical in form (cf. the modern English word 'capsule'). Murals with *capsae* have been found at Pompeii and in the Roman Catacombs.

Codex

From the Latin *Caudex/Codex* (wooden block, tree-trunk), the technical term for a volume of papyrus, vellum or parchment sheets with writing on both sides, bound together in the form of a number of single or folded pages like a modern book.

Dead Sea Scrolls

This expression is commonly used to refer to the scrolls and fragments of scrolls in Hebrew and Aramaic discovered in eleven caves near the settlement of Qumran on the Dead Sea, between 1947 and 1956. This usage is slightly incorrect, however, since there are places and areas elsewhere at the Dead Sea where manuscripts have been found – e.g., in the Nahal Hever, the Wadi Murraba'at, and on Masada. The first reference to a cave with scrolls can be found in a text by the Christian author Origen at the beginning of the third century AD: he informs his readers that he used one such scroll, found in a cave 'near Jericho', for the Hebrew text of his edition of the Bible, the Hexapla. It is one of the many mysteries of Dead Sea Scroll studies that no archaeologist took this information seriously and that it was left to Bedouins accidentally to discover caves containing scrolls. While most scholars assume that the scrolls found near Qumran were written by the orthodox Essene community, there is also a consensus that the twenty-five Greek texts found in Cave 4 (six) and 7 (nineteen) came from outside Qumran. Cave 7, just beneath Cave 4, with exclusively Greek texts entirely on papyrus, is an exception among the eleven caves with texts.

Diacritical signs

Critical or diacritical signs are marks used by scribes or editors to distinguish particular readings or variants and editorial decisions. The obelus (-) and the asterisk (*) are two examples. The system was introduced by Aristarchus at the library of Alexandria in the second century BC. (Dia)critical signs were also occasionally used to help readers to find their way in manuscripts which in antiquity were normally written without gaps between words (*scriptio continua*) and without punctuation marks. For example, a high point or dot, the *stigme teleía*, could be used like a full stop. A horizontal line underneath the beginning of a line (*'paragraphus'*) could be used to indicate the end of a passage in the same line, where a small gap (*'spatium'*) averaging the width of between two and nine letters would specify the exact place.

Form criticism

The attempt to examine a text and its development on the basis of literary forms, oral predecessors, their units, and their *Sitz im Leben* (setting in the life of a community), introduced and developed by the German scholars K. L. Schmidt, M. Dibelius and R. Bultmann.

Gnosticism / Gnosis

Derived from the Greek word *gignoskein*, 'to know', these terms cover all sorts of 'heretical' movements from the mid-first to the fourth centuries. A common trait of such sectarian groups is the attempt to gain knowledge of spiritual secrets by mystical and mythological speculation, relinquishing the role of faith, thereby seeing the true nature of God and finding salvation. Adherents of gnostic teaching thought themselves superior to ordinary, scripture-orientated Christians. St Paul attacks gnostic tendencies in 1 Corinthians and other letters. The most important collection of such texts was found by two peasants in Nag Hammadi, Upper Egypt, in 1945.

Häkchenstil

Also called 'hooked style', or *Häkchen* in German, because of the 'hooks' which characterize letters written in it. It is one of many terms used to differentiate between ancient types of handwriting. More often than not, such styles vary, and any one manuscript may present a combination of elements derived from different styles which occasionally should rather be called 'mannerisms' of an individual scribe. However, if not used categorically, these terms help to differentiate between individual hands and their periods. *Häkchen* are an indicator of an earlier rather than a later period of uncial papyri.

Herculanean style

A similar general term to the above-mentioned *Häkchenstil*, used to describe common characteristics of manuscripts found at Herculaneum. Since the site was destroyed by the eruption of Vesuvius in AD 79, there is a certain upper limit to the dates of texts found at Herculaneum. But since not all manuscripts discovered at this site were also written there – they could have come from practically anywhere in the Roman Empire – the term is helpful mainly to describe manuscripts collected at a particular period and in a particular place.

Membranae

Membrana, 'skin' or 'parchment', was the Latin technical term for a (parchment) notebook and is used in Greek transcription by St Paul in the plural, *membranai* (2 Timothy 4:13), to describe the notebooks he wants Timothy to bring. The reference in 2 Timothy is the earliest Greek occurrence of this word. The *membranae* were, technically speaking, precursors of the codex.

Nomen sacrum / Nomina sacra

Literally 'holy name' or 'holy names', a term introduced to describe words like 'God', 'Lord', 'Jesus', 'Son', 'Spirit' for the persons of the Trinity which were, as a rule, abbreviated in Christian biblical manuscripts, probably from the introduction of the codex onwards. The most common system was the use of the first and last character, in certain words with the addition of a middle letter. It seems that Christian scribes and the authorities behind them introduced the *nomina sacra* to emulate the Jewish custom of writing the holy, unpronounceable name of God with the Hebrew consonants JHWH which in Greek manuscripts had the visual effect of an abbreviation.

Ostracon/ostraca

A Greek word to describe potsherds used for writing. Often employed for brief notices, larger pieces sometimes carried whole literary texts. In ancient Greece, such *ostraca* were used to vote on the banishment of people – hence the English word 'to ostracize' someone.

Oxyrhynchus

One of the Egyptian sites where papyri were discovered by archaeologists or peasants – others include Fayyûm and Nag Hammadi. Among biblical scholars, Oxyrhynchus became famous for its numerous New Testament papyri – to such an extent that the expression 'the Oxyrhynchus New Testament' could be coined. Debates about dates notwithstanding, the New Testament fragments found at Oxyrhynchus cover a period from the early second century AD to *c.* AD 600.

Palaeography

From Greek *palaios*, 'old', and *graphe*, 'writing'. The science of studying, analysing and describing the handwriting and its characteristics, their forms and dates, in ancient manuscripts. It is not always clearly distinguished from papyrology, which is the more general term, additionally comprising all other aspects of ancient manuscripts.

Papyrus

A tall aquatic plant cultivated, in antiquity, in the Egyptian Nile marshes, and later, during the early Middle Ages, also grown in Palestine, Sicily, and elsewhere. In papyrology, the term refers to the writing material produced from its stem pith. The method was described by Pliny the Elder in his *Natural History*, Book 13, before AD 79.

Paragraphus

See 'Diacritical signs'.

Parchment

A refined form of prepared animal skin used as writing material, developed at Pergamum – hence its name.

Pericope

From the Greek *'perikope'*, 'a piece cut out', used to describe a selected passage from a book; in Christianity, a text set aside for a reading in a service, or for study.

Philology, Classical

The study of the languages and literatures of classical Greek and Latin antiquity, including the New Testamental period. Classical philologists for a long time neglected the New Testament documents as much as New Testament scholars have neglected the context of non-Christian language and literature. One of the legacies of this erroneous attitude is the mistake in teaching 'New Testament Greek' as though this was a different language or dialect, which of course it is not.

'Q'

In all-encompassing term derived from the German word *Quelle* (source), and used to embrace numerous, often conflicting theories about a source or sources behind the Gospels. Thus, if Matthew and Luke contain material that is nonexistent in the earliest Gospel, Mark, such material could have come from 'Q'. Any answer to the popular question 'Did "Q" ever exist?' depends on a clear definition. The most likely answer is, of course, that 'Q' as such never existed – and therefore cannot be reconstructed, since there was more than one collection of sayings and other material was used by the Gospel writers. St Luke himself says as much in the prologue to his Gospel (1:2–3), and St John states that not all the material available to him was incorporated into his Gospel (21:25). The theologian and historian Papias, writing in about AD 110, refers to *logia* of Jesus collected by St Matthew in Aramaic. Provided that *logia* here means, literally, 'sayings', St Matthew could himself have provided 'Q' for his own later, complete Gospel, and for that of St Luke (which is dependent upon Matthew as much as on Mark). In any case, no papyrus with any trace of what might be called 'Q' has survived.

Quire

From Latin *quaternio*, a set of four. Usually four sheets folded to yield eight leaves or sixteen pages.

Qumran

See 'Dead Sea Scrolls'.

Recto

From Latin *rectus*, right. The right or front side of a leaf; in papyri, mainly used to describe the side where the fibres run horizontally. Because of the folding system in codices, the text on the verso or back could precede the text on the recto. This is the case with the Magdalen Papyrus.

Scriptio continua

See 'Diacritical signs'.

Scroll

Used in preference to 'roll' to describe rolls made of parchment, leather, vellum, or papyrus by gluing, occasionally stitching, leaves together and rolling them up. Scrolls were often purpose-made, but could not be endless; twelve metres is an above-average length. In the New Testament, the two books by St Luke, his Gospel and Acts, were published in two scrolls prior to the introduction of the codex, where they would easily fit inside one such 'book'.

Septuagint

From Latin *septuaginta*, 'seventy', the oldest complete Greek translation of the Hebrew/Aramaic Old Testament of about 250 BC, including the Apocrypha. The name was derived from the legend that seventy, or rather seventy-two, scholars translated the texts in seventy days. Its practical purpose was the necessity to provide an Old Testament for the growing number of Jews who were unable to read and understand Hebrew. In New Testament times, the Septuagint was used throughout the Roman Empire and is the version quoted in the New Testament. Its common abbreviation is 'LXX'.

Sittybos

Sittybos or *sillybos* is the Greek technical term for a tag, usually made of parchment or papyrus, that was attached to the handle or back of a scroll in order to identify its contents without unrolling it. The name of the work inside, perhaps a short description, and, if there was more than one work of the same title (such as *euangelion* or 'Gospel'), the name of the author also, were written on this *sittybos*. Several ancient examples have survived. For the textual tradition of the New Testament, the common and necessary use of these tags guarantees the correct identification of the Gospel authors during the early stages of the Gospels on scrolls.

Spatium

See 'Diacritical signs'.

Stichometry

From the Greek *stichos*, 'line' or 'row'. It is used to describe a line or verse of writing; ancient scribes were normally paid according to the number of *stichoi* they wrote or copied. Stichometry refers to the technique of measuring books. The length of a *stichos* is an important element in the decipherment, identification and editing of papyri: the average length of a line is a yardstick for the completion of fragmentary lines. Two of the papyri discussed in this book, the Magdalen Papyrus, P64, and 7Q5 from Qumran, offer far-reaching examples of this procedure.

Synoptic Gospels

Mark, Matthew and Luke, so called because the first three Gospel writers share a 'common view' (Greek, *syn-opsis*) in their portrayal of Jesus, despite all their differences, whereas John offers a distinctively different approach to the selection of sayings, narratives, and chronology. The traditional tendency to prefer the Synoptic Gospels for their historical value had to be abandoned in view of the increasing evidence supporting the accuracy and trustworthiness of John in his own right; it is no longer possible to play them off against each other.

Tachygraphy

From Greek *tachys*, 'sharp', and *graphe*, 'writing', for different systems of ancient shorthand writing common in New Testament times and before, throughout the Roman Empire.

Torah

From the Hebrew for 'precept', 'law': the Pentateuch, that is, the five first books of the Old Testament, ascribed to Moses, and, in a more narrow sense, the law of the 'Old Testament'.

Vellum

From Old French, *velin*, calf. Writing material made from the skin of young calves and other, often unborn animals to yield extra-fine quality.

Verso

From Latin *vertere*, 'to turn'. The term is usually employed to describe the back (or rather reverse), left, side of a leaf, where the fibres run vertically. On parchment, vellum or leather manuscripts, the system of differentiating between *recto* and *verso* could be applied by referring to the lighter 'flesh' side and the darker 'hair' side.

Zierstil

German for 'decorated style', a term introduced by the German papyrologist Wilhelm Schubart to describe a style of handwriting not unlike the '*Häkchenstil*', with decorative roundels and small lines at the extremities of a main stroke in a letter (also called serifs). Schubart assumed that this style was common during the first centuries BC and AD, whereas the British papyrologist E. G. Turner felt that the term was too vague to be useful for dating purposes. For the limitations of such characterizations see above, '*Häkchenstil*'.

NOTES

1: Portrait of a Papyrologist: the Revd Charles B. Huleatt, Victorian Missionary and Scholar

1) G. W. Steevens, *Egypt in 1898* (London, 1898), p. 225–6.
2) The authors are deeply indebted to Captain Julian Williams and Thomas Huleatt-James, both indirect descendants of Charles Bousfield Huleatt, for their help in the writing of this chapter.
3) See W. G. Rutherford, *St Paul's Epistles to the Thessalonians and to the Corinthians* (London, 1908). This posthumous publication includes a helpful prefatory memoir by Spenser Wilkinson.
4) 21 January 1909, p. 132.
5) W. G. Rutherford, *St Paul's Epistles to the Romans – A New Translation, with a Brief Analysis* (London, 1900), p. xi.
6) This aspect of the university's history is well explored in Richard Symonds, *Oxford and Empire: The Last Lost Cause?* (London, 1986).
7) Thomas Hughes, *Tom Brown at Oxford* (1861), quoted in Malcolm Graham, *Images of Victorian Oxford* (Oxford, 1992).
8) J. R. Green, *Oxford Studies* (1901), p. xi, cited in Graham, op. cit., p. 9.
9) See Laurie Magnus, *Herbert Warren of Magdalen – President and Friend 1853–1930* (London, 1932); T. Herbert Warren, *Magdalen College, Oxford* (London, 1907); H. A. Wilson, *Magdalen College, Oxford* (London, 1899); for a fictional portrait of Magdalen during the Warren era, see Compton Mackenzie's 1913 novel, *Sinister Street*.
10) Magnus, op. cit., pp. 86, 55.
11) *Lecture Given by T. H. Warren to Undergraduates of Magd. on the Last Sunday of the Summer Term of 1885* (Oxford, 1885).
12) Guildhall Library MS.
13) *The Greater Britain Messenger*, 1909, p. 21.
14) For a useful account of Strauss's work and influence see Stephen Neill, *The Interpretation of the New Testament 1861–1961* (London, 1964), p. 12ff.
15) Cited in Neill, op. cit., p. 194.

16) Cited in Bernard M. G. Reardon, *Religious Thought in the Victorian Age: A Survey from Coleridge to Gore* (London, 1980), p. 259.

17) Cited in Neill, op. cit., p. 193.

18) *Anglican Church Magazine*, 1904, pp. 15–17.

19) Ibid., 1906, pp. 44–5, 70–72.

20) *Annual Report of the C&CCS*, 1898–9.

21) *Annual Report of the C&CCS*, 1906–7.

22) See J. S. Reynolds, *The Evangelicals at Oxford 1735–1871: A Record of an Unchronicled Movement* (Oxford, 1953); the authors are grateful to the Reverend Reynolds for his assistance on Huleatt's years at Wycliffe Hall.

23) Ibid., p. 159.

24) See F. W. B. Bullock, *The History of Ridley Hall, Cambridge* 2 vols (Cambridge, 1941, 1953) for the origins of both halls.

25) *Wycliffe Hall, Oxford* (Oxford, 1878).

26) See Symonds, op. cit., Chapter 11.

27) For an account of a near contemporary of Huleatt's who became a missionary in Egypt, see C. E. Padwick, *Temple Gairdner of Cairo* (London, 1929).

28) Symonds, op. cit., p. 227.

29) For a survey of the society's history, see Brian Underwood, *Faith at the Frontiers: Anglican Evangelicals and their Countrymen Overseas* (London, 1974).

30) *The Greater Britain Messenger*, 1891.

31) Minutes of the C&CCS, 29 July 1891.

32) *Programme of Cook's International Tickets to Egypt 1898–9*.

33) See Piers Brendon, *Thomas Cook – 150 Years of Popular Tourism* (London, 1991).

34) Charles A. Cooper, *Seeking the Sun: An Egyptian Holiday* (Edinburgh, 1892), pp. 97–8.

35) *The Times*, 21 May 1909, p. 12.

36) Quoted in Ian Wilson, *Jesus the Evidence* (London, 1984), p. 16.

37) This contrast is still a striking feature of modern papyrology. The Isaiah scroll discovered at Qumran is more than seven metres long, while the oldest extant fragment of Virgil found on Masada is only 16 × 8 cm.

38) See A. H. Sayce, *Reminiscences* (London, 1923).

39) Sayce, A. H., *The Egypt of the Hebrews and Herodotos* (London, 1896).

40) Quoted in Anthony Sattin, *Lifting the Veil: British Society in Egypt 1768–1956* (London, 1988).

41) See, for instance, Sayce, op. cit., pp. 332–4.

42) Magdalen College Librarian's Report, 1901.

43) C. Roberts, 'An Early Papyrus of the First Gospel', *Harvard Theological Review*, 46 (1953), pp. 233–7.

44) *Annual Report of the C&CCS*, 1901–2.

45) *Anglican Church Magazine*, 1909.

46) *Annual Report of the C&CCS*, 1903–4.

47) Obituary notice in the *Guardian*, 13 January 1909.

48) For an account of the earthquake, see J. W. Wilson and Roger Perkins, *Angels in Blue Jackets: The Navy at Messina, 1908* (Chippenham, 1985); for Collins's part in it, see his account in the *Anglican Church Magazine*, March–April 1909, and Arthur James Mason, *Life of William Edward Collins, Bishop of Gibraltar* (London, 1912).

2: Dates and Controversies: St Matthew and the Debate About the Origins of the New Testament

1) Martin Hengel, *Studies in the Gospel of Mark* (London, 1985), pp. 85–113.

2) There are no historical writings without an 'interest' in antiquity; the Gospels are certainly not any more tendentious than, say, the Roman historian Tacitus with his book *Agricola*, a selective biography of his father-in-law Cn. Iulius Agricola written in AD 98. The first four sentences are an uninhibited declaration of partisanship. At the beginning of his history of Rome, *Ab urbe condita*, c. AD 9, Livy states that he writes in order to praise the glorious deeds of the one people 'leading on earth' – i.e., the Romans. It was customary to admit one's interests – and to have them in the first place. St Luke, writing that he published his gospel so that Theophilus 'may know the truth concerning the things of which you have been informed' (Luke 1:4, RSV), was in the very best company of ancient historians.

3) Hengel, op. cit., p. 110.

4) A widespread misunderstanding of this verse has been caused by the expression 'some of those standing here who will not taste death . . .', as though it was stressing the word 'some'. Jesus does not imply that others will die. All the sentence does say is that some, not all of those present, will see a revelation of his glory. And indeed, only a few of them were present at the Transfiguration.

5) This is a literal translation from the original Greek.

6) Cf. Romans 11:26!

7) Interestingly, the Greek word used in Matthew 10:23 for this act of 'completing', *teléo*, is used in exactly the same sense at the beginning of St Luke's Gospel: 'When his parents had completed everything which the Law of the Lord prescribes, they returned to Galilee, to their town of Nazareth.'

8) See Chapter 3.

9) Theodor Zahn, *Das Evangelium des Matthäus* (Leipzig/Erlangen 1903; 4th edn 1922; repr. Wuppertal/Zürich, 1984), p. 407.

10) 'Awake or asleep' = 'whether we live or die'; cf. Romans 14:8. In other words, Paul himself was prepared for death prior to the Second Coming, as others had died before – including such eminent figures as Stephen, the leader of the Hellenists among the Christian community at Jerusalem as early as *c*. AD 33 – an event Paul had witnessed and supported before his conversion.

An alternative explanation assumes that the Second Coming had already happened fifty days after Easter, at Pentecost, in the outpouring of the Holy Spirit, the 'paraclete' or 'helper' prophesied by Jesus in John 14:16–26, 15:26, and 16:9–11.

11) Nestle-Aland *Novum Testamentum Graece*, (27th rev. edn, 1993), p. 453.

12) St Mark is sometimes excepted from this 'rule', as the prophecy is slightly abbreviated, less detailed, than in the others. Thus, 'generous' scholars would grant St Mark a date of 'about AD 70'. Remarkably, the late Günther Zuntz, Professor of Hellenistic Greek (which is the period including the New Testament) at Manchester University, and an internationally recognized authority on the subject, thought nothing of such artificial arguments and opted for the other end of the spectrum: the most likely date of composition of St Mark was, for him, AD 40 (see G. Zuntz, 'Wann wurde das Evangelium Marci geschrieben' and *idem*, 'Ein Heide las das Markusevangelium', in H. Cancik, ed., *Markus-Philologie. Historische, literargeschichtliche und stilistische Untersuchungen zum zweiten Evangelium* (Tübingen, 1984), pp. 47–71 and pp. 205–22).

For St Matthew's Gospel, the earliest dates suggested by scholars who were not impressed by the theory of a prophecy made up after the event are *c*. AD 40–60 (J. A. T. Robinson, *Redating the New Testament*, London, 1976); *c*. AD 43 (B. Orchard and H. Riley, *The Order of the Synoptics*, Macon, Ga, 1987); and *c*. AD 50–64 (B. Reicke, 'Synoptic Prophecies on the Destruction of Jerusalem, in D. E. Aune, ed., *Studies in New Testament and*

Early Christian Literature. Essays in Honour of Allen P. Wikgren (Leiden, 1972), pp. 121–34).

13) As the Anchor Bible, vol. 26, W. F. Albright and C. S. Mann, *Matthew: Introduction, Translation and Notes* (New York, 1971), puts it: 'A Messiah without a Messianic Community would have been unthinkable to any Jew', p. 195.

14) Hengel, op. cit., pp. 64–84.

15) See, e.g., Theodor Birt, *Die Buchrolle in der Kunst* (Leipzig, 1907, repr. 1976); E. Schmalzriedt, *Peri Physeos. Zur Frühgeschichte der Buchtitel* (München, 1970); and G. Cavallo, *Libri, Scritture, Scribi a Ercolaneo* (Naples, 1983).

16) Hengel, op. cit., pp. 81–2.

17) For the archaeology of Capernaum with its enormous, surfaced jetty (700 m. long and 2 m. wide), see M. Nun, *Anchorages and Harbours Around the Sea of Galilee* (En Gev, 1988), pp. 24–6; cf. also B. Pixner, *Wege des Messias und Stätten der Urkirche. Jesus und das Judenchristentum im Licht neuer archäologischer Erkenntnisse*, ed. R. Riesner 2nd, enl. edn, Giessen 1994), pp. 65–6.

18) See F. Herrenbrück, *Jesus und die Zöllner* (Tübingen, 1990).

19) C. F. D. Moule, 'St Matthew's Gospel: Some Neglected Features', in *idem*, *Essays in New Testament Interpretation* (Cambridge, 1982), pp. 67–74, here pp. 73–4. Moule does not think that this disciple then went on to write the whole Gospel himself, but he argues in favour of his role in the collection of the original source material.

20) Quoted by Eusebius in his *Church History* of, 39, 16 (written *c.* AD 324/5). See Chapters 3 and 6 of our book.

21) Told by Clement of Alexandria (*c.* AD 150–219), *Stromateis*, 4, 9.

22) An excellent, exhaustive survey of opinions and publications on this Gospel and all New Testament writings can be found in the most comprehensive study of the New Testament, the 1,160 pages of D. Guthrie's *New Testament Introduction* 4th rev. edn (Leicester, 1990).

23) J. A. T. Robinson, *The Priority of John* (London, 1985), pp. 1–122.

24) K. Berger, *Theologiegeschichte des Urchristentums. Theologie des Neuen Testaments* (Tübingen/Basel, 1994), here in particular pp. 653–7 (on St John) and pp. 568–71 (on Revelation). Berger remains more conservative and closer to the traditional consensus on the dates of other New Testament writings, mainly without going into chronological details.

25) A. H. N. Green-Armytage, *Jesus Who Saw* (London, 1952), pp. 12–13.

26) D. L. Sayers, 'A Vote of Thanks to Cyrus', in *idem, Unpopular Opinions* (London, 1946; 2nd edn, 1951), pp. 23–8, here p. 25.

3: The Jesus Papyrus in Context: the Science of Papyrology and Christianity at Qumran

1) A story preserved by the German papyrologist U. Wilcken, *Die griechischen Papyrusurkunden* (Berlin, 1897), p. 10.
2) Most of the Codex Sinaiticus is now at the British Library in London; several leaves are kept at the University Library of Leipzig (von Tischendorf's home university), and a further twelve, recently discovered at the monastery, have so far remained there. The other, equally important codex, also of a mid-fourth-century date, is the Codex Vaticanus, at the Vatican Library.
3) A good description of the technique can be found in P. W. Pestman, *The New Papyrological Primer* (Leiden/New York, 1990).
4) Gaius Plinius Secundus, *Natural History*, 13, 70–82.
5) See I. Gallo, *Greek and Latin Papyrology*, Classical Handbook 1 (London, 1986), p. 14, and Chapter 5 of this book.
6) For this and for further material, cf. Theodor Birt, *Die Buchrolle in der Kunst* (Leipzig, 1907, reprinted 1976), here pp. 254 and 326.
7) Thus, the later the Pastoral Epistles are dated, the more likely it becomes, theoretically at least, that *biblia* already means codices rather than scrolls. Against the tendency to post-date 2 Timothy to the late-first or early-to-mid-second century, see recently (among others) G. D. Fee, *1 and 2 Timothy, Titus* (San Francisco, 1984) and M. Prior, *Paul the Letter-Writer and the Second Letter to Timothy* (Sheffield, 1989).
8) C. H. Roberts and T. C. Skeat, *The Birth of the Christian Codex* (London, 1983), pp. 21–3, here p. 22.
9) See J. Genoth-Bismuth, *Un Homme nommé Salut. Genèse d'une 'hérésie' à Jérusalem* (2nd edn, Paris, 1995), pp. 205–7, here p. 205, analysing the tracts Sabbat 16:1 and 116a.
10) J. O'Callaghan, 'Papiros neotestamentarios en la cueva 7 de Qumrân?', *Biblica*, 53 (1972), pp. 91–100; authorized English translation by W. L. Holladay in *Journal of Biblical Literature*, 91 (1972), Suppl., pp. 1–14. O'Callaghan published in-depth studies of the 7Q papyri in many subsequent issues of specialist journals, answering his opponents. A good summary of his investigations is contained in his monograph *Los Papiros*

Griegos de la Cueva 7 de Qumrân (Madrid, 1974). See also his *Los primeros testimonios del Nuevo Testamento* (Córdoba, 1995), pp. 95–145.

11) For the recent debate about this date and the deficient nature of attempts to question it, see Chapter 5, n. 18.

12) K. Schubert, 'Die Religion der Qumranleute', in J. B. Bauer, J. Fink, H. D. Galter, eds., *Qumran, Ein Symposion* (Graz, 1993), pp. 73–85, here pp. 84–5.

13) For further literature and sources, see J. A. Fitzmyer, *The Dead Sea Scrolls: Major Publications and Tools for Studies* (rev. edn, Atlanta, 1990), and in this book Chapter 5, n. 18.

14) C. P. Thiede, '7Q – Eine Rückkehr zu den neutestamentlichen Papyrusfunden in der siebten Höhle von Qumran', *Biblica*, 65 (1984), pp. 538–59.

15) C. P. Thiede's latest monograph in English, a full discussion of the arguments 'pro and con', is *The Earliest Gospel Manuscript? The Qumran Fragment 7Q5 and its Significance for New Testament Studies* (Exeter/Carlisle, 1992). See also the most up-to-date summary in C. P. Thiede, '7Q5 – Facts or Fiction?', *Westminster Theological Journal*, 57 (1995), pp. 471–4.

16) S. Talmon, 'Streit um die Rollen von Qumran', *Zur Debatte*, 22/5 (1992), pp. 1–3.

17) 'No credo possano esserci dubbi circa l'identificazione del 7Q5'; O. Montevecchi, 'Ricerchiamo senza pregiudizi' ('Let us research without prejudices'), interview with S. Paci, *30 Giorni*, XII/7–8 (1994), pp. 75–6.

18) G. Stanton, *Gospel Truth? New Light on Jesus and the Gospels* (London, 1995), pp. 20–32 and pp. 11–20 respectively.

19) M. Baillet, J. T. Milik and R. de Vaux, eds, *Discoveries in the Judaean Desert of Jordan*, III: *Les 'Petites Grottes' de Qumrân*, 2 vols (Oxford, 1962).

20) H. Hunger, '7Q5: Markus 6, 52–53 – oder? Die Meinung des Papyrologen', in B. Mayer, *Christen und Christliches in Qumran?* (Regensburg, 1992), pp. 33–56, here p. 39.

21) Comparatively speaking, omissions (or rather, non-inclusions) can be found in other very early papyri, such as in the P46 or, in a particularly striking case, in the oldest known papyrus of St John's Gospel, the famous P52 at the John Rylands University Library, Manchester (Gr. P. 457). Chapter 18:37 has only one *eis touto* ('for this') instead of two, which is the case in all other St John manuscripts without exception. A singular phenomenon, and yet no one has batted an eyelid – indeed, it is not even mentioned in the apparatus of the critical Greek New Testament editions.

22) P. Segal, 'The Penalty of the Warning Inscription from the Temple of

Jerusalem', *Israel Exploration Journal*, 39 (1989), pp. 79–84.

23) H.-U. Rosenbaum, 'Cave 7Q! Gegen die erneute Inanspruchnahme des Qumran-Fragments 7Q5 als Bruchstück der ältesten Evangelien-Hand-scrift', *Biblische Zeitschrift*, 51 (1987), pp. 189–205, here p. 200. Rosenbaum's paper is marked by factual errors, invectives and lack of expert knowledge.

24) F. T. Gignac, *Grammar of the Greek Papyri of the Roman and Byzantine Periods*, vol. 1: *Phonology* (Milan, 1976), pp. 80–3.

25) Hunger, op. cit.

26) The official report on this investigation was published by C. P. Thiede, 'Bericht über die kriminaltechnische Untersuchung des Fragments 7Q5 in Jerusalem', in Mayer, op. cit., pp. 239–45, with 4 plates, including a video printout of the *nu* detail.

27) Stanton, op. cit., Plate 8. On pp. 28–9 he claims, in italics, that 'although it is most unlikely that an early copy of Mark's Gospel found its way to Cave 7, this is not completely impossible. The theory that 7Q5 is part of Mark's Gospel does not collapse for this reason, but simply because the crucial damaged letter on line 2 of 7Q5 *cannot* be a *nu*.' As Chapter 3 demonstrates at length, an early copy of St Mark's Gospel at Qumran is anything but unlikely, and Stanton would even be prepared to accept this, it seems. So why does he insist on the impossibility of the *nu*, in the face of the Jerusalem microscope and of Hunger's comparative analysis? His belittling of the perfectly clear evidence from Jerusalem is incomprehensible, all the more so as he himself quotes from a letter received from the critical American Qumran scholar J. A. Fitzmyer who has been impressed by the evidence of the photograph of the Jerusalem analysis (Stanton, p. 198, n. 16).

28) F. Rohrhirsch, 'Das Qumranfragment 7Q5', *Novum Testamentum*, 30/2 (1988), pp. 97–9; idem, *Markus in Qumran? Eine Auseinandersetzung mit den Argumenten für und gegen das Fragment 7Q5 mit Hilfe des methodischen Fallibilismusprinzips* (Wuppertal/Zurich, 1990).

29) The latest two attempts, imaginative but unrelated to the visible evidence on the papyrus, came from Vittoria Spottorno and Daniel B. Wallace; see C. P. Thiede, 'Greek Qumran Fragment 7Q5: Possibilities and Impossibilities', *Biblica*, 75 (1994), pp. 394–8, and idem '7Q5 – Facts or Fiction?', Westminster Theological Journal 57 (1995) pp. 471–4.

30) See C. P. Thiede, 'Papyrologische Anfragen an 7Q5 im Umfeld antiker Handschriften', in Mayer, op. cit., note 20, pp. 57–72.

31) E. G. Turner, 'Menander, *Samia* 385–390 Austin (170–175 Koe)', *Aegyptus*, 47 (1967), pp. 187–90.

32) F. H. Sandbach, *Menandri Reliquiae Selectae* (rev. edn, Oxford, 1990).

33) H. M. Cotton and J. Geiger, eds, *Masada II. The Latin and Greek Documents* (Jerusalem, 1989), pp. 31–4, with plate.

34) K. Aland, 'Über die Möglichkeit der Identifikation kleiner Fragmente neutestamentlicher Handschriften mit Hilfe des Computers', in J. K. Elliott, ed., *Studies in New Testament Language and Text* (Leiden, 1976), pp. 14–38, here pp. 21–2 and 32–3, and subsequent literature.

35) Albert Dou, Professor of Mathematics at Madrid University and member of the Royal Academy of Sciences, has recently added yet another element to the corroboration of 7Q5 = Mark 6:52–3. Having analysed every single possible (and impossible) reading of complete and fragmentary letters on 7Q5, and considered every attempt at identifying the fragment, regardless of the papyrological plausibility, and on the basis of the available stichometry, he came to a truly breathtaking conclusion: the possibility that 7Q5 is *not* identical with Mark 6:52–53 is 1:900 thousand million (A. Dou, 'El cálculo de probabilidades y las posibles identificaciones de 7Q5', in J. O'Callaghan, *Los primeros testimonios del Nuevo Testamento* (Córdoba, 1995) pp. 116–39.

36) This is not the place to discuss the other fragments in Cave 7, one of which has been identified as 1 Timothy 3:16–4:3; see J. O'Callaghan, *Los Papiros Griegos de la Cueva 7 de Qumran*; C. P. Thiede, 'Papyrologische Anfragen an 7Q5 im Umfeld antiker Handschriften', in Mayer, op. cit., pp. 57–72, here pp. 59–65; *idem, The Earliest Gospel Manuscript?*, pp. 46–54; *idem*, 'Das unbeachtete Qumrân – Fragment 7Q19 und die Herkunft der Höhle 7', *Aegyptus*, 74 (1994), pp. 123–8.

4: The Earliest Christian Book – the Magdalen Papyrus Examined

1) Reported by Hegesippus and quoted by Eusebius, *Church History*, 2, 23, 3–18.

2) Tacitus, *Annals*, 15, 38–44.

3) Cf. Acts 18:2; Suetonius, *Claudius*, 25, 4; Dio Cassius, *History*, 60, 6, 6.

4) For a summary of the archaeological evidence and the date, see É. Puech, 'La synagogue judéo-chrétienne du Mont Sion', *Le Monde de la Bible*, 57 (1989), pp. 18–20; B. Pixner, *Wege des Messias und Stätten der Urkirche. Jesus und das Judenchristentum im Licht neuer archäologischer Erkenntnisse*,

ed. R. Riesner, (2nd enl. edn., Giessen 1994), pp. 287–326. Recently, J. E. Taylor launched an attempt at doubting most early, Jewish Christian sites in Jerusalem (*Christians and Holy Places: The Myth of Jewish Christian Origins*, Oxford, 1993). However, her methods and results are based on a deficient historical and linguistic awareness of the sources and their meaning, and a lack of archaeological carefulness. See B. Pixner, *Wege des Messias*, Chapter 32, 'Bemerkungen zum Weiterbestehen judenchristlicher Gruppen in Jerusalem', pp. 402–11.

5) For the date and the historical context, see the most circumspect study on the subject, F. Manns, *John and Jamnia: How the Break Occurred Between Jews and Christians* (Jerusalem, 1988), in particular pp. 15–30.

6) Cicero refers to copies of letters preserved in such notebooks: *Epistulae ad Familiares*, 9, 26, 1; cf. E. R. Richards, *The Secretary in the Letters of Paul* (Tübingen, 1991), pp. 3–4, 65, 164. For the role of the Roman poet Martial in the spreading of the codex in classical literature, see Chap. 5.

7) The manifold advantages of the codex for the early Christians have been described and analysed by many scholars and from various viewpoints; see, e.g., C. H. Roberts and T. C. Skeat, *The Birth of the Christian Codex* (London, 1983); G. Cavallo, 'Codice e storia dei test greci antichi. Qualque riflessione sulla fase primitiva del fenomeno', *Bibliologia*, 9 (1989), pp. 13–35; T. C. Skeat, 'The Origin of the Christian Codex', *Zeitschrift für Papyrologie und Epigraphik*, 102 (1994), pp. 263–8; S. R. Lewellyn and R. A. Kearsley, *New Documents Illustrating Early Christianity* (Sydney, 1994), vol. 7, pp. 250–6, and many others.

8) Eusebius, *Church History*, 2, 15, 2.

9) C. H. Roberts, 'An Early Papyrus of the First Gospel', *Harvard Theological Review*, 46 (1953), pp. 233–7.

10) C. P. Thiede, 'Papyrus Magdalen Greek 17 (Gregory-Aland P64). A Reappraisal', *Zeitschrift für Papyrologie und Epigraphik*, 105 (1995), pp. 13–20 and Plate IX, here p. 19.

11) The outstanding importance of P37 for the textual tradition of the New Testament was recently emphasized by D. C. Parker's monograph, *Codex Bezae. An Early Christian manuscript and its text* (Cambridge, 1992).

12) *Nuevo Testamento Trilingüe* (3rd edn, Madrid, 1994), p. 152.

13) The order of the Magdalen Papyrus, *autōn* before *meti*, is also favoured, albeit in brackets, by the main text of A. Merk, *Novum Testamentum Graece et Latine* (11th edn, Rome, 1992), p. 94.

14) In fact, Wachtel's article was apparently written under pressure to mount

an immediate counter-attack without paying sufficient attention to detail. His palaeographical description of the Magdalen Papyrus and some Qumran scrolls from Cave 4, and hence his conclusions as to the dating of these scripts, are marred by factual errors which can only be attributed to undue haste. As for Matthew 26:22, we might indeed make allowances for his misjudgment on the basis of his ignorance of the microscopal analysis of the line. K. Wachtel, 'P64/P67: Fragmente des Matthäusevangeliums aus dem 1. Jahrhundert?', *Zeitschrift für Papyrologie und Epigraphik*, 107 (1995), pp. 73–80.

B. Aland, director of the Münster Institute, emphasized the hesitancy in coming to terms with the textual challenge of the earliest papyri, in a recent, otherwise useful essay published before the redating of the Magdalen Papyrus and its textual reappraisal: B. Aland, 'Das Zeugnis der frühen Papyri für den Text der Evangelien diskutiert am Matthäusevangelium', in F. Van Segbroeck / C. M. Tuckett / G. Van Belle / K. Verheyden (eds), The Four Gospels 1992. Festschrift Frans Neirynck, Leuven 1992, vol. III, pp. 325–35.

15) C. H. Roberts, 'Complementary Note' (dated 9.6.60), in R. Roca-Puig, *Un Papiro Griego del Evangelio de San Mateo* (Barcelona, 1962), pp. 58–60.

16) For stichometrical reasons only, Roca-Puig assumed that 'father' (*patéra*) was abbreviated 'PRA' in line 2 of fragment 1, verso. This is unlikely, since 'Father' may be treated as a holy name, but originally only if it refers to God himself, not to Abraham as it does in Matthew 3:9. A full, unabbreviated *pater* could easily be fitted into the stichometrical structure of the papyrus if the word was divided between lines 1 and 2. Conversely, 'God' (*theos*) would have been abbreviated by the first and last letters, *theta + sigma*, in a reconstructed line 5 (Matthew 3:9) – a line of which only one letter, a *tau*, is legible; and on the recto of the same fragment, we may assume for the same reason that *Iesous* in line 2 (Matthew 3:15) was abbreviated to read IS.

17) See Roca-Puig, *Un Papiro Griego*, p. 55.

18) C. P. Thiede, 'Papyrus Bodmer L. Das neutestamentliche Papyrusfragment p[73] = Mt 25:43/26:2–3', *Museum Helveticum*, 47/1 (1990), pp. 35–40, with plate.

19) See P. A. Kuhlmann, *Die Giessener literarischen Papyri und die Caracalla-Erlasse. Edition, Übersetzung und Kommentar* (Giessen, 1994), pp. 116–30.

20) K. Aland, 'Neue Neutestamentliche Papyri II', *New Testament Studies*, 12 (1965/6), here pp. 193–5.

21) J. van Haelst, *Catalogue des Papyrus littéraires juifs et chrétiens* (Paris, 1976), p. 146; C. H. Roberts and T. C. Skeat, *The Birth of the Codex* (London, 1983), pp. 40–1, 65–6.

22) K. Aland, *Studien zur Überlieferung des Neuen Testaments und seines Texts* (Berlin, 1967), p. 109.

23) K. Aland and B. Aland, *Der Text des Neuen Testaments* (Stuttgart, 1981; 2nd enl. edn 1989), pp. 105, 106, 110.

24) P. W. Comfort, *The Quest for the Original Text of the New Testament* (Grand Rapids, Mich., 1992), pp. 81–3.

25) P. W. Comfort, 'Exploring the Common Identification of Three Manuscripts: P4, P64, and P67', *Tyndale Bulletin*, 46:1 (1995), pp. 43–54; C. P. Thiede, 'Notes on P4 = Bibliothèque Nationale Paris, Supplementum Graecum 1120/5', *Tyndale Bulletin*, 46:1 (1995), pp. 55–7. Comfort's paper is also most valuable for its summary of arguments in favour of the undisputed codex identity of the Magdalen and the Barcelona papyri.

26) J. Morell, 'Nouveaux fragments du papyrus 4', *Revue Biblique*, 47 (1938), pp. 5–22 and plates I–VIII.

27) For the importance of the *tau*, cf. also Comfort, 'Exploring the Common Identification of Three Manuscripts: P4, P64, and P67', p. 50.

28) This material was first published and annotated by C. P. Thiede in his paper 'Die Datierung von antiken Handschriften als Beispiel für interdisziplinäre Zusammenarbeit in der Papyrologie', in C. P. Thiede and G. Masuch, *Wissenschaftstheorie und Wissenschaftspraxis. Reichweiten und Zukunftsperspektiven interdisziplinärer Forschung* (Paderborn, 1995), pp. 205–21, with six photographs. The material presented in that paper is fully integrated and expanded in Chapter 5 of this book.

5: The Jesus Papyrus Redated

1) Y.-K. Kim, 'Palaeographic Dating of P46 to the later First Century', *Biblica*, 69 (1988), pp. 248–57. Commonly dated to '*c.* 200', the P46 is the oldest surviving codex of a complete collection of St Paul's letters which could – historically speaking – easily have existed more than one century earlier. For a critique of Kim's position, see B. M. Metzger, *The Text of the New Testament. Its Transmission, Corruption and Restoration* (3rd enl. edn, Oxford, 1992), pp. 256–66, and Thiede's critique of Metzger in his re-edition of the Magdalen Papyrus, 'Papyrus Magdalen Greek 17 (Gregory-

Aland P64). A Reappraisal', *Zeitschrift für Papyrologie und Epigraphik*, 105 (1995), p. 18, n. 32.

2) H. Hunger, 'Zur Datierung des Papyrus Bodmer II (P66)', *Anzeiger der Österreichischen Akademie der Wissenschaften, Phil.-hist. Klasse*, 4 (1960), pp. 12–23. This important papyrus, the oldest surviving near-complete codex of St John's Gospel, is commonly dated to '*c.* 200', three-quarters of a century later than the date arrived at by Hunger.

3) See P. W. Comfort, *The Quest for the Original Text of the New Testament* (Grand Rapids, Mich., 1992), pp. 31–3.

4) G. Bonani, M. Broshi, I. Carmi, S. Ivy, J. Strugnell and W. Woelfli, 'Radiocarbon Dating of the Dead Sea Scrolls', *Atiqot*, 20 (1991), pp. 27–32; G. A. Rodley, 'An Assessment of the Radiocarbon Dating of the Dead Sea Scrolls', *Radiocarbon*, 35 (1993), pp. 335–8.

Recently, eighteen further Dead Sea Scrolls were radiocarbon dated, using ragged parts of the top or bottom edges and two pieces of linen that had allegedly wrapped the scrolls. This new test confirmed previous datings, but caused one major upheaval: a scroll fragment from Cave 4, 4Q258, had previously been dated to *c.* 100 BC by palaeographical means, whereas the Carbon-14 result was 'AD 119–245'. This dating, archaeologically and palaeographically impossible and therefore to be ruled out straight away, is 'difficult to explain', according to a preliminary report (see 'New Carbon-14 Results Leave Room for Debate', *Biblical Archaeology Review*, 24, 4 (July/August, 1995), p. 61). The explanation, however, is as simple as it is well-known: even allowing for the general effectiveness of 'calibration' (the empirical adjustment of the data on the basis of independent information), external influences on the state of a piece of papyrus or leather may hopelessly distort the C-14 result. Given such vagaries (who knows what kind of influence a fragment was subjected to, when and how?), and the almost useless time-span inherent in the method (even the latest analysis allowed for a range of 170 years in one case), radiocarbon dating can, at best, be used as a control mechanism and definitely not as a tool for conclusive results in papyrology.

5) H. C. Youtie, *The Textual Criticism of Documentary Papyri. Prolegomena* (2nd edn, London, 1974), p. 66.

6) *The Oxyrhynchus Papyri*, Part I (London, 1898), pp. 59–60, kept at the British Library, London, under the inventory number P. 745.

7) Librarian's Report, 1901, Archives of Magdalen College, Oxford. Hunt may have been influenced by the lack of corroborative codices from the

first century; he and Grenfell had already misdated the fragment from the 'History of the Macedonian Wars' for the same reason. Given the popularity of the Latin codex at the end of the first century and into the early second century, during Martial's lifetime (with codex 'paperback' editions of classics like Homer, Virgil, Cicero, Livy, Martial and Ovid, all mentioned by Martial himself), one may indeed ask why it did not catch on during the second and third centuries, and why it was only in the mid to late fourth century that the codex format became the preferred format for non-Christian literature as well. The answer probably lies in the very fact that the codex was being used by the Christians to such an extent that it was identified with them: the codex was *the* Christian format. Decent Roman '*litterati*' would not want to be seen copying the scribal habits of an illicit religion. Only with Constantine and the Christianization of the Roman Empire would the codex begin to enjoy an accepted and acceptable position.

A similar phenomenon occurred at the same time, the late first, early second century, when the Jews began to discontinue the use of their own Greek translation of the Old Testament, the Septuagint of the third century BC. The Christians had been using it, for quotations and in their missionary activities, to such an extent that it had become Christian property in Jewish eyes. Alternative Jewish translations were produced so that the 'soiled' Septuagint could be avoided.

8) Masada papyrus 721A: one line of fifteen fragmentary letters, containing *Aeneid*, 4, 9, and dated to AD 73/74. Edited by H. M. Cotton and J. Geiger, *Masada II: The Latin and Greek Documents* (Jerusalem, 1989) pp. 31–5, and plate I, 721 a/b.

For the use of Latin in first-century Palestine, particularly among New Testament authors, see A. Millard, 'Latin in First-Century Palestine', in Z. Zevit / S. Gitin / M. Sokoloff (eds), *Solving Riddles and Untying Knots. Biblical, Epigraphic, and Semitic Studies in Honor of Jonas C. Greenfield* (Winona Lake, 1995), pp. 451–8.

9) In a major treatise, *Against the Heresies*, the second-century theologian Irenaeus recorded the information that St Mark wrote his Gospel after the *exodos* of St Peter (and St Paul). Many commentators have assumed that Irenaeus was referring to St Peter's death – comparatively late, in other words, some time after AD 65/67 – rather than to an event during his lifetime. G. Stanton, in his latest monograph, *Gospel Truth? New Light on Jesus and the Gospels* (London, 1995), pp. 49–50, repeats this old

mistake. *Exodos* can, in fact, mean 'death' although most examples in biblical Greek mean 'departure', as in the title of the second book of the Old Testament. In 1991 the American scholar E. Earle Ellis presented a paper at the International Qumran Congress, Eichstätt University, demonstrating from a computer analysis of Irenaeus's works that he always used *thanatos* (or, in Latin, *mors*) when he meant death, and that he was thus in complete agreement with other early church historians like Eusebius that St Mark's Gospel was written during the lifetime of St Peter. (E. E. Ellis, 'Entstehungszeit und Herkunft des Markus-Evangeliums', in B. Mayer, *Christen und Christliches in Qumran* (Regensburg, 1992), pp. 195–212, here 198–201.)

10) Eusebius, *Church History*, 2, 15, 2.

11) *The Times* (London), 24 December 1994.

12) O. Murray, P. Parsons, T. W. Potter and P. Roberts, 'A "stork-vase" from the Mola di Monte Gelato', *Papers of the British School of Rome*, vol. LIX (London, 1991), pp. 177–95, here p. 195.

13) See above, p. 193.

14) G. Cavallo, *Ricerche sulla maiuscola biblica* (Florence, 1967). There are of course other important handbooks with useful material, such as C. Roberts's *Greek Literary Hands, 350* BC–AD *400* (Oxford, 1955); E. G. Turner's *Greek Manuscripts of the Ancient World* (Oxford/Princeton, 1971; 2nd enl. edn rev. by P. Parsons, London, 1987); the indispensable R. Seider, *Paläographie der griechischen Papyri*, I/II (Stuttgart, 1967/1970); G. Cavallo and H. Maehler, *Greek Bookhands of the Early Byzantine Period*, AD *300–800* (London, 1987), and many, many others.

15) G. Stanton, in *Gospel Truth?* p. 14, states that he cannot see the reasons why Thiede 'was no longer satisfied by the arguments advanced by Roberts in favour of a late second-century date'. In fact, the reasons are clearly set out. But Stanton in any case misses the point of the original article, which was to explore fresh arguments rather than to criticize old ones.

16) C. H. Roberts, 'An Early Papyrus of the First Gospel', *Harvard Theological Review*, 46 (1953), pp. 233–7, here p. 237.

17) R. Roca-Puig, *Un Papiro Griego del Evangelio de San Mateo*, (Barcelona, 2nd ed, 1962), with C. H. Roberts's 'Complementary Note' (dated 9.6.60) on pp. 59–60.

18) This year, AD 68, has been accepted by scholars since the publication of the archaeological report by the leader of the excavation team, Roland

de Vaux (*Archaeology and the Dead Sea*, London, 1973). Occasionally doubts have been raised, but without solid archaeological or historical foundation. For a reliable summary, see J. Murphy-O'Connor, 'Qumran', in *The Anchor Bible Dictionary*, vol. 5 (New York, 1992), pp. 590–4, and O. Betz and R. Riesner, *Jesus, Qumran and the Vatican: Clarifications* (London, 1994), pp. 50–68.

19) See Roberts's monograph *Manuscripts, Society and Belief in Early Christian Egypt* (London, 1979), pp. 26–48, here p. 46.

20) The historicity of the so-called 'Flight to Pella', mentioned by the church historian Eusebius (*Church History*, 3, 5, 3), has been doubted by sceptics; the debate and the conclusive arguments in its favour are summed up in B. Wander, *Trennungsprozesse zwischen Frühem Christentum und Judentum im 1. Jahrhundert n.Chr.* (Tübingen/Basel, 1994), pp. 272–5.

21) I. Gallo, *Greek and Latin Papyrology* (London, 1986), p. 14.

22) P. W. Skehan, E. Ulrich and J. E. Sanderson, eds, *Discoveries in the Judaean Desert*, IX: *Qumran Cave 4* (Oxford, 1992).

23) Ibid., p. 8.

24) 7 April 30 appears to be the only date that fulfils all relevant criteria for the day of the Crucifixion. There are minority votes in other directions, such as AD 28 or, more vigorously, AD 33. But even these variations would not decisively deflect from the short span that determines the period after which the first papyrus of a completed Gospel could be expected.

25) The papyri from Cave 7 were first published in 1962: M. Baillet, J. T. Milik, R. de Vaux, eds, *Discoveries in the Judaean Desert, III: Les 'Petites Grottes' de Qumrân* (Oxford, 1962).

26) This, at any rate, is the present majority consensus expressed, among others, by D. Barthélemy, W. Schubart, E. Würthwein, C. H. Roberts, E. Hanhart. See E. Würthwein, *Der Text des Alten Testaments* (5th edn, Stuttgart, 1988), p. 184, with plate; W. H. Schmidt, W. Thiel and R. Hanhart, *Altes Testament* (Stuttgart, 1989), pp. 194–5, with plate. Peter Parsons, again commenting on the date on behalf of the Dead Sea Scrolls editorial team, did not object to it but somewhat hesitatingly preferred a date towards the end of the first century BC: E. Tov, ed., *The Greek Minor Prophets Scroll 8HevXIIgr* (Oxford, 1990), pp. 19–26.

27) H. M. Cotton and J. Geiger, eds, *Masada II. The Latin and Greek Documents* (Jerusalem, 1989), pp. 123–4 and plate 15, no. 784.

28) An example of inappropriate and palpably wrong statements on palaeographical details, meant to serve the purpose of refuting Carsten Thiede's

redating, can be found in K. Wachtel's paper, 'P⁶⁴/⁶⁷: Fragmente des Matthäusevangeliums aus dem 1. Jahrhundert?' *Zeitschrift für Papyrologie und Epigraphik*, 107 (1995), pp. 73–80, here pp. 76–9.

29) A. M. Farrer, *The Revelation of St John the Divine* (Oxford, 1964), p. 37.

30) A. E. Housman, 'The Application of Thought to Textual Criticism', *Proceedings of the Classical Association*, August 1921, 18 (1922), here pp. 68–9; reprinted in J. Carter, ed., *A. E. Housman, Selected Prose* (Cambridge, 1961), pp. 131–50, here pp. 132–3.

31) P. Oxy. II 246, Plate VII, now at the Cambridge University Library.

32) L. Ingrams, P. Kingston, P. J. Parsons and J. R. Rea, in *Oxyrhynchus Papyri XXXIV* (London, 1968), pp. 1–3, with two plates; P. W. Comfort, *The Quest for the Original Text of the New Testament* (Grand Rapids, Mich., 1992), p. 188.

33) See B. P. Grenfell and A. S. Hunt, *Oxyrhynchus Papyri I* (London, 1898), pp. 4–7, with one plate; E. M. Schofield, 'The Papyrus Fragments of the Greek New Testament', unpublished Ph.D. thesis, Southern Baptist Theological Seminary, Louisville (1936), pp. 86–91.

34) B. P. Grenfell and A. S. Hunt, *Oxyrhynchus Papyri II* (London, 1899), pp. 1–8, and *Oxyrhynchus Papyri XV* (London, 1922), pp. 8–12.

35) E. Lobel, C. H. Roberts, E. G. Turner and J. W. R. Barns, in *Oxyrhynchus Papyri XXIV* (London, 1957), pp. 1–4, with one plate; K. Aland, 'Alter und Entstehung des D-Textes im Neuen Testament. Betrachtungen zu P⁶⁹ und 0171', in J. Janeras, ed., *Miscelánea papirológica Ramón Roca-Puig* (Barcelona, 1987), pp. 37–61.

36) T. C. Skeat, in *Oxyrhynchus Papyri L* (London, 1983), pp. 3–8, with one plate.

6: Scribes, Gospel Readers and the Dawn of Christianity

1) K. Laub, AP, 'City linked to Jesus is unearthed', *Philadelphia Inquirer*, 2 July 1995.

2) This is the only philologically correct understanding of the term and the point St Mark is trying to make. The common modern translation, 'she was a pagan' or 'she was a gentile', would be a nonsensical pleonasm if applied to a woman explicitly described as a Syro-Phoenician. Cf. J. N. Sevenster, *Do You Know Greek? How Much Greek Could the First Jewish Christians Have Known?* (Leiden, 1967), p. 190; M. Hengel, *Studies in the Gospel of Mark* (London, 1985), p. 29; R. Riesner, *Jesus als Lehrer. Eine*

Untersuchung zum Ursprung der Evangelien-Überlieferung (3rd enl. edn, Tübingen, 1988), p. 391. Riesner also refers to the dialogues of Jesus with Pilate, in the apparent absence of an interpreter.

3) B. Schwank, 'Ein griechiches Jesuslogion?', in N. Brox et al., eds, *Anfänge der Theologie* (Graz, 1987), pp. 61–3.

4) As always in New Testament criticism, there are those who prefer to think that such historical cameos are legends, made up by the author. But even if we were to assume, for the sake of argument and in contradiction to the comparative experience of historiography, that St Luke (or whoever wrote the Gospel) made it all up, we would still have to live with the fact that a first-century Christian document has Jesus quoting from a classical play.

5) R. O. P. Taylor, *The Groundwork of the Gospels* (Oxford, 1946), pp. 21–30.

6) Other examples include 1 Corinthians 1:1 ('Paul ... and Sosthenes'); 2 Corinthians 1:1 ('Paul ... and Timothy'); Philippians 1:1 ('Paul and Timothy'); Colossians 1:1 ('From Paul ... and from our brother Timothy'); 1 Thessalonians 1:1 ('Paul, Silvanus and Timothy'); 2 Thessalonians 1:1 ('Paul, Silvanus and Timothy'); and Philemon 1:1 ('From Paul ... and from our brother Timothy').

7) G. Burge, 'The Real Writer of Romans', *Christian History*, 47/XI, no. 3 (1995), p. 29.

8) The best recent investigative summary of this difficult subject can be found in E. R. Richards, *The Secretary in the Letters of Paul* (Tübingen, 1991), pp. 26–47, 169–72. Richards suggests that the shorthand qualities of Tertius may have qualified him for the job of taking down and editing the long letter to the Romans (p. 171), but he does not comment on the Greek Old Testament reference to shorthand writing (Psalm 45:1), nor on St Matthew's qualifications in this respect, analysed by others – see below.

9) On St Matthew (Levi-Matthew) as shorthand writer see, among others, E. J. Goodspeed, *Matthew, Apostle and Evangelist* (Philadelphia, 1959), pp. 16–17 and R. H. Gundry, *The Use of the Old Testament in St Matthew's Gospel* (Leiden, 1967), pp. 182–4; on shorthand writing behind St Mark's Gospel, see B. Orchard and H. Riley, *The Order of the Synoptics* (Macon, Ga, 1987), pp. 269–73.

10) A useful commentary on this verse in its stenographical context can be found in A. Wikenhauser's 'Der heilige Hieronymus über Psalm 45(44):2', *Archiv für Stenographie*, 59/III (1908), pp. 187–9.

11) P. Benoit, J. T. Milik, R. de Vaux, eds., *Discoveries in the Judaean Desert of Jordan*, II: *Les grottes de Murraba'at* (Oxford, 1961), pp. 275–9.

12) When Carsten Thiede, having seen the original years ago, applied for its loan to an archaeological exhibition in Italy which he is helping to prepare, at the time of writing, as president of the scientific committee, he was told by the John Rockefeller Museum, Jerusalem, where it is kept, that it has been put aside for restoration.

13) Most people almost automatically assume that the Christ monogram was introduced by Emperor Constantine, through his vision prior to the decisive battle against Maxentius in AD 312 (Lactantius, *On the Deaths of the Persecutors*, 44, 5; Eusebius, *Life of Constantine*, 1, 28). However, the 'chi-rho' had been popular long before, and the vision merely authorized it, as it were, persuading Constantine to 'affix Christ to the shields' of his soldiers ('Facit ut iussus est et transversa X littera summo capite circumflexo, *Christum in scutis notat*', Lactantius).

14) See, e.g., J. Finegan, *Encountering New Testament Manuscripts. A Working Introduction to Textual Criticism* (Grand Rapids, Mich., 1974), p. 32.

15) See Chapter 5, n. 2.

16) See, recently, B. M. Metzger, *The Canon of the New Testament: Its Origin, Development, and Significance* (Oxford, 1987), pp. 167–9; J. Jeremias and W. Schneemelcher, 'Papyrus Egerton 2', in W. Schneemelcher, ed., *Neutestamentliche Apokryphen in deutscher Übersetzung* (5th edn, Tübingen, 1987), pp. 82–5. A few years ago, a new fragment unknown to H. I. Bell and T. C. Skeat, the first editors of the Egerton Papyrus in 1935, was discovered and edited as part of the Cologne collection of papyri, P. Köln No. 255; the new fragment confirmed the palaeographical similarities with P66 (St John) which, according to H. Hunger, must be dated *c*. AD 125.

17) Examples and comparisons with biblical usage can be found in E. Nachmanson, 'Die schriftliche Kontraktion auf den griechischen Inschriften', *Eranos*, 10 (1910), pp. 100–41, G. Rudberg, *Neutestamentlicher Text und Nomina Sacra* (Uppsala, 1915), and other publications, particularly by Rudberg.

18) L. Traube, *Nomina Sacra: Versuch einer Geschichte der christlichen Kürzung* (Munich, 1907). For the technical differences between 'abbreviation', 'contraction' and 'suspension', further material and occasionally differing assessments, see also A. H. R. E. Paap, *Nomina Sacra in the Greek Papyri of the First Four Centuries A.D. – The Sources and Some Deductions* (Leiden,

1959). Cf. also F. Bedodi, 'I "nomina sacra" nei papiri greci vet-
erotestamentari precristiani', *Studia Papyrologica*, 13 (1974), pp. 89–103,
and A. Pietersma, 'Kyrios or Tetragram: A Renewed Quest for the Original
LXX', in A. Pietersma and C. Cox, eds, *De Septuaginta. Studies in Honour
of John William Wevers* (Mississauga, Ont., 1984), pp. 85–101. See also A.
Millard, 'Ancient Abbreviations and the *Nomina Sacra*', in A. Leany and
E. J. Eyre, eds, *An Unbroken Reed. Essays in Honour of A. F. Shore* (London
1995), pp. 221–6.

19) For a summary of the debate, see C. P. Thiede, 'Papyrologische Anfragen
an 7Q5 im Umfeld antiker Handschriften', in B. Mayer, *Christen und
Christliches in Qumran?* (Regensburg, 1992), pp. 57–72, here pp. 59–64;
and *idem, The Earliest Gospel Manuscript? The Qumran Fragment 7Q5 and
Its Significance for New Testament Studies* (Exeter/Carlisle, 1992), pp. 48–
52, with plate.

20) An objective case in point is the statement of Émile Puech, one of the
leading members of the official Dead Sea Scrolls editorial team; he is
convinced that there are 'conclusive reasons' for identifying 7Q4 as a
fragment from 1 Timothy: B. Pixner, *Wege des Messias und Stätten der
Urkirche, Jesus und das Judenchristentum im Licht neuer archäologischer Erkenntnisse*, ed. R. Riesner (2nd enl. edn, Giessen, 1994), p. 386.

Pixner, in a comment on Puech's statement, notes the chronological
problems – by which he probably means the current *communis opinio*
among New Testament scholars: that 1 Timothy was not written by St
Paul and is perhaps as late as the second century. Apart from the fact that
there is a continuous debate about the dating of this epistle and the
'Pastorals' in general, which is wavering enough to exclude any firm,
definitive statements about the earliest possible date, we must keep in
mind that St Paul died in AD 64/65, or in AD 67 at the very latest – which
would allow a pupil of his time to complete and distribute the letter
before it could have reached Qumran by AD 68. For the controversy about
the date of 1 Timothy, and a reliable summary of arguments for a pre-AD
68 date, see D. Guthrie, *New Testament Introduction* (4th rev. edn, Leicester,
1990), pp. 607–52.

21) J. O'Callaghan, '1 Timothy 3, 16; 4, 1.3 en 7Q4?', *Biblica*, 53 (1972), pp.
362–7.

22) Fragment 20, line 4 (Leviticus 4:27: 'If any one of the common people
sins unwittingly in doing any one of the things which IAO has commanded not to be done ...' RSV) See P. W. Skehan, E. Ulrich and J. E.

Sanderson, eds, *Discovery in the Judaean Desert, Qumran Cave 4* (Oxford, 1992), p. 174 and Plate 120. For an analysis of the handwriting on Pap4QLXXLev^b and its date, see Chapter 5 of this book.

23) S. Brown, 'Concerning the Origin of the *Nomina Sacra*', *Studia Papyrologica*, 9 (1970), pp. 7–19, here p. 19.

24) Cf. J. O'Callaghan, *'Nomina sacra' in papyris graecis saeculi III neotestamentariis* (Rome, 1970). This book is an indispensable tool for anyone trying to trace *nomina sacra* in the oldest papyri.

25) C. H. Roberts, *Manuscript, Society and Belief in Early Christian Egypt* (London, 1979), p. 46.

26) Ibid.

27) The triangle as a symbol for the Trinity was apparently particularly popular in early northern African Christianity, but there are very few traces of it in early Christian inscriptions, etc. This scarcity is accounted for not only by decay, destruction and so on, but also by the doctrine of St Augustine. He condemned its use, since it had been usurped by gnostic Manichaeans, a sect whose popularity had become dangerous to the Christians in certain regions of the Empire (*Contra Faustum*, 20, 6). After that, only very few Christian writers dared to use it and write about it. A noteworthy exception is St (or 'Mar') Saba (AD 437–532), whose monastery in the desert near Bethlehem still houses some priceless manuscripts. He wrote a whole treatise about the trinitarian triangle, which has been preserved in a Coptic copy. The enduring influence of St Augustine prevented its reoccurrence in Christian literature and art until the Middle Ages.

28) Whole bookshelves have been filled with learned debates about the text Jesus might have written (Exodus 23:7, 'Have nothing to do with a false charge'? [NIV]). There is a minority school of scholars, led by Marta Sordi of the University of Milan, who think that Jesus *did* write a letter, not preserved in the New Testament but elsewhere, based on the tradition about the historical King Abgar V Ukama of Edessa (AD 13–50) and his correspondence with Jesus. Eusebius quotes the texts and makes it explicitly clear that he has seen the letters, coming from the royal archives of Edessa (*Church History*, 1, 13). However, even if we subscribe to this view, we would still not know if Jesus had written the letter in his own hand. Eusebius himself points out that the letters in the Edessa archive were in Syriac, a language not previously associated with the historical Jesus. However, this letter of Jesus was so popular that it was copied on

to numerous papyri, *ostraca* (potsherds), and even appeared on inscriptions and amulets, some of them in Greek, in a version which is different (i.e., independent) from the text transmitted by Eusebius.

29) See also 2 John 12, where parchment and ink are mentioned, and 3 John 13, with a reference to stylus and ink.

30) For an English translation of the fragments, see E. Hennecke, ed., *New Testament Apocrypha*, vol. 2 (London, 1965), pp. 276–322, and M. R. James, *The Apocryphal New Testament* (London, 1924, repr. 1955), pp. 300–36; for a critical edition, see L. Vouaux, *Les Actes de Pierre. Introduction, Textes, Traduction et Commentaires* (Paris, 1922).

31) One commentator, G. Ficker, suggested that this Marcellus was the Granius Marcellus mentioned by Tacitus, *Annals*, 1, 74: G. Ficker, *Die Petrusakten. Beiträge zu ihrem Verständnis* (Leipzig, 1903), pp. 38–9.

32) Needless to say, the mere hint at the thought that St Peter could have written 2 Peter will cause an outcry of indignation among most New Testament scholars; and this is not the place to take sides. Suffice it to say that the question is still far from being answered conclusively. Two examples may indicate the direction of recent thinking: E. Earle Ellis offered persuasive arguments for a date of St Jude's Letter prior to AD 62 ('Prophecy and Hermeneutics in Jude', in *idem, Prophecy and Hermeneutics in Early Christianity* (Tübingen, 1978), pp. 221–36); and J. Crehan argued, on text-critical grounds, for the dependency of Jude on 2 Peter ('New Light on 2 Peter from the Bodmer Papyrus', in E. A. Livingstone, ed., *Studia Evangelica*, vol. VII (Berlin, 1982), pp. 145–9).

7: Fragments of the Truth – the Jesus Papyrus in Our Times

1) William Hamilton, *A Quest for the Post-Historical Jesus* (London, 1993).

2) Cited in Marcus J. Borg, *Jesus in Contemporary Scholarship* (1994), p. 185; for this debate in general, see Stephen Neill and Tom Wright, *The Interpretation of the New Testament 1861–1986,* 2nd ed (Oxford, 1988).

3) Neill, op. cit., pp. 4–5.

4) See especially R. Bultmann, *The History of the Synoptic Tradition* (rev. edn, Oxford, 1972).

5) For a fine review of this 'third quest' literature, see Borg, op. cit.

6) See N. T. Wright, *Who Was Jesus?* (London, 1992).

7) Borg, op. cit., p. 183.

8) See John P. Meier, *A Marginal Jew: Rethinking the Historical Jesus*, 2 vols (New York/London, 1991 and 1993).

9) Paul Tillich, *Dynamics of Faith* (London, 1957), pp. 51–3.

10) J. A. T. Robinson, *Redating the New Testament* (London, 1976), p. 336.

11) Robinson, op. cit., p. 355.

12) X. Leon-Dufour in *In Search of the Historical Jesus*, ed. Harvey K. McArthur (London, 1970), p. 61.

13) See, for instance, 1 Corinthians 11:2; 2 Thessalonians 2:15.

14) B. Gerhardsson, *The Origins of the Gospel Tradition* (London, 1979), p. 28.

15) Gerhardsson, op. cit., p. 64.

16) The most recent scholar to develop this line of investigation is Rainer Riesner, *Jesus als Lehrer Eine Untersuchung zum Orsprung der Evangelien-Überlieferrung* (3rd enl. edn, Tübingen, 1992).

17) It is interesting to note how much information the Evangelists took for granted. Mark 1 assumes the reader knows who John the Baptist is; Mark 5 assumes similar knowledge of Pilate.

18) See, in particular, Richard A. Burridge, *What Are the Gospels? A Comparison with Graeco-Roman Biography* (Cambridge, 1992).

19) Burridge, op. cit., p. 258. '. . . because this is a life of an historical person written within the lifetime of his contemporaries, there are limits on free composition'.

20) Cited in Dennis Nineham, *The Use and Abuse of the Bible* (London, 1976), p. 49.

21) See Erich Auerbach's masterly account of this subject: *Mimesis. The Representation of Reality in Western Literature* (Bern, 1946).

22) In fact, the writers of the New Testament were well aware of the difference between empirical fact and myth. The careful use of the word *mythos* (1 Timothy 1:4 and 4:7; 2 Timothy 4:4; Titus 1:14; 2 Peter 1:16) makes this very clear.

Conclusion: the Magdalen Papyrus and Faith

1) And as Robinson argued before Berger in 1976.

INDEX

The letter 'e' after a page reference indicates an epigraph. A number in parentheses after a page reference is a note number. The notes have been indexed when they introduce subjects that are not mentioned in the corresponding passage of the main text.

The controversial
remnants: a Greek *Nu*?

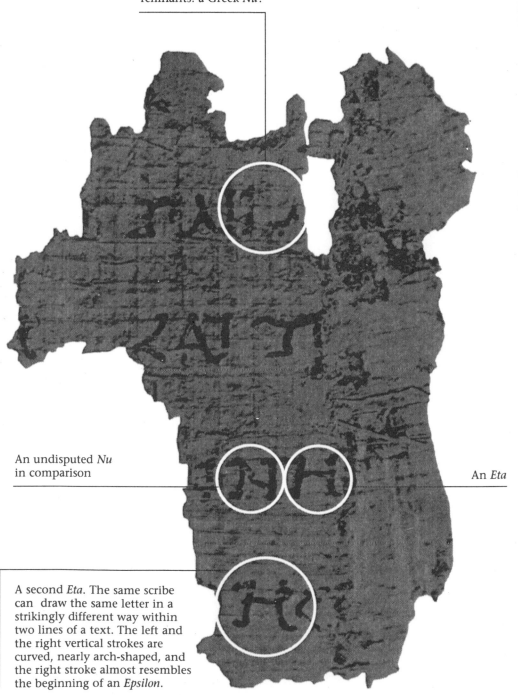

An undisputed *Nu*
in comparison

An *Eta*

A second *Eta*. The same scribe
can draw the same letter in a
strikingly different way within
two lines of a text. The left and
the right vertical strokes are
curved, nearly arch-shaped, and
the right stroke almost resembles
the beginning of an *Epsilon*.